Norbert Elia and Human Interdependencies

C000153122

EDITED BY
THOMAS SALUMETS

McGill-Queen's University Press
Montreal & Kingston · London · Ithaca

© McGill-Queen's University Press 2001
ISBN 0-7735-2196-8 (cloth)
ISBN 0-7735-2266-2 (paper)

Legal deposit third quarter 2001
Bibliothèque nationale du Québec

Printed in Canada on acid-free paper

This book has been published with the help of a grant
from the German Academic Exchange Service (DAAD)
and financial support from the University of British
Columbia.

McGill-Queen's University Press acknowledges the
financial support of the Government of Canada through
the Book Publishing Industry Development Program
(BPIDP) for its activities. It also acknowledges the
support of the Canada Council for the Arts for its
publishing program.

Chapter 3, Cas Wouters, "The Integration of Classes and
Sexes in the Twentieth Century: Etiquette Books and
Emotion Management," is published with permission
from the *Journal of Social History*, where it appeared
in volume 29 (1995) as "Etiquette Books and Emotion
Management in the 20th Century: Part One – The
Integration of Social Classes" (107–24) and "Part Two –
The Integration of the Sexes" (325–40).

Canadian Cataloguing in Publication Data

Main entry under title:
  Norbert Elias and human interdependencies
  Papers presented at a conference held in Vancouver,
  Mar. 20–22, 1997.
  Includes bibliographical references and index.
  ISBN 0-7735-2196-8 (bound) –
  ISBN 0-7735-2266-2 (pbk.)
  1. Elias, Norbert – Congresses. 2. Sociology –
Congresses. 3. Civilization, Modern – Congresses.
1. Salumets, Thomas
HM479.E38N66 2001   301   C00-901707-0

Typeset in Sabon 10/12
by Caractéra inc., Quebec City

Norbert Elias and Human Interdependencies

Contents

Preface

The first in a series of conferences marking the centenary of Norbert Elias's birth on 22 June 1897 was held in Vancouver on 20–22 March 1997. The distinction of its being the first conference in North America devoted to Elias's work added a particular historical significance to this event. Most of the chapters in this volume had their origin in that conference.

The publication of this book would not have been possible without the financial support of the Social Sciences and Humanities Research Council of Canada, the German Academic Exchange Service (New York), the University of British Columbia, and the former Goethe-Institut in Vancouver. Many people helped in various ways; in particular, I would like to mention Alan Tully, Errol Durbach, Stephen Mennell, Hermann Korte, Caroline Goeltsch, Benjamin Ellison, Julia Feesey, Elizabeth Hulse, and the staff at McGill-Queen's University Press. Finally, I wish to thank the contributors. It was a pleasure to work with them and to share in their knowledge of Norbert Elias and human interdependencies.

Contributors

JORGE ARDITI is an associate professor of sociology at the State University of New York in Buffalo. His book *A Genealogy of Manners: Transformations of Social Relations in France and England from the Fourteenth to the Eighteenth Century* was recently published by the University of Chicago Press. He has authored articles on the sociology of knowledge, agency and identity, the transformation of manners and changing infrastructures of social relations, and post-structuralism. He is now engaged in a study of forms of subjectivity in non-Western societies and the ethical implications of post-structuralism.

GODFRIED VAN BENTHEM VAN DEN BERGH was until 1998 professor of international relations at Erasmus University in Rotterdam as well as an associate of the Institute of Social Studies in The Hague. His most recent book, *The Nuclear Revolution and the End of the Cold War: Forced Restraint* (Basingstoke), was published in 1992. His present research interests are the development of nationalism, comparative study of state formation, and the spread of nuclear weapons in the world state system. He is chairman of the board of the Netherlands Association for International Affairs and a member of the Executive Board of the Advisory Council for International Affairs of the Dutch Ministries of Foreign Affairs and Defence.

REINHARD BLOMERT teaches sociology at Humboldt University in Berlin and at Karl-Franzens University in Graz, Austria. He is the editor of several books and the author of *Psyche und Zivilisation: Zur theoretischen Konstruktion bei Norbert Elias* (2d ed., 1991) and *Intellektuelle im Aufbruch: Karl Mannheim, Alfred Weber, Norbert Elias und die Heidelberger Sozialwissenschaften in der Zwischenkriegszeit* (1999). He has published numerous articles and currently is a member of the Zivilisation und Gesellschaft research group.

STEPHEN GUY-BRAY teaches at the University of Calgary. He has published articles on the Earl of Surrey, Christopher Marlowe, John Dryden, Robert Duncan, and Daryl Hine. He is currently writing a book-length study of the homoeroticism of the English elegaic tradition.

THOMAS M. KEMPLE is assistant professor in the Department of Anthropology and Sociology at the University of British Columbia in Vancouver. Most recently he is the author *of Reading Marx Writing: Melodrama, the Market, and the "Grundrisse"* (Stanford, 1995), and he is currently writing a companion volume on Max Weber. In the past he has worked at Concordia University in Montreal and York University in Toronto, and has written several articles for sociological publications.

HERMANN KORTE is professor emeritus of sociology at the University of Hamburg. He is the author of ten books, including *Über Norbert Elias: Das Werden eines Menschenwissenschaftlers* (1988–97), *Einführung in die Geschichte der Soziologie* (1998), and *Utopia. Das Himmelreich auf Erden?* (1999). His research interests focus on civilization processes and theory of social processes, urban sociology, demography, and the theoretical and political problems of international labour migration. He is co-editor of three volumes of essays on the civilization theory of Norbert Elias and is one of the three trustees of the Norbert Elias Foundation in Amsterdam. Professor Korte is also a member of PEN.

HELMUT KUZMICS is currently professor of sociology at the University of Graz in Austria. In 1989 he authored *Der Preis der Zivilisation: Die Zwänge der Moderne im theoretischen Vergleich*. In addition, in 1991 he co-edited *Der unendliche Prozess der Zivilisation: Zur Kultursoziologie der Moderne nach Norbert Elias* and in 1993 *Transformationen des Wir-Gefühls: Studien zum nationalen Habitus*. He was a visiting scholar at the University of Hanover in 1990 and at the University of Cambridge in 1990–91. His current interests include a comparison of Austrian and English character and the relationship between literature and sociology.

STEPHEN MENNELL is professor of sociology and director of the Institute for the Study of Social Change at the National University of Ireland in Dublin, and since 1997 he has been one of the three trustees of the Norbert Elias Foundation in Amsterdam. He studied at Cambridge and Harvard Universities and took his doctorate at the University of Amsterdam. Professor Mennell is the author of the standard work *Norbert Elias: An Introduction* and with Johan Goudsblom has edited two selections from Elias's work, *Norbert Elias on Civilisation: Power and Knowledge* and *The Norbert Elias Reader: A Biographical Selection*, both published in 1998. His numerous other books include *All Manners of Food* (1985).

THOMAS SALUMETS is associate professor of Germanic studies at the University of British Columbia in Vancouver. He took his doctorate at Princeton University, and he is a fellow of the Alexander von Humboldt Foundation. With Sander L. Gilman, he is an editor of the novels and aphorisms of F.M. Klinger. He is also the author of numerous articles on German and Estonian literary and cultural history. In 1996 Professor Salumets, with J. Roche, published the multi-author volume *Germanics under Construction*. In 1995–97 he chaired the Programme in Comparative Literature at the University of British Columbia. Currently, he is the editor of the *Journal of Baltic Studies* and acting head of the Department of Germanic Studies at UBC. Among his present research interests are Norbert Elias, foreign literature didactics, and European cultural studies.

THOMAS J. SCHEFF is professor emeritus of sociology at the University of California in Santa Barbara. He is the author of *Being Mentally Ill* (3d ed., 1999), *Microsociology* (1990), *Emotions and Violence* (with Suzanne Retzinger; 1991), *Bloody Revenge* (1994), *Emotions, the Social Bond, and Human Reality* (1997), and other books and articles. He is a former chair of the section on the sociology of emotions of the American Sociological Association and former president of the Pacific Sociological Association. His fields of research are social psychology, emotions, mental illness, and new approaches to theory and method. His current studies concern popular music, solidarity-alienation, and emotional expression in the mass media.

ULRICH C. TEUCHER previously worked as a pediatric oncology nurse at the university hospital in Hamburg, Germany, before entering the doctoral program in comparative literature at the University of British Columbia in Vancouver. His dissertation is entitled "Writing the Unspeakable: Metaphor in Cancer Narratives," and it investigates the poetics of English and German autobiographical cancer narratives. As part of his project he assists in a relaxation group at the Cancer Agency in Vancouver.

ANNETTE TREIBEL is professor of sociology at the Pedagogical University of Karlsruhe. She is the author of *Migration in modernen Gesellschaften* (2d ed., 1999) and *Einführung in soziologische Theorien der Gegenwart* (5th ed., 2000). She has written numerous essays in the field of figurational sociology and Norbert Elias scholarship; with Reinhard Blomert and Helmut Kuzmics she co-edited two volumes, *Transformationen des Wir-Gefühls* (1993) and *Zivilisationstheorie in der Bilanz. Beiträge zum 100: Geburtstag von Norbert Elias* (2000). Since 1995 Professor Treibel has been a member of the Elias Editorial Board. She is currrently interested in sociological theory, migration, figurational sociology, and gender studies.

CAS WOUTERS is a researcher at the Faculty of Social Sciences at Utrecht University in the Netherlands. He co-authored with Bram van Stolk the 1987 work *Frauen im Zwiespalt*, and in 1990 he published *Van Minnen en Sterven* (On loving and dying). As well, he has written numerous articles on the sociology of emotion management and on the twentieth-century process of "informalization." His research project entitled "Informalization and the Civilizing of Emotions" focuses on how changes in dominant social codes are connected to changes in emotion management and habitus in twentieth-century Holland, Germany, England, and the United States.

Norbert Elias and Human Interdependencies

Introduction

THOMAS SALUMETS

> We are not "independent" ... We are mutually dependent.
> Norbert Elias, *Reflections on a Life*

For Norbert Elias (1897–1990) there were few, if any, more urgent tasks than learning about human interdependencies. Early on, he argued the need for a more open and fuller consideration of the complex and continually changing ways in which we are connected. In his view, there "can be no 'I' without 'he,' 'she,' 'we,' 'you' or 'they.' It is plainly very misleading to use such concepts as 'I' or ego independently of their position within the web of relationships to which the rest of the pronouns refer" (1978c, 124). Yet in the course of the "civilizing process," as Elias saw it unfold, the self-image of the *homo clausus*, the apparently closed-off individual, was mistaken for reality. To correct this error, he focused his efforts on human interdependencies. The ensuing quest for long-term continuities of change in human relations dominated his entire adult life. It culminated in a wealth of publications, all of them in their own right issuing compelling challenges to what in his view amounted to a self-defeating anachronism, a leftover of our geocentric past – the myth of the isolated ego.

For a variety of reasons, ranging from his unconventional style of writing to his background as a German Jew, recognition for his achievements came late, not until well after his formal retirement from the University of Leicester in 1962 and subsequent brief period as chair of sociology at the University of Ghana (1962–64). And even then, interest in his work was initially largely confined to a small group of admirers and loyal supporters (mostly in Germany and the Netherlands). Elias did not give up, but the lack of wider acknowledgment over all those years was especially difficult for him. It touched the core of his work. Although he firmly believed in his project, he was also convinced that "the meaning of everything a person does lies in what he or she means to others," as he put it in *The Loneliness of the Dying* (1985b, 33). Interdependence was crucial to both Elias the person and Elias the human scientist. Life without recognition, he argued in his study of Mozart, is "the kind of meaninglessness that someone can die of" (1993, 6).

Although it perhaps never reached the point that he himself had wished for and came rather late in his long life, Elias, unlike Mozart, lived to see his popularity soar. He was almost eighty years of age when the years of wider recognition were about to begin. In 1976 *The Civilizing Process* was republished (the first edition had appeared in 1939). The paperback edition of his magnum opus turned into a best-seller in Germany, the country he had fled shortly after the Nazis came to power. A host of books, many lectures and honours, interviews, and an increasing number of publications with Elias and his work as their subject followed. He had finally arrived.

When Norbert Elias died on 1 August 1990 in Amsterdam, he was well known throughout central Europe. His books have since been translated into many languages, and his exceptional contributions to our knowledge of human interdependencies have earned him – the long-time outsider – the distinction of belonging to the great sociologists of the twentieth century. Among his publications available in English are the following books: *The Court Society* (1983), *The Loneliness of the Dying* (1985b), *Quest for Excitement: Sport and Leisure in the Civilizing Process* (Elias and Dunning 1986), *Involvement and Detachment* (1987b), *The Society of Individuals* (1991a), *The Symbol Theory* (1991b), *Time: An Essay* (1992), *Mozart: Portrait of a Genius* (1993), *Reflections on a Life* (1994a), *The Established and the Outsiders* (Elias and Scotson 1995), and *The Germans: Power Struggles and the Development of Habitus in the Nineteenth and Twentieth Centuries* (1996a). In addition, since 1998 there are two Elias readers available: *The Norbert Elias Reader: A Biographical Selection* (1998a) and *Norbert Elias: On Civilization, Power, and Knowledge: Selected Writings* (1998b).

Recently, a new edition of Elias's masterpiece, *The Civilizing Process*, was published (2000). The editors, Eric Dunning, Johan Goudsblom, and Stephen Mennell, revised the original English version and restructured the book. Book-length English-language publications devoted to Elias and his process (figurational) sociology include the standard introductions by Stephen Mennell (1989 and 1992b) and Robert Krieken's critical guide, written for the Routledge Key Sociologists series (1998). Mennell's and Krieken's books complement an already relatively well established, largely central European body of literature on Elias (such as Baumgart and Eichener 1991; Blomert 1991; Bogner 1989; Fletcher 1997; Gleichmann 1984; Goudsblom 1994; Hackeschmidt 1997; Korte 1988; Kuzmics 1989; M. Schröter 1997; and Wouters 1999). But the interest in him is not limited to Europe. It is ever widening and increasingly includes North America.

Norbert Elias and Human Interdependencies affirms Elias's by now entrenched European presence, but it also points to and participates in his discovery in North America, in both the sciences and the humanities. Yet important as this focus is, the book is not only about Elias. It is also about human interdependencies – interdependencies as they emerge from the individual contributions published here. The perspectives offered are correspondingly various and cover a wide range of subjects, from the World Wide Web to medieval poetry, nations and gender, cancer narratives and money, emotion management and the financial markets, and the American civilizing process and the repression of shame. As distinct as they are, they all bear witness to Elias's innovative achievements and his ability to inspire confidence in the mutual dependence of human beings.

The first part of this book centres on the three broad patterns of social change that have had a defining influence on figurational sociology: the civilizing, decivilizing, and informalizing processes. The aim of the first chapter is to introduce Norbert Elias and his theory of the civilizing process. Chapters 2 and 3 are devoted to the discussion of decivilizing and informalizing processes.

The first chapter, written by Hermann Korte, traces Norbert Elias's life from Breslau (today, Wrocław), Elias's hometown, to Heidelberg and Frankfurt and eventually to his exile years in England, where he stayed from 1935 until the early 1960s. According to Korte, it was the relative powerlessness of the individual in society that captured Elias's imagination early on. *The Civilizing Process*, he argues, bears witness to this and also contains the main theses that were to inform his subsequent publications; they cover a wide range of topics in areas such as sports, literature, art, knowledge, and the sciences. As a central concern of Elias's best-known book, *The Civilizing Process,* Korte identifies the long-term transformations of external constraints (*Fremdzwänge*) into self-constraints (*Selbstzwänge*). It is, according to Elias, a blind but structured process involving the unplanned consequences of planned actions. In other words, figurations – the continuously shifting and competing networks of human interdependencies – determine the civilizing process. As an ultimately unintended but human-made process, it must be, according to Elias, open-ended. Therein, Korte concludes, lies the appeal of Elias's theory. It is meant neither to celebrate nor to condemn the history of the European West. Rather than rendering us helpless, however, his theory simply and much more importantly "leaves us the hope of intervening, of making changes, in the course of history" (Korte).

While we are not defenselessly trapped, decivilizing pressures nevertheless loom large. They are, as Stephen Mennell reminds us in the next chapter, sometimes more, sometimes less hidden behind the scenes but always present. Civilizing and decivilizing processes represent, Mennell argues, two sides of the same coin. If we are indeed dealing with a "tension balance between conflicting pressures" (Mennell), how are we to know, he asks, whether civilizing or decivilizing tendencies dominate? And does not their coexistence with civilizing processes disprove Elias's theory? In his effort to unravel the various strands of this complicated issue, Mennell looks at short-term decivilizing processes such the Holocaust in Nazi Germany and the perceived increase in violent crimes in the Western world today, as well as the "permissive society" – the trend towards more variety and leniency, more "psychologizing" than "moralizing" behaviour. He also addresses the issue of *long-term* decivilizing processes. A long-term perspective would allow for a more meaningful comparison since Elias's theory of the civilizing process involves changes in habitus and state formation spanning several centuries. Mennell concedes that more research into decivilizing processes is needed. Yet present evidence, he concludes, does not lead to a "refutation of Elias's theory." On the contrary, at least in the often-cited instance of the "permissive society," it has been suggested that more informal behaviour requires a higher degree of habitual self-control and not less. "Informalization" thus supports, rather than undermines, the long-term patterned change suggested by Elias's pioneering work. Cas Wouters, in the next chapter, provides a more detailed analysis of the "informalizing" process.

Investigating twentieth-century American, Dutch, English, and German etiquette books, Wouters advances the hypothesis that "major directional trends in dominant codes and ideals of behaviour and feeling ... are closely connected with trends in power relationships and emotion management." All four countries share three interconnected patterns of change, he suggests. They are the lessening of inequalities, increasing interdependence, and rising demands for self-regulation and emotion management. Wouters's aim is to specify this general trend with respect to class and gender. He notes that across classes both social and psychic distance is diminishing. As a result, he argues, there is an "increasing social constraint towards 'unconstrained self-restraint.'" Part 2 of this chapter focuses on the social and psychic distance between the sexes. Here too, according to Wouters, mutually expected self-control is on the rise. More informal behaviour and increased integration has, on balance, not led to diminished self-control. Instead, the pressure to be more flexible and accommodating is growing. Can the same be said for human relations elsewhere, such as in the fast-growing digital world of cyberspace?

In the next chapter, Jorge Arditi examines the growing literature on "netiquette," the Internet equivalent of socially desirable behaviour. What social structures are emerging, and can they be placed in Elias's theory of the civilizing process? The hiding-behind-the-scenes of the body that Elias describes in *The Civilizing Process* seems to have reached an absolute point in cyberspace. While the body has not disappeared, it is not present either. It is completely detached. This phenomenon, Arditi suggests, goes hand in hand with a need to remind users of the Internet that they are still dealing with human beings. Human relations in cyberspace are different from relations in material space, but they are still real, not virtual. Far from the widespread impression of chaos in cyberspace, Arditi argues, an "order of things" particular to the Internet is emerging: with the detachment of the body, both aggression *and* intimacy levels are rising. Does this mean that the civilizing process has gone into reverse? Are we dealing with a decivilizing process? Self-control is, after all, weakening. Arditi contends that these developments cannot be properly understood either as a simple continuation of the civilizing process or as decivilization. In the case of human relations in cyberspace, he suggests, it thus "would seem more accurate to speak of new processes of figuration and reconfiguration."

Thomas Scheff, in his chapter "Unpacking the Civilizing Process: Interdependence and Shame," underscores the importance of "interdependence" as a core concept in Elias's work. According to Scheff, Elias uses the technical conception of the term in contrast to "independence" and "dependence" and closely relates it to his arguments concerning foresight, psychologization, and mutual identification. His notion of interdependence thus allows for a "clearly articulated dissection of relationships within and between groups" (Scheff) and may prove useful in arriving at a better understanding of "solidarity" and "alienation." This is why Scheff argues for a shift in emphasis from the value-laden term "civilizing process" to the more neutral and, in Scheff's view, productive "interdependence." Such a change, he insists, would be of great benefit, especially to Westerners, since it is they who, in his opinion, suffer most from a suppression of interdependence. Scheff credits Elias not only with bringing interdependence out into the open but also with drawing our attention to "shame"; it too has been driven underground. "Unlike Freud or anyone else, Elias documents *step by step* the sequence of events that led to the repression of emotions in modern civilization" (Scheff).

Norbert Elias's interest in long-term and unintended but structured consequences of planned actions as they emerge from figurations, the changing patterns of human relations, extends from sports to the sociology of knowledge, including, in complicated and critical ways, imaginative literature. His relatively frequent use of literary texts in his scholarly publications bears witness to the importance that he assigned to imaginative literature (Salumets 1999). The spectrum of literary texts used by Elias in one way or another ranges from relatively obscure to very well known texts and includes prose, poetry, and references to drama and even science fiction. In his *The Civilizing Process*, an entire section is entitled "Literary Examples of the Relationship of the German Middle-Class Intelligentsia to the Court" (1994b, 18–24) and an interpretation of the *Minnesang* in relation to the habitus and social position of medieval knights (323–34). In *The Loneliness of the Dying* he quotes and discusses a poem by the Silesian baroque poet Hofmann von Hofmannswaldau (1985b, 19–23). The notes to part 1 of *The Society of Individuals* contain quotations from poems by Rilke and Goethe (1991a, 64–6). A short case study published in the German edition of his *The Established and Outsiders* (Elias and Scotson 1990, 295–305) is based almost exclusively on his reading of Harper Lee's novel *To Kill a Mockingbird*. Edgar Allan Poe's story "A Descent into the Maelstrom" is used in Elias's discussion of the double bind in his *Involvement and Detachment* (1987b, 75–184, in particular 79–80). In his *The Germans* he incorporates passages from two little-known novels by Walter Bloem entitled *Der krasse Fuchs* (The crass fox; 1996a, 109–11) and *Volk wider Volk* (Nation against nation; 181–2). There are many more examples, including Elias's use of texts by the controversial expressionist-realist writer Ernst Jünger and of French literature in *The Court Society* (1983). What is more, throughout most of his life, Elias himself wrote poetry. In 1987, on the occasion of his ninetieth birthday, a collection of his poems was published in Germany (1987d). It contains forty poems – most of them in German, some in English – ten so-called *Nachdichtungen* (adaptations and/or translations), and a ballad ("Die Ballade vom armen Jakob") about the fate of outsiders as Elias saw it. This ballad about "poor Jacob" the Jew, which Elias wrote in an internment camp on the Isle of Man in 1941, has been published separately (1996b).

It is this kind of crossing and joining of the boundaries between fiction and figurations, so characteristic of Elias and his work, that informs the following four chapters. Helmut Kuzmics is primarily concerned with the relationship between sociology and literature as it emerges from Elias's work. He situates his discussion of Elias's use of literary texts within a broad context. It ranges from the measurement-oriented scientific approach and traditional literary criticism and hermeneutics to deconstruction. With Elias, Kuzmics suggests, it is possible to give fiction its due weight without relegating it to mere source material for sociological research or reducing it to an expression of arbitrariness. Instead, literary texts can co-determine sociological theory and provide access to otherwise hidden emotional structures. A more dynamic relational and correspondingly less-static and reductionist pattern of human interdependencies can thus become visible. This, Kuzmics argues, is the primary value that Elias the human scientist assigned to literature. Using literature in this way is part of Elias's consistent criticism of a particular self-image that has dominated Western thought for centuries: the isolated ego, the "we-less I," or *homo clausus*, as Elias often referred to it.

Thomas Kemple, in his account of the sociogenesis of the modern self, turns to a classic literary treatment and prefiguration of the *homo clausus* image: Homunculus, the disembodied individual in Goethe's *Faust*. He symbolizes "the peculiarly Western invention of the pure knowing self, abstracted from time and space" (Kemple). Kemple discusses differences and similarities in the sociological projects of Max Weber and Elias. He focuses on Weber's concern with *Faust* and Elias's critique of the pressures to locate the individual without reference to other human beings. Elias, Kemple argues, "provides us with both a vivid picture of our own self-imposed technique of confinement and an image for their transformation." Here Kemple calls attention to Elias's conception of *homines aperti*. It gives expression to the understanding that human beings are "open," rather than "closed," personalities always co-determining one another both in co-operation and in conflict.

That the stakes are indeed high in making these distinctions, as Kemple concludes, becomes particularly evident in dealing with a life-threatening illness, the subject of the next chapter. Ulrich Teucher's "Writing in the Face of Death: Norbert Elias and Autobiographies of Cancer" is an exploration of Elias's *The Loneliness of the Dying* and the role of literature in societies where people largely live in denial of illness and death – where the dying are, in Elias's sense of the term, the "outsiders" in a community of "established," the living. Literature, Teucher concludes from his research of English and German cancer narratives, can assist us in decreasing the power differentials that exist between the living and the dying in very specific ways: It helps us to break the code of silence, the air of embarrassment that still surrounds cancer, and we learn to communicate in more productive ways *about* death and *in the face* of death. As a result, we are not as often at a loss for words; we can become more involved, show and express our feelings more openly when we are needed most. Because of autobiographies of cancer, life with the disease can become a less isolating experience, both for the living and for the dying.

The potential significance of writing as a social event is at issue in the next chapter as well, but Stephen Guy-Bray is concerned with tension balances of a different kind. His focus is on gender relations and the ways in which human drives become subject to the civilizing process. In Guy-Bray's reading of Marie de France's lay *Le Chaitivel* (written in approximately 1180), writing and text are seen as part of the conflict between the sexes. When a member of the knightly class is unable to control a woman's sexuality, Guy-Bray argues, he attempts to control her writing, her textuality. Yet, though the medieval knights enjoy the monopoly on violence and the balance of power is clearly tilted in their favour, it is in this instance a female author who has the "monopoly on how events are perceived and remembered" (Guy-Bray). Poetry thus turns into one of those rare opportunities at "the great feudal courts of the twelfth century," as Elias put it in his *The Civilizing Process*, "to overcome male dominance and attain equal status with men" (1994b, 326).

Despite Elias's interest in the subject, gender perception and performance does not figure prominently in his work. As a matter of fact, gender remained a largely static term for him. Nevertheless, his discussion of power balances, Annette Treibel suggests in the next chapter, is well suited to gender studies. Only on the surface, she says, is there a clear general trend towards gender equality in Western societies. Scrutiny of less-visible domains reveals a much more traditional male habitus. To put it differently, "figurational ideals" of both men and women have changed, "but the figurational patterns themselves have not changed very much" (Treibel). How does Elias's concept of "power balances" and power as an attribute of human relations (rather than as an object, a commodity) help to explain this contradiction? Treibel asks. First and foremost, it draws attention to the interdependence of men and women. It brings into view that male resistance to changes in the power balance between men and women is itself a sign of the gains that women have made. It draws attention to the fact that conflicts are inevitable in this process and that, in addition to covert male resistance to female emancipation, women often help to perpetuate their own inequality.

The concluding chapters are concerned with larger survival units and the closely related concepts of "nation" and "state," the powerful force of money in large-scale integration processes, and the American civilizing process. The chapter entitled "Symbol and Integration Process: Two Meanings of the Concept 'Nation,'" written by Godfried van Benthem van den Bergh, aims at the changing meaning of the concept of "nation" in western Europe. The author traces the transformation of dynasties into nation-states and is able to identify eight different kinds of nationalisms. They do not, however, solve the vexing problem of defining nations. Instead of thinking about nations in static, unchanging terms, the author proposes to address the conceptual confusion by seeing nations either as symbols supported by myths or as processes of integration.

Using Elias's observations on the change in western Europe from a warrior to a courtier society as point of departure, Reinhard Blomert describes developments in the banking business of the twentieth century as another civilizing process. In his investigation of the increasing interdependence of national currencies, he shows how and why the desire for currency autonomy gave way to the acceptance of increasingly global and more restrained standards of behaviour in the financial markets of industrial countries.

The final chapter, written by Stephen Mennell, concerns the American civilizing process. Provoked by the question of why is there no "Eliasism" in the United States, Mennell takes the main sections of *The Civilizing Process* as points of departure and relates them to aspects of American history. He discusses, first, the notions of "civilization" and "culture" in American society from Thomas Jefferson onwards; then the history of American manners, paying particular attention to Peter Stearns's *American Cool* (1994); and finally, the connections between habitus- and state-formation processes in America, an aspect, Mennell argues, that to date has not received systematic scholarly attention. While Elias was primarily concerned with the western European courtly civilizing process, the relevant issues that he discusses are nevertheless, Mennell concludes, part and parcel of American consciousness. What is still missing, he suggests, is the story of the various human interdependencies as they inform the American civilizing process. It has yet to be told in the productive ways known to us through the work of Elias.

Nevertheless, the general awareness of interdependencies has undoubtedly grown; it has perhaps even become a commonplace that everything and everyone is connected. It is as if we are not caught anymore in the powerful essentialist drift of what is often referred to as Western analytical thought, the main subject of Elias's critique. Yet as much as we appear to *know* that the isolated ego is a myth, our ability to recognize interdependencies and, more important, to act accordingly is necessarily limited. Despite the prevailing rhetoric that suggests otherwise, the challenge thus remains: we need to find out more about the complex and changing ways in which we are connected.

The more we engage in this task and are prepared to deal with the consequences – this is the seemingly paradoxical promise – the less dependent we become.

Few can match Norbert Elias's contributions to this compelling project. The authors of this book acknowledge this fact and pay tribute to his achievements. At the same time, they carry on with his explorations of human interdependencies, extend them into other areas, and issue their own wide-ranging and penetrating challenges to the myth of the isolated ego. In the process, they too change what we know about our mutual dependence.

1 Perspectives on a Long Life: Norbert Elias and the Process of Civilization

HERMANN KORTE

Norbert Elias was born in 1897, at the end of the nineteenth century, in Breslau, Silesia. He died in 1990, towards the end of the twentieth century, in Amsterdam. He spent a third of his life in London and Leicester in bitter exile. From 1962 to 1964 Elias taught at the University of Ghana in Accra. He made his first extended visit to Germany in 1965, teaching first as a visiting professor in Münster, Westphalia, and later at Konstanz and Aachen. Finally, he spent the years from 1978 to 1984 at the Centre for Interdisciplinary Research in Bielefeld.

The list of towns in which Norbert Elias lived for extended periods must also include Heidelberg and Frankfurt. Each of these places is linked to his biography in a very specific way. For each stay, one can describe a particular phase in the relationship between the histories of society, of his work, and of his personal life. However, none of these phases can be understood without those that preceded it. The development of individual human beings is just as unplanned as that of the societies they form with other human beings. But the direction that this development has taken and the structure it has had can be recomposed – both for individuals and for societies – by comparing their different phases.

As a sociologist, I concentrate as a rule on the ever-changing mechanisms of social interweaving, the figurations that human beings form together. But a biography is generally concerned with only *one* person. As a consequence, the subject of a biography of Norbert Elias would be his person and its social context, or quite generally the relationships between one individual and society. I am concerned here primarily with three periods of his life: his youth and student years in Breslau, his time in Heidelberg and Frankfurt, and his exile in England.

YOUTH AND STUDIES IN BRESLAU

The image that appears to us before the First World War is one of a carefree and protected childhood and youth. Norbert Elias did not set foot in a school until he was nine. Until then the only child of Hermann and Sophie Elias, née Galevski, had been brought up and taught by governesses and a private tutor. He attended the Städtische Johannes-Gymnasium from the first to the sixth forms. This was the school for the sons of the better society of Jewish Breslau. The third largest Jewish community in Germany, after Berlin and Frankfurt, lived in this city. A number of Jewish city councillors in the Liberal party looked after the affairs of the school, and this was the reason that Jewish teachers and a rabbi were allowed to teach there.

The Jewish community kept to itself. At the school, which was a renowned humanistic establishment, conflicts with German pupils hardly arose, and anti-Semitic incidents were largely absent. Any occasional incidents that took place were not regarded seriously, being dismissed as the "misdemeanor of uneducated hooligans," as Elias put it in *Reflections on a Life* (1994a, 126). However, when little Norbert was taken out for walks by his nanny, "street urchins" had called "Jewboy, Jewboy" after him (1994a, 12). At age fifteen or sixteen, when the pupils' career plans were being discussed in class, he said that he wanted to be a university professor. One of his classmates objected, "*That* career was cut off for you at birth" (1994a, 12). Everyone laughed, teachers and pupils alike. But such experiences did nothing to shake Elias's self-confidence. If the Jews of Breslau occasionally found themselves in the position of outsiders, this obstacle was perceived through the veil of "the thoroughly secure life we [the Jews] led physically, economically and culturally" (1994a, 126). They were prosperous, and they felt "[c]ompletely" safe (1994a, 13).

But then the First World War broke out. Elias and his classmates took the *Abitur* on 8 June 1915. He quickly enrolled as a student of philosophy and German language and literature at the University of Breslau. Then, like all his classmates, he volunteered for war service. Doing so was taken for granted. Elias had just turned eighteen when he became a soldier. He first trained as a telegraph operator in Breslau and then was deployed behind the lines on the Eastern Front. After about six months his unit was moved to the Western Front, where he fought at the battle of the Somme, with its enormous losses, until he was wounded.

In all the autobiographical statements by Elias that I know, he tells graphically and factually about the horrors of war, although about his own wounding he is unable to speak. In *Reflections on a Life* he relates the shock that he suffered: "I have a vivid recollection of going to the front, of dead horses and a few dead bodies and that underground shelter ... Then there is some feeling of a big shock, but I cannot recollect. I cannot even remember how I got back" (1994a, 27). When he was asked, "Do you remember losing any comrades in your group?" he answered, "No, not losing them. I mean, one saw ... For that, I think I should have to go into analysis" (1994a, 26). Elias could not remember the end of the war. Nor did he know how he got back to Breslau: "I have no idea how I got there. First seeing the city and meeting my parents again – all that has gone" (1994a, 27).

The veil through which he had experienced the world up to then had been torn aside. The young man who had been cared for and protected until then had become a different person: "Then the war changed everything. When I came back, it was no longer my world ... For I had also changed myself" (1994a:15). However, it was not violence and death that left the most lasting impression on Elias but, as he noted explicitly in his *Reflections on a Life*, "the relative powerlessness of the individual in the social structure" (101). And he experienced anti-Semitism directly and brutally. When he found a fellow soldier lying in his bed, which happened to be the best one, he tried to throw him out. "Now he, too, lost his temper, and in this situation – that was very characteristic – he started insulting me, 'Jewboy! Clear off, Jewish pig!'" (1994a, 23)

In the chapter "Notes on the Jews as Part of an Established-Outsider Relationship" in his *Reflections on a Life*, Elias writes: "What I have to say here about the Jews is really part of my account of my apprenticeship, of what learning taught me. It is a singular experience to belong to a stigmatized minority while at the same time being wholly embedded in the cultural flow and the political and social fate of the stigmatizing majority" (1994a, 121). And he goes on, "I cannot say that the problems of identity arising from belonging simultaneously to a German and a Jewish tradition have ever worried me unduly" (1994a, 121). I regard this last comment as a later rationalization, for on his return from the war in November 1917, he immediately took up a post as a leader of the Zionist Blau-Weiss hiking association. The protected only child, relatively untouched by political events, opened himself to an obligation arising from his membership in a minority group.

An interpretation of Elias that we hear or read frequently is that his experience of violence and death in the First World War and the murderous terror under National Socialism preoccupied him throughout his life and had a determining influence on his scholarly work. I have always doubted such an unambiguous connection. It may be that his interest in topical political questions increased in later years, but in 1918 it was very different. In the interview already mentioned, Elias had no recollection of political events such as the murders of Rathenau and Erzberger. He did not know how he had reacted at the time. "It is very strange ... my own feeling of that time is a blank" (1994a, 28). Nor did he join a political party or align himself with the pacifist movement. His truly pivotal experience of the war was that of the relative powerlessness of the individual in society. The question that concerned him after that time was "Why am I forced to live in a certain way, distinguished from my contemporaries and different from my parents' generation and from my forefathers?" That became his lifelong theme, which he was to work on for the next seventy years.

In 1917 Elias first began studying medicine to please his father. His attachment to a battalion of convalescents allowed him to do so. But in 1919, soon after the *Physikum* (the intermediate preclinical examination), he switched from medicine to philosophy. In the summer semester that year he studied in Heidelberg, partly so that he could attend lectures by Karl Jaspers, and in 1920 he went to Freiburg, where he took part in Edmund Husserl's seminar on Goethe. He began writing a philosophical dissertation on the subject "Idea and Individual: A Critical Study of the Concept of History" under the neo-Kantian Richard Hönigswald. This study drew on his war experiences and at the same time inaugurated the sociological approach specific to Elias. In *Reflections on a Life* he himself draws the connection between the experiences of war and inflation and the relative powerlessness of the individual within the social structure. The war experiences must have been in the foreground at that time, as his experiences of the inflationary period only began, according to his own reports, when the dissertation had already been written.

It was the place of the individual in history that interested Elias. He had already begun to question the figure of the "isolated human being," the traditional subject of knowledge. He himself saw this doubt in the context of "my experience of social life itself, for example, in the war; book-learning was certainly not central to it" (1994a, 100). His rejection of the neo-Kantian position was therefore predictable, almost a priori. How one lives as an individual in society cannot be prescribed in a universally binding way if the individual is to have any chance of at least partially escaping social compulsions. "I could no longer ignore the fact that all that Kant regarded as timeless and as given prior to all experience, whether it be the idea of causal connections or of time or of natural and moral laws, together with the words that went with them, had to be learned from other people" (1994a, 91).

This realization led to Elias's well-known quarrel with Hönigswald, but that was of rather marginal importance. What is more significant is that in the dissertation, he had already begun to discuss the thesis of a sequential order "within which a later event arises from a specific sequence of earlier events" (1994a, 152). And for him this meant posing the somewhat involved question, How does it come about that I and the group to which I belong are forced to behave in a certain way which is entirely distinguishable from the enforced behaviour of other people and groups?

The text of the dissertation of 1922 is couched in abstract, philosophical language. Nevertheless, we can already discern in it the themes to which Elias was later to devote his work as a sociologist. But these early indications of his scholarly orientation can be seen far more clearly in a twelve-page contribution that he published in mid-1921 in the journal of the Jewish hikers' association, Blau-Weiss. The article, entitled "Vom Sehen in der Natur" (How we look at nature) is, curiously, one of the first texts documenting Norbert Elias's academic development. Many of the theses that are later presented in a more developed way are formulated here for the first time.

This is especially clear when he touches on problems of historical development. The divergence from the neo-Kantian position of Hönigswald is also apparent. In inquiring factually into the historicity of our way of looking at nature, Elias sets himself apart from philosophical a priori thinking. His observation that the Greeks had a different understanding of nature and that a structured evolution of such understanding can be demonstrated from the Renaissance up to the present is diametrically opposed to the ahistorical thinking of his philosophy teacher.

In pointing to the long-term developments of certain patterns of perception, behaviour, and evaluation, Elias had also discovered the theme of his life's work. Of course, the approach that he formulated here for the first time was still a fragmentary one, but the foundations for later questions, including those about the development of consciousness, had already been laid. His basic attitude, which was to lead him away from both abstract metaphysics and a relativistic, personifying historiography, can already be recognized. In the article he writes: "The danger with a historical investigation is always the following: either the investigator interprets the earlier world in terms of himself and his own world or he goes to the opposite extreme, prematurely disconnecting himself from it as soon as he encounters anything alien or unfamiliar, and declaring that the way to any understanding is blocked. Yet careful, reflective work might be able to bring much fruitful information to light from precisely such unfamiliar material" (1921, 136).

We shall come across this way of approaching history again and again: at the annual meeting of the German Sociological Association in Zürich in 1928, in the *Habilitationsschrift* (the thesis qualifying him as a university lecturer) of 1933, and in his central work, *The Civilizing Process*. In his first essay in 1921, Elias still lacked knowledge and technical means. In the elaboration of his theory of civilization he acquired the historical, sociological, and psychological knowledge and instruments that enabled him to demonstrate the reasons for longer-term changes and for more limited and abrupt advances of historical development. Even at that early stage, he had a clear idea of the necessary preconditions for his approach: "Only someone who is aware of developments in neighbouring disciplines will be able to find more correct answers to questions on his own – someone who 'in careful work, familiarizes himself with the foundations and the advancing results of scholarship, that is, with the actual development of knowledge'" (Korte 1997, 85).[1]

The article of 1921 ends with a Greek quotation that can be translated as "Let us pass each other the torches" (Korte 1997, 85). In my view, this motto can be seen as the guiding principle of all of Norbert Elias's scholarly work. It is given its clearest expression fifty-six years later, in a speech delivered in the Frankfurt Paulskirche, when he accepted the Adorno Prize: "Work in the human sciences, as in other sciences, is a torch race: we take the torch from the preceding generation, carry it some distance further, and pass it to the next generation, so that they can go beyond us. The work of the preceding generation is not abolished thereby – it is the precondition for the ability of later generations to surpass it" (1977, 67).

In this way the young Elias gathered his experiences: the Jewish parental home, the humanistic education, the necessity of hard intellectual work and self-disciple. He also learned that one must endure conflict with someone more powerful if the matter at hand demands it, and that intellectual honesty can lead to success.

But his years of apprenticeship were not yet completed. After the examination for his doctorate in 1922, Elias could no longer count on the financial support of his parents. Inflation during the economic crisis had eaten up the interest that his father received from his savings. So the son was forced to earn his own living. Through connections, he received a position in a firm making small iron parts (such as stove flaps and valves). The director, a Herr Mehrländer, was looking for a junior manager with academic qualifications, preferably a doctorate. Elias was such a man.

He began his work by spending a short time in all the departments of this medium-sized firm, which, as he recalled, employed about eight hundred workers. He then became head of the export department. In this capacity he went on extended journeys to Scandinavia, among other places, to recruit representatives and agents for the firm. His work for the factory was a very important experience for Elias, since it helped him to breach the wall of the academic ivory tower, which had already been seriously weakened by his military service and his disputes with his philosophy teacher. His experience of the horrors of war was joined now, as he saw it later, by that of the wretchedness of the working class during the economic crisis of 1922–23.

Because of his work in industry, the position of university teacher, which Elias had been aiming for since his early school days, had receded far into the distance. He had not yet given up his life's goal, a professorship – how could he? – since he saw it as his true vocation. He now had his first experience of waiting, but he did not give up hope. During his long journeys he trained his mind by translating Greek anecdotes and jokes into German and then summarizing them. He sent a small selection of these to the *Berliner Illustrierte*, which, to his great surprise, printed five of the comical stories in July 1924 and even sent him a small fee. That was the signal for the man of letters to move on. Elias resigned his post in the iron-goods factory, where the charm of novelty had worn off in any case, and set off for Heidelberg in the naive belief that he would be able to earn money by writing and in the hope of a university career.

HEIDELBERG

In Heidelberg Elias devoted himself finally to sociology, which was dominated at that university by two people, the cultural sociologist Alfred Weber and the young lecturer Karl Mannheim. Elias came into contact with both. He soon made friends with Mannheim, who was about his own age and for whom he acted as a kind of assistant and go-between with the students. Elias, some years older than the students and already holding a doctorate, soon found himself at the centre of a group of students, including such individuals as Hans Gerth, Richard Löwenthal, Heinrich Taut, Svend Riemer, and Suse and Georg Schwarzenberger. On the other hand, the incumbent professor was Alfred Weber, whose support Elias needed for his *Habilitation*. So it came about that he attended the advanced seminars held by both Alfred Weber and Karl Mannheim.

In sociological terms, there was a clear antithesis between the idealistic position of Weber and the materialist stance of Mannheim. In day-to-day life in Heidelberg none of this came to the surface. Weber's institutional position was far too lofty, and it was not in the solid Heidelberg style to carry on subliminal feuds. The differences only came into the open at the sixth annual meeting of the German Sociological Association, held in Zürich in 1928. At the conference, Mannheim, in his lecture entitled "The Meaning of Competition in the Intellectual

Sphere," had placed the sociology of knowledge and the critique of ideology crucial to his own work at the centre of debate. He had added further incendiary material by directly attacking Weber's liberalism. In the course of this debate, following the privy councillors and doctors as the hierarchy of the time required, Norbert Elias voiced his own opinion.

On the one hand, he opposed Weber's approach, which was both individualistic and idealistic. But at the same time he made it clear that Mannheim's relativistic standpoint, with its critique of ideology, also stood in need of revision, because of the one-sided stress that it placed on the sphere of knowledge and the importance it gave to the single creative individual. Elias said: "Anyone who places the 'creative human being' at the centre of his discussion still has really the feeling of existing alone, of forming, in a sense, a beginning and an end. But someone who places the historical movement of human societies at the centre, must know that he himself is neither a beginning nor an end, but, if I may put it that way, a link in the chain. And it is clear that this awareness confers on its bearer a very different importance than the former" (1929, 111). Although this verbal contribution lacks a certain precision, it does signal a sociological program to which Elias remained committed, and on which he was to work for long years under very difficult conditions.

In 1928 he could look to the future with confidence and hope that despite the handicap of his Jewish origin, he would one day receive a professorship at a German university. He had shown, after all, that he could hold his own in debate with well-known and influential figures. He had delivered his first piece of apprenticeship work scarcely four years after taking up sociology as both academic discipline and career path. But the path to a professorship was still a long one, as he was fourth or fifth on Alfred Weber's list of future *Habilitation* candidates, and this would have meant a wait of at least ten years.

But then about a year after the Zürich conference, Mannheim was appointed to the chair of sociology at Frankfurt. He offered to take Elias with him as his assistant. Elias, to whom nothing mattered more than his *Habilitation,* agreed once Mannheim had promised to let him enter for this qualification after three years as an *Assistent* (a position corresponding roughly to that of assistant lecturer). Seeing this as a way of shortening the path to academic qualification, he followed Mannheim to Frankfurt.

FRANKFURT

In the spring of 1930 Elias, full of hope and energy, took up his work in the sociology department at Frankfurt, headed by Karl Mannheim.

The department was on the ground floor of the Institut für Sozialfor-schung, the director of which was Max Horkheimer. This proximity did not mean that the two directors co-operated with regard to subject matter. Mannheim thought Horkheimer too far to the left, while Horkheimer considered Mannheim too far to the right. All the same, there was a good deal of collaboration over the daily business of teaching which was carried out or mediated by the two assistants, Leo Löwenthal and Norbert Elias.

There are a number of reports on Elias's work as an *Assistent*. In Heidelberg he had already acted as a screen between the students and Mannheim, to the benefit of both, for Mannheim not only wanted to be left in peace but was generally regarded as difficult in his dealings with his juniors. In a revealing passage in her autobiography, Margarete Freudenthal writes: "Professor Mannheim had brought an assistant with him from Heidelberg, who had exactly what Mannheim lacked. Dr Elias was thorough, methodical, and full of unselfish willingness to help us all. If we had not understood something in a lecture, he explained it to us. If we got stuck in our essays, he took an interest in our problems as if they were his own. We all assumed that he would be made Mannheim's *Privatdozent*" (Sallis-Freudenthal 1977, 109).

That was indeed the plan. Elias soon started work on his *Habilita-tion* treatise, which was eventually to be published in enlarged form as *Die Höfische Gesellschaft* (in English, *The Court Society*) by Luchterhand in 1969, more than thirty-five years later. In this book Elias describes and explains the processes that turned the court society into the elite formation of the French absolutist state.

The slow transformation of a warrior and landowning nobility founded primarily on a barter economy into an aristocracy based primarily on a money economy as the leading stratum had not happened in a planned way, but had emerged from the ambivalent power relationships between the king and the nobility. The nobility needed the king to maintain its privileges and a lifestyle in keeping with its rank, while the king needed the nobility as an indispensable weight to balance tensions between the classes over which he ruled. Concepts such as feudal nobility and aristocracy thus take on an empirico-theoretical meaning; that is to say, their relationships to each other and the structural changes of society as a whole are more clearly revealed, allowing a better understanding of the professional-bourgeois, urban, industrial society that followed this last non-bourgeois figuration.

A further part of the sociological content of this theory is the observation that not only do the forms of organization change but also those involved in them, the people woven together in the long-term process. Although the behavioural changes of people are not yet at the centre of Elias's study, this psychogenic aspect of the developmental process of human society is already present. He shows how the behaviour, speech, lives, and taste of the people involved in the society changed, and how all this finally turned into the etiquette that members of the court had to follow, though they sometimes found it burdensome.

In tracing the immanent structure of a past epoch, Elias was distancing himself somewhat from the political controversies of his day. When he contrasted professional bourgeois society to the cultural makeup of court society, he wanted also to give access to a better understanding of currently existing cultures and civilizing forms of communal life. This is an important difference from some publications of his contemporaries, such as Herbert Marcuse, who also dealt with problems of culture and society, but located the discussion centrally within capitalism.

Although Elias bypassed contemporary problems up to the 1980s, that does not mean that his empirico-theoretical models were not suited to explaining them or showing possible solutions. In his books *Humana Conditio* and *The Germans* he demonstrated that he was quite capable of applying his analyses of past epochs to current problems of world politics. And the community study he carried out at Leicester, which was published with the title *The Established and the Outsiders*, shows clearly that the ambivalent power relationships between various powerful groups and persons can be found not only at the court of Louis xiv but also between more established groups of residents and the less powerful.

The thesis was indeed finished three years after Elias's arrival in Frankfurt. The examination procedure was set in motion and took a positive course, and after the district president had approved the *venia legendi* (the entitlement to teach at a university), only the inaugural lecture remained to be held. But that was not to happen. After the National Socialists had assumed power early in 1933, they immediately began "cleansing" the universities of Jews and critical scholars. Elias waited for a few weeks, unsure what to do with himself and his so-hopefully-begun career. But finally he could no longer ignore the gravity of the situation, and in March 1933 he fled to France with a little luggage and a portable typewriter; in the autumn of 1935 he moved from there to England, where he remained until the early 1960s.

EXILE

Elias did not like the word "emigration," with good reason. "Exile" is a more fitting word, implying so much free choice and even sometimes an element of comfort. But now he, so very nearly a lecturer at the University of Frankfurt, sat in the reading room of the British Museum, that tradition-steeped chamber where Karl Marx had written *Das Kapital*, in the midst of a people whose language he did not speak and of whose customs he was ignorant, trying to escape the dejection of exile through scholarly work. The result was the two volumes of *The Civilizing Process: Sociogenetic and Psychogenetic Investigations*.

Elias sometimes described how he came to start writing the work. In his studies in the British Museum reading room he had come across books on etiquette more or less by chance. The various editions from different periods placed very differing demands on good behaviour. That fact interested him, and by finding out about rules of etiquette and demonstrable changes in manners, he gained access to the scientific problem of how to obtain a better understanding and explanation of the unplanned and long-term changes in the societies which people form when they come together.

It must be added, however, that the question about the reasons for changes in social conditions had been central to sociology since the beginnings of the discipline, and especially since Marx. Elias was therefore doing what his colleagues of the same age, as well as those older and younger than him, were also doing. He was trying to explain why certain social changes had taken place in Europe, whether they were something accidental or whether a structural principle could be discovered behind them. Since the start of his sociological work in Heidelberg, he had known of the questions around which everything in sociology revolved; he knew the materials and the sources.

Out of them Elias made something new. He got away from the paradigms and their schools and founded a position of his own. That he used empirical material such as table manners and rules of etiquette for this does not surprise his reader for long, for he was able to show the development of different precepts in such a way that the social reasons for the changes became visible.

Whereas etiquette manuals from the thirteenth to eighteenth century are central to the first volume, subtitled (in the German edition) *Changes of Behaviour in the Secular Upper Strata of the West*, in the second volume, *Changes in Society*, he concentrates on the process of state formation. Here the starting point is the question of how it was possible that, from the sixteenth century, absolutist states could come into being, some of them territorially very large, in which one person, usually a man, was able to acquire such great power that all his subjects without exception, including the aristocracy, had to obey him. The civilizing process was closely bound up with the process of the formation of states; its was a process lasting centuries, in which knights were turned into courtiers.

The first volume of the *Civilizing Process* was finished by 1936, and everything seemed to be taking a positive turn. A small scholarship from a refugees' organization enabled Elias to live, and his parents in far-off Breslau were still able to help, especially when it was a matter of getting the work, which was written in German, printed. They financed the preprinting of the first volume, which was produced in Germany by a minor publisher in Gräfenheinichen, a small town between Wittenberg and Bitterfeld. In a carefully targeted way, Elias sent copies to friends and possible reviewers. We know from many reports and also from correspondence found among Walter Benjamin's posthumous papers that through this marketing campaign Elias was preparing for the publication of the whole work, which was to appear in 1938 with the imprint of a Czech publishing house.

After the occupation of Czechoslovakia, however, this book by a Jewish author could no longer be published in Prague. The printing plates were secretly moved to Switzerland. There in 1939 *The Civilizing Process: Sociogenetic and Psychogenetic Investigations* was issued in two volumes by the Haus zum Falken, a publishing firm founded by another German in exile, Fritz Karger, in Basel. Elias again sent out carefully targeted copies. Thomas Mann, for example, received both volumes in the summer of 1939 while on holiday at the Dutch seaside resort of Nordwijk. He mentioned the book several times in his diary, noting on 8 August, now back in Zürich, "Elias's book has more merit than I thought. In particular, the pictures from the late Middle Ages and the waning era of chivalry" (1980, 440).

Elias had to wait a long time for his first academic appointment. In 1954, after years of bitter exile, he, at the age of fifty-seven, finally received a teaching post in the newly founded Department of Sociology at the University of Leicester, where he taught until 1962. Many of the current British professors of sociology studied under him at that time, Martin Albrow and Anthony Giddens among others. After a two-year stint as visiting professor at the University of Ghana, Elias returned to Germany in 1965, for the first time since his exile, as visiting professor at the University of Münster.

But even at that time *The Civilizing Process* was still largely unknown, except to the cognoscenti. Nor did a second edition in 1969 make any difference. The reason was not only the prohibitively high price of the hardcover edition but, above all, the very unreceptive climate at that time. In West Germany, social scientists – and not only social scientists – were preoccupied with assimilating Marx. Only when the explanatory power of analyses based on historical materialism turned out to be far less than had been believed in the first euphoria was *The Civilizing Process* able to move into their field of vision.

When the Suhrkamp Verlag published a low-cost paperback edition in 1976, more than 20,000 copies were sold within a few months. The sales success of the book has continued until today and has been extended by translation into more than twenty languages.

It was not quite so surprising, therefore, that the first Adorno Prize went to Norbert Elias. He received many honours after that, but the Adorno Prize had special importance for him. Intended as a tribute to his life's work, it spurred the eighty-year-old scholar to continue writing indefatigably and to teach in all parts of the world until shortly before his death on 1 August 1990.[2]

The range of his œuvre is very wide: from the sociology of knowledge to questions of world society, from analyses of the German catastrophe to the sociology of art, from investigations of society at the court of Louis xiv to urban studies. But he developed the central theses of all these works in the 1930s in *The Civilizing Process*. These ideas are dealt with in the following section.

THE CIVILIZING PROCESS

Anyone starting to read the book may be slightly surprised by the empirical material that Elias uses. He takes, above all, handbooks on manners as the empirical basis of his arguments. But from chapter to chapter he succeeds in clarifying for the reader the connection existing between changes in table manners and other rules of etiquette and individual and social changes. A particularly telling example is the question of why we now no longer eat with our fingers but with a fork.

The Example of the Fork

In the chapter "On the Use of the Fork at Table," Elias sensitively explores the question of why we now see it as uncivilized, ill-bred, and in some way barbaric to lift food to the mouth with one's fingers. On the surface, the reason is obvious: such behaviour is unhygienic and unappetizing. These are reasons, as Elias tells us, that belong in the category of feelings of embarrassment and shame. "The fork is nothing other than the embodiment of a specific standard of emotions and a specific level of revulsion. Behind the change in eating techniques between the Middle Ages and modern times appears the same process that emerged in the analysis of other incarnations of this kind: a change in the structure of drives and emotions" (1994b, 103).[3]

At the end of this short section we find – and this is a fundamental characteristic of Elias's mode of argumentation – two general comments. First, he points out that this civilizing of manners, first formed within a "narrow circle," was slowly extended to the whole of society, so that it was instilled from above to below. And secondly, he notes that this long-term civilizing process is today repeated in the socialization of children. But this happens in such a way that behaviour, in being forced into the same mould and in the same direction, appears to growing children almost as something "inward, implanted in them by nature" (105).

The standard brought into being as part of a process is now no longer understood as an external compulsion but becomes a self-restraint; this is a characteristic of the civilizing process. The upholding of this standard is taken over by individual control mechanisms that only occasionally need support from outside. That this process never comes to an end and includes long-term changes is self-evident, for any observation of its result does not refer to the end of a process but to a historical or a current phase of a long-term process.

Sociogenesis and Psychogenesis

At the end of the short section "On the Use of the Fork at Table" there is also a summary that reveals much about the aims and results of the work: "Thus the socio-historical process of centuries, in the course of which the standard of what is felt to be shameful and offensive is slowly raised, is re-enacted in abbreviated form in the life of the individual human being. If one wished to express recurrent processes of this kind in the form of laws, one could speak, as a parallel to the laws of biogenesis, of a fundamental law of sociogenesis and psychogenesis" (105).

The preceding quotation makes plain one of the basic rules by which Elias proceeds. Social rules and individual behaviour, both in their content and form and in their changes, can only be adequately studied and understood if a central place is given to the *long-term* nature of the "socio-historical process of centuries." However, it cannot be said that this is merely a basic rule of methodology, since that would wrongly restrict our insight into the necessity of investigating long-term social changes to a single aspect, though one that certainly exists. Elias's approach involves both the observation of an empirical situation and, at the same time, a theoretical statement about it.

That long-term developments can be summed up by general process models is a viewpoint by no means shared by all sociologists. The same is true of the implied observation that changes in society are normal and are not deviations from the social norm, as structural functionalism asserts. In the introduction to the second edition of 1969, Elias writes, not without irony and vexation, that sociology could have spared itself the wrong turning represented by North American systems theory, as espoused by structural functionalism, if it had listened earlier to his arguments of the 1930s.

He presents the change in human behaviour, feelings, and affects as *one* part of the civilizing process. Civilization is, first and foremost, the long-term transformation of external constraints into internal ones. It is a long-term process that does not run in a directional way according to a rational plan, but its structure and direction up to now can be investigated, described, and made use of in analyzing and diagnosing present phases and predicting future phases of social development.

The discovery of this civilizing process and the model of the long-term transformation of affects and drives would in themselves have been a pioneering achievement and must have been regarded as a major innovation in the history of sociology. For a time there was a tendency to be content with evaluating Elias's approach in these terms. The reason, probably, was that it seemed to give sociology access to psychoanalysis in a way which was certainly desired and which did not need to implicate the psyche of the individual scholar. But these attempts, usually by younger sociologists, did not prove long-lasting. Psychoanalysis cannot be absorbed as simply and neatly as that. It soon became clear also that, despite establishing this important model of the civilizing process, Elias's real achievement lay in having established the relation, in his theory of social processes, between long-term changes in the behaviour of individual people and long-term changes in the society that they form together.

Moreover, the term "relation" is not enough to designate adequately the situation that Elias described. To formulate it more exactly, one would need to talk of a mesh, a *figuration*, for the word "relation" misleads us into prematurely assuming one-sided relationships, hierarchical or temporal sequences of the order of "firstly/secondly" or "important/less important". The situation he addresses, however, is that changes in the standard of behaviour of individual people are interwoven with particular changes in the structure of human society – and conversely (to make sure that this formulation, too, is not misinterpreted). I should like to clarify this distinction by means of an example that makes up part of the second volume of *The Civilizing Process*: the emergence of stable central organs of government in the form of monopolies of violence and taxation.

Competition and Interdependence

The emergence of stable central organs of government involves a process of the socio-economic division of functions and of state formation that could also be characterized by the terms "competition" and "interdependence." The development of medieval feudal society into the European absolutist states is a segment of the long-term, structured, unplanned process of civilization. If Elias starts his analysis of state formation in the West with the central European feudal societies of the early Middle Ages, this should not be understood as if it were the starting point of the development, the zero point. This stage of development, too, had its forerunners, so that it is difficult to identify a beginning.

The early developmental phase, as compared to later phases of European development, is characterized by the dominance of the barter economy, by the low degree of the use of money, trade networks, and the division of labour, and by a low level of state formation and pacification. This relatively unpacified situation is in turn characterized by a low degree of monopolization of physical force and a correspondingly high level of bodily threat and permanent insecurity for the individual. In this historical situation the king or a comparable central ruler cannot dominate the territorial rulers because of his limited military and economic strength.

Anyone who is permanently threatened will not plan for the long term; for anyone who constantly has to fight, the civilizing of the aggressive urge can be dangerous or even fatal. At this stage of development, external compulsions determine the lives of people. But it is precisely the need to fight, the competition with others, that gives rise to a developmental dynamic. This dynamic, however, cannot be guided in a planned way by the individual participants, who are enmeshed in it, interwoven with it. The developmental dynamic inherent in the situation of competition can only achieve its long-term effect because the people concerned are interdependent. They cannot think or act without other people.

The long-term, unplanned social process of state formation in Europe leads first to a reduction in the number of competitors, then to a monopoly position of individual princes, and finally to the emergence of the absolutist state with the monopolization of physical violence by the institutions of the monarchy. The process of state formation is interwoven with the processes of the socio-economic division of functions, the transition from the barter to the money economy, the increased division of labour, trading interconnections, urbanization, and thus the social rise of the middle classes, the third estate. But it is also interwoven with the other strand of the civilizing process, the transformation of the psychological structures of the people concerned.

From now on, people have to *plan rather than fight*. The state's monopoly on violence permits a long-term view and thus long chains of actions. On the other hand, the reining-back of affects makes possible an enlarging of the scope for thought and action. The court people are the first to practise a behaviour based on long-term views, on calculation and self-control. They are, seen in this way, the first "modern" people of a new epoch.

SOCIOLOGICAL RESULTS

Long-term changes in the behaviour of individual people and the social figurations they form together – in other words, what Elias calls the civilizing process – take their driving force from competition between interdependent people, and groups of people, for *power*. He writes, "fear of loss or reduction of social prestige is one of the most powerful motive forces in the transformation of constraints through others into self-restraints" (473). It is therefore the interdependence of people that determines the civilizing process, imposing on it, as Elias notes, "an order *sui generis*." This is "an order more compelling and stronger than the will and reason of the individual people composing it. It is this order of interweaving human impulses and strivings, this social order, which determines the course of historical change; it underlies the civilizing process" (444). And therefore, we must add, it underlies all social changes.

A number of conclusions follow for sociology, the most important of which is that human beings and the social meshes they form together must stand at the centre of all research: "The 'circumstances' which change are not something which comes upon men from 'outside': they are the relationships between people themselves" (480).

Elias's importance for sociology, in the narrower sense, and for the social sciences, in the broader sense, lies in the fact that he points the way to concepts which are richer in content and more adequate to their objects. He thereby opens up the possibility of attaining a better understanding of human societies at a higher level of synthesis. In speaking no longer of monopoly capitalism and the mechanisms attributed to it but of the process of monopolization, he reaches a higher level of synthesis, which, on one hand, includes earlier explanations but, on the other, enlarges and transcends them.

Furthermore, Elias breaks with the traditional sociological mode of conceptualization, which is, at the same time, an expression of certain conceptions of the societies formed by people together. The outstanding feature of these differences is that he draws no conceptual distinction between individual and society. He breaks with the long-held idea that there is "society" and also "the self-sufficient individual." For his studies in *The Society of Individuals*, the distinction between the levels of structural functionalism and of action theory is no longer needed.

A text entitled *The Society of Individuals* had been announced by a Swedish journal as early as 1939, in an advertisement for the first edition of *The Civilizing Process*, but it did not appear at that time. Elias repeatedly reworked the text in the 1940s and 1950s, and in this period he developed a second section to the book. There is also a third part, dating from 1986. The subject of all three texts is a fundamental question of sociology: How far, and why, is the organizational level of society more than the sum of the individuals who form this society together? If the three texts are compared, it can be seen how, in a productive output spanning almost fifty years, the viewpoint in terms of long-term developments becomes more and more central. It might also be said that the *sociological theory of processes* moves further and further into the foreground. By transcending the classical conceptual antithesis between action and structure, Elias attains a higher level of synthesis.

CRITICAL DEBATES ABOUT ELIAS'S WORK

The more widely that Elias's works penetrated the social sciences and many adjacent disciplines, the more there arose critical debates concerning his theoretical projects and his empirical material. As always in such cases, one can distinguish between internal criticism of detail and rejection in principle. One of the most important internal objections is that Elias neglects the bourgeoisie and the phase of capitalism, the main fields of sociological interest since the mid-nineteenth century. With regard to this criticism, it should be pointed out that when he makes feudalism and the aristocracy the focus of his attention, his aim is primarily polemical.

In tracing the immanent structure of a past epoch, Elias distances himself somewhat from current political controversies. But in contrast to professional bourgeois society, the civilizing and cultural makeup of the court society serves to give access to a better understanding of currently existing cultures and civilizing forms of community. By renouncing a frontal approach to current developments, Elias avoids addressing the unprepared reader directly. This is a major difference from the practice of many of his contemporaries, such as Herbert Marcuse, who were also concerned with problems of culture and society, but whose central interest was in their application to capitalism. Although Elias avoided contemporary problems even in his eighties, this does not mean that his empirical and theoretical models were not suited to explaining them or offering possible solutions. With his books *Humana Conditio* and *The Germans* he has shown that it is possible to throw light on current problems of world politics through long-term analyses of past epochs. The study he wrote during his time at Leicester, published as *The Established and the Outsiders*, also shows clearly that the ambivalent tensions in the relationships between various powerful groups and people can be demonstrated to exist not only at the court of Louis xiv but also between any established groups of citizens and a less powerful group.

There is by now no area of sociology where the sociological theory of process is not being used to try to formulate and answer research problems. The theory has become, in the 1990s more than ever before, a fixed part of the repertory of European sociology. This development has partly to do with the fact that, following Elias's death, his theory can now be canonized without the danger of one's finding oneself publicly corrected by its author. More generally, however, it is the theory's emphatic focus on social processes that makes it attractive, especially to younger social scientists. The quotation "Civilization has not yet ended" is found on the title page of the first and second editions of *The Civilizing Process*. The same words make up the final sentence in the second volume. They mean that our future is open, both for individuals and for the societies they form together. Nothing is definitive, nothing fixed.

On this point Elias differs from predecessors and contemporaries. Georg Simmel lamented the "tragedy of culture," Max Weber saw himself and society as trapped in a "steel cage," and Max Horkheimer and Theodor W. Adorno found their words overtaken by the Holocaust. The theory of civilization leaves us with a chance, and therein, aside from the scholarly reasons, lies its appeal: it leaves us the hope of intervening, of making changes, in the course of history.

NOTES

I am grateful to Nina Baur for her help with this contribution. It was translated into English by Edmund Jephcott.

1 In the original text, this quotation is footnoted (44) and refers to "Vom Sehen in der Natur" (1921, 139–40).

2 For further biographical information, see Elias's *Reflections on a Life* (1994a).

3 All page references to Elias's *The Civilizing Process* are to the one-volume paperback edition from Blackwell (1994b).

2 The Other Side of the Coin: Decivilizing Processes

STEPHEN MENNELL

Decivilizing processes are what happen when civilizing processes go into reverse. But that is a deceptively simple statement. As usual when working with Norbert Elias's theories, we need to think in terms of a tension balance between conflicting pressures. It could be argued that decivilizing trends, or decivilizing pressures, are *always* present. Indeed, civilizing processes arise (as blind, unplanned processes) out of people's struggles to solve the problems posed to them in their lives by decivilizing pressures – for example, the threat of violence and insecurity. So we need to think of civilizing and decivilizing pressures as pushing against each other, just as, under Elias's influence, we have learned to think in terms of centrifugal and centripetal forces contending against each other in state-formation processes. The question is, Which forces gain the upper hand in the short term or the long term: centrifugal or centripetal, civilizing or decivilizing? But what does it mean to say that civilizing or decivilizing forces have become dominant?

Elias speaks of civilizing processes occurring on two levels. The first is the individual level and is relatively uncontroversial: infants and children have to acquire through learning the adult standards of behaviour and feeling prevalent in their society. To speak of this as a civilizing process is more or less to use another term for "socialization," and that this process has a typical structure and sequence is not disputed. (Researchers from Freud and Piaget onwards have debated the details of the sequence of childhood development, but few would question that there *is* a sequence.) But the second level is more controversial. Where did these standards come from? They have not always existed; nor have they always been the same. Elias argues that it is possible to identify long-term civilizing processes in the shaping of standards of behaviour and feeling over many generations within particular cultures. Again, the idea that these standards *change* is not controversial; what generates debate is that the changes take the form of structured processes of change, with a discernible – though unplanned – direction over time. This problem of direction is crucial, for the notion of a decivilizing process as a *reversal* of a civilizing process only makes sense if one can be confident that the process was previously moving in a structured way in a recognizable direction.[1]

To avoid any misunderstanding whatsoever, we must recognize the linguistic nuances of what is happening. In English, and even more so in French, the word "direction" has two meanings. It can convey the sense of conscious and intentional management and steering of affairs, as in the term *direction d'un entreprise*. That is not at all what I mean here by "the problem of direction." Rather, we are concerned with blind processes that are not the outcome of the plans and intentions of any particular individual people, but are the unintended products of the interweaving of many people's plans and intentions. Such "undirected" interweaving can give rise to processes that have direction in a sense more akin to physicists' concepts of "vector" and "momentum" (Mennell 1992a).

DECIVILIZING PROCESSES: SOME CANDIDATES FOR THE LABEL

Nothing appears to undermine the plausibility of the civilizing-process thesis more than the widespread perception that, whatever may have been the trend in Europe from the Middle Ages to the nineteenth century, the twentieth century has seen a reversal in many of those trends. I shall examine three issues about which there has been dispute: the Holocaust in Nazi Germany, whether violent crime is becoming more prevalent in contemporary society, and how the "permissive society" of the mid-twentieth century is to be interpreted. I shall then briefly raise the question of longer-term decivilizing processes affecting whole societies over periods of several generations. These four topics are in no sense intended as a typology of decivilizing processes.

The Holocaust

Sir Edmund Leach alleged that at the very time that Elias was formulating his thesis, "Hitler was refuting the argument on the grandest scale." This contention, though crudely expressed, does raise a genuine problem. Almost worse than its crudity is its implication that Elias, writing as a Jewish refugee from Hitler's Germany in the 1930s, was a naive optimist. Yet he was anything but naive. True, he had completed *The Civilizing Process* before the "Final Solution" had taken final form, but something of the character of the Nazi regime was already clear. In fact, as he explained in the preface, "the issues raised by the book have their origins less in scholarly tradition, in the narrower sense of the word, than in the experiences in whose shadow we all live, experiences of the crisis and transformation of Western civilization as it has existed hitherto" (1994b, xvi). While Elias, like virtually everyone else, no doubt failed to foresee the full extent of the killings, a sense of foreboding is often evident. And there are many elements in his own thinking that help to clarify the serious problems posed by the Holocaust and other instances of humans' inhumanity to fellow humans.

It is a crass misreading of the theory of civilizing processes to see it as a model of "progress," let alone inevitable progress.[2] On the contrary, the process of internal pacification of territory was a highly contingent and precarious one. Elias had his eyes wide open to the ever-present threat of violence within states. His theory of state formation begins from Max Weber's definition of the state as "an organization which successfully upholds a claim to binding rule-making over a territory, by virtue of commanding a monopoly of the legitimate use of violence" (Weber 1978, 1:54), but Elias bypasses the problematic red herring of "legitimacy" by linking a rising level of internal security and calculability in everyday life directly to the formation of people's social habitus.[3] The nub of his argument, linking the theory of state formation to that of the civilizing process proper, is contained in the statement that "if in a particular region, the power of central authority grows, if over a larger or smaller area people are *forced* to live at peace with one another, the molding of the affects and the standards of the demands made upon emotional management are very gradually changed as well" (1994b, 165, italics added and translation modified).

The means of violence continue to play a part, even in the most internally pacified society, though – like defecation, urination, nakedness, and other aspects of manners – they may over time come to be increasingly hidden behind the scenes of social life. They may lurk in the shadows, but they are still there. The gradually established social control of dangers was a precondition for the more "civilized" standard of conduct, but the "armor of civilized conduct would crumble very rapidly if, through a change in society, the degree of insecurity that existed earlier were to break in upon us again, and if danger became as incalculable as once it was. Corresponding fears would burst the limits set to them today" (1994b, 253n). In other words, civilized conduct takes a long time to construct, but it remains contingent upon the maintenance of a high level of internal pacification, and it can be destroyed rather quickly. That, I think, is one of the central problems with the whole theory: at first glance Elias does appear to want to have his cake and eat it too.

At this point, however, a more detailed reading of his work than critics such as Leach were prepared to accord it soon provides clarification. First, in *The Civilizing Process*, as well as in many of his writings towards the end of his life (Haferkamp 1987; Mennell 1987), Elias constantly emphasized that the curbing of affects, including impulses towards the use of violence, is contingent on internal pacification *within* the territory of emerging state societies. The use of violence *between* states showed few signs of diminishing. The release of the affects in battle – the sheer enjoyment of fighting (*Angriffslust*) which had been evident among early medieval warriors – had perhaps become a little curbed, but that change had been offset by the increasing scale of warfare as, over the centuries, battles between territorially larger states had come to be fought out by larger numbers of people over larger geographical areas.

In struggles between members of different "survival units" (tribes or, later, states) there is, historically speaking, nothing very unusual about the mass murder of defeated enemies or about pogroms of outsider groups. They were long taken for granted.[4] In Europe, however, there had gradually emerged a system of states which, in world perspective, were territorially relatively small but also relatively effective. Even there, only gradually in the course of state-formation processes did outbreaks of violence and cruelty by one social group towards another diminish in frequency and ruthlessness. That they did so at all was, Elias argued, because spreading webs of interdependence tend to be associated with relatively more equal power ratios and "functional democratization," resulting in more and more reciprocal controls being established between more and more social groups. Less abstractly, "more people are forced more often to pay more attention to more other people" (Goudsblom 1989, 722). This shift produces pressures towards greater consideration of the consequences of one's own actions for other people on whom one is more or less dependent, and there tends in consequence to be an increase in mutual identification. This idea is not new to Elias – it was expressed very clearly by Alexis de Tocqueville[5] – but it has a very direct bearing on matters of violence and cruelty.

At this point, Elias's theory of established-outsider relations becomes highly relevant. This concept was first explicitly developed in the limited context of a fairly conventional study of a small community in the English Midlands in Elias and Scotson's analysis of 1965. It focused especially on relations between two neighbourhoods, both occupied mainly by outwardly similar working-class families. However, the idea of established and outsider groups was already implicit in *The Civilizing Process*, in the discussion both of the "colonization and repulsion" mechanism by which new standards of behaviour were developed and disseminated and of the differing trends in violence between interstate and intrastate tensions. Even earlier, Elias had broached some of these themes in one of his first published essays (1935), on the expulsion of the Huguenots from France; there is no doubt at all that, from first to last, the connecting thread was his concern with the position of the Jews in Germany.[6] In later work by Elias and others, the ideas have been extended in their application to class relations in cities, to race and ethnic relations, to the power balances between men and women and between heterosexuals and homosexuals, and to many other contexts (Mennell 1989, 115–39).

In inventing the concept of established-outsider relations, Elias was seeking categories which, though simpler in themselves than the familiar terms of Marxist and Weberian debates, would yet enable him to grapple better with the complexities of identity and inequality actually observed within the flux of social interdependencies. Looked at singly, the people of the two different neighbourhoods in the community that Elias studied differed very little from each other: they had similar occupations and similar houses, and most lived similarly respectable lives. The principal difference between them as groups was that the houses in one neighbourhood (the "Village") were several decades older than those in the other (the "Estate"), and a number of key families in the former were long established and formed a closely-knit network. They monopolized the key positions in local churches, associations, and other focuses of community life, in which the residents of the Estate played little part. This ascendancy had come about in an unplanned way over the years. But the established group developed an "ideology" which represented the outsiders as rough, uncouth, dirty, and delinquent, although in fact only a very small minority of the Estate families were other than thoroughly respectable. In this process, gossip played a vital part. Gossip is highly selective and distorting. Through it, people compete in demonstrating their fervent adherence to their own group norms by expressing their shock and horror at the behaviour of those who do not conform. Only the items of news least flattering to the outsider group ("blame gossip") were relayed; the perfectly acceptable behaviour of the great majority was not news. Blame gossip conveyed a highly simplified presentation of social realities based on a "minority of the worst." Members of the established group also gossiped about themselves, a practice that in itself was a powerful source of social control restraining potential infringements of their own norms of respectability. But in this gossip about themselves, selectivity tended to operate in the opposite direction: it tended to be "praise gossip," based on a "minority of the best." A general conclusion from this case study, of wider relevance, is that, as Elias and Scotson note, "By and large ... the more secure the members of a group feel in their own superiority and their pride, the less great is the distortion, the gap between image and reality, likely to be; and the more threatened and insecure they feel, the more likely is it that internal pressure, and as part of it, internal competition, will drive common beliefs towards extremes of illusion and rigidity"(1965, 95).

Of course, the pressures inherent in the process of functional democratization which tend towards increasing the level of mutual identification are never sufficient to eradicate established-outsider conflicts altogether. Indeed, these same processes of differentiation create problems of coordination. Larger-scale organization in state and economy forces groups of people together in closer interdependencies than formerly, and these new patterns create new concentrations of power resources, new inequalities, new opportunities for established-outsider struggles. All the same, if these struggles take place *within* a relatively effective state, we would generally expect a high probability of them most often being pursued by non-violent means.

We can now return to the problem of the Holocaust and begin to see that Elias's ideas, far from being refuted by it, actually help in the frightful task of understanding how and why it happened. The Jews had always been an outsider group within German society,[7] but, as Elias himself emphasizes in his autobiographical reflections, in the Kaiserzeit they generally felt perfectly secure. Though they were conscious of the disadvantage imposed on them by the German establishment, it was the kind of undramatic disadvantage that Elias later depicted among the residents of the Estate. Pogroms were something that happened away to the east. Anti-Semitism might be widespread in Germany, but a high level of civilized constraints could be largely taken for granted. So what changed?

Elias thinks of civilizing processes as involving a change in the balance between external constraints (*Fremdzwänge*, constraints by *other people*) and self-constraints (*Selbstzwänge*), the balance tilting towards the latter in the control of behaviour in the average person. Decivilizing processes may be defined as a tilting of the balance back in favour of external constraints. But in neither case will the operation of self-constraints remain unchanged if changes take place in the patterning of external constraints – the behaviour of other people. Calculation of the external constraints always plays a part in the steering of conduct, and if the calculations suddenly or gradually yield different outcomes, behaviour will change.

Still more will it change if the outcomes become, as Elias said in the remark quoted above, more incalculable: the pattern of people's fears responds to changes in the dangers they face. And one of the distinguishing characteristics of decivilizing trends is a rise in the level of danger and a fall in its calculability. During times of social crisis – military defeats, political revolutions, rampant inflation, soaring unemployment, separately or, as happened in Germany after the First World War, in rapid sequence – fears rise because control of social events has declined. Rising fears make it still more difficult to control events. Thus people become still more susceptible to wish fantasies about means of alleviating the situation. A vicious circle or "double–bind process" is set up, and a process of that kind can be clearly seen in Germany after 1918, helping to explain the rise of the Nazis and the appeal of racial beliefs, one instance of the more general category of fantasy-laden beliefs.[8] The Weimar period plainly provided fertile soil for such beliefs. In The Germans, Elias (1996a, 214–23) himself wrote about the decline of the state's monopoly of violence under the Weimar Republic, and Jonathan Fletcher (1997) has argued that it was then, rather than subsequently under the Nazi regime, that decivilizing forces were most clearly dominant. The grim paradox is that it was the return to a highly effective state monopolization of the means of violence (though somewhat less "behind the scenes" than formerly) under Hitler, together with the renewed dangers and fears provided by the Second World War, that permitted the Holocaust to be so effectively organized.

It is striking how hard the Nazi regime had to strive to diminish the identification that many Germans felt with their fellow Germans, the Jews (which was evident, for instance, in the popular reaction to Kristallnacht in 1938). It was not merely a matter of propaganda, whipping up a sense of danger. The Jews were first removed to ghettos, breaking their personal contacts with their non-Jewish neighbours. Then, under the official pretext of "resettlement in the east," they were removed to transit camps, labour camps, and finally extermination camps far "behind the scenes" of metropolitan Germany. The regime remained apprehensive of German public opinion even at this stage (Noakes and Pridham 1988, 3:997–1208). "Mutual identification" was apparently not negligible, but it was successfully bypassed. Its bypassing, as well as the mass murders themselves and all the innumerable actions of lesser cruelty that led up to them, were triumphs of rational organization. Modern social organization vastly multiplied the technical capacity to kill.

It is the sheer rationality of the Holocaust that has led many to see it as a refutation of the theory of civilizing processes. Zygmunt Bauman writes:

the major lesson of the Holocaust is the necessity ... to expand the theoretical model of the civilizing process, so as to include the latter's tendency to demote, exprobate and delegitimize the ethical motivations of social action. We need to take stock of the evidence that the civilizing process is, among other things, a process of divesting the use and deployment of violence from moral calculus, and of emancipating the desiderata of rationality from interference of ethical norms and moral inhibitions. As the promotion of rationality to the exclusion of alternative criteria of action, and in particular the tendency to subordinate the use of violence to rational calculus, has been long ago acknowledged as a constitutive feature of modern civilization, Holocaust-style phenomena must be recognized as legitimate outcomes of the civilizing tendency, and its constant potential. (1989, 28)

But the theory needs to be expanded much less that Bauman imagines. Rationalization is an important component of the theory as originally formulated by Elias. Steadily lengthening and interweaving chains of interdependence, he contended, exert increasing pressure on the people caught up in them to exercise a greater degree of self-constraint and foresight, and one form that this takes is rationalization (1994b, 457–60).

"Rationality," warns Elias, has no absolute beginning in human history. Just as there was no point at which human beings suddenly began to possess a "conscience," so there is none before which they were completely "irrational." Still more misleading is it to think of rationality as some kind of property of individual minds in isolation from each other: "There is not actually a ratio, there is at most rationalization (1994b, 480). What actually changes is the way that people are bonded with each other in society, and in consequence the moulding of personality structure. Elias's argument is that the forms of behaviour we call "rationality" are produced within a social figuration in which extensive transformation of external compulsions into internal compulsions takes place. He says: "The complementary concepts of 'rationality' and 'irrationality' refer to the relative parts played by short-term affects and long-term conceptual models of observable reality in individual behaviour. The greater the importance of the latter in the delicate balance between affective and reality-orientated commands, the more 'rational' is behaviour" (1983, 92).

The very long chains of interdependence and division of social functions that play such a part in the civilizing process were also essential to implementing the Final Solution. And ironically, as Elias argues, "civilized" controls in turn play their part in making possible those long chains of organized and coordinated activities, especially through rational bureaucratic organization. The emotional detachment of an Eichmann, sitting in an office working out timetables for trains to Auschwitz, is one aspect of this phenomenon. Here there is no disagreement between Elias and Bauman, although one has to recognize, not for the first time, that the use of the word "civilization" as a technical term in Elias's sociology is a positive invitation to misunderstandings of this kind.

It should be noted that Bauman uses the term "civilizing process" in a sense only loosely related to Elias's work. He is certainly mistaken if he thinks that Elias "restated the familiar self-definition of civilized society" or that he "celebrates with such relish" the "mellowing of manners" (Bauman 1989, 107). The single most powerful influence on Elias's early work, after all, was Freud, in whose *Civilization and Its Discontents* (as in many other discussions during that period) civilization is by no means seen as an unalloyed good or as "progress." And if Elias did not much discuss the "process of divesting the use and deployment of violence from moral calculus," it is because systems of ethics and morals as such have never played much part in his theory; indeed, he has often been criticized for playing down the role of the church and moral teachings.

The Holocaust refuted the theory of the European civilizing process in much the same way that the Black Death cast doubt on the long-term tendency for the continent's population to grow. That comment is not facetious, nor is it an attempt to immunize the theory against falsification. It still leaves a great deal to be explained. But the fact is that, for all the horrific suffering which the Holocaust involved, civilizing tendencies regained dominance after a relatively few years; whether and how they would have done so without external military intervention we can only speculate.

Is Contemporary Society Becoming More Violent?

Highly involved in the practical problems of their own everyday lives, people today often find it difficult not to believe that they are living in a world which is more violent than a generation or two ago. And the image of a peaceful agrarian society in the more remote past ("Merrie England") also persists strongly.

The perception that "law and order" are breaking down in the cities of the Western world, and that the level of danger in everyday life there is rising, cannot be taken at face value. In the case of Britain, for example, Pearson has shown how, for hundreds of years, successive generations have voiced similar fears of escalating violence, moral decline, and the destruction of "the British way of life." At the same time, the perception cannot be dismissed out of hand. Certainly, there seem to be short-term fluctuations in violence, in response to rising and falling tensions. Yet there is very little hard historical evidence for a rising curve of violence over terms longer than one or two generations. Admittedly, trends are difficult to study even in the short-term, since a rise in officially recorded or publicly reported incidents of violence may at least partly reflect an increase in the effectiveness of the police, or indeed, a diminished tolerance of minor violence. However, such evidence as we have of long-term trends in violent crime over many generations, notably the quantitative studies of Gurr and Stone, appears to support Elias's case rather than otherwise.

Over a shorter time scale and once more in the specific case of Britain, Dunning and his Leicester colleagues have investigated trends in violent disorders between 1900 and 1975. They classify reported incidents of violence into four categories: disorders connected with politics, with industrial disputes, with sports and leisure, and with the community in general, the last serving as a catch-all for episodes of street fighting not clearly belonging in the other categories (Dunning et al. 1987). Except in the sports-related category, the trend over the period as a whole was downwards. On the other hand, the graphs do show an upward turn in the 1960s and 1970s. It is not easy to say whether this represents simply a minor short-term fluctuation or a more definite reversal of a long-term trend, but the latter possibility has led Dunning, Murphy, and Williams to speculate that Britain is experiencing an actual "decivilizing" upsurge in violence (1988, 242–5). The explanation that they tentatively offer for this pattern introduces an interesting qualification into the theory of civilizing processes. They suggest that functional democratization, as one of the central components of the civilizing process, produces consequences which are, on balance, "civilizing" in its early stages, but that when a certain level has been reached, it produces effects which are decivilizing and promote disruptive conflict. Functional democratization has perhaps proceeded far enough for the demands of outsider groups to be expressed strongly but not far enough, in Britain at least, to break down rigidities that prevent their demands being met fully. At any rate, Dunning and his colleagues admit that "we do not fully understand the periodicity and ups and downs ... the conditions under which a society moves, on balance, in a 'civilizing' direction and the conditions under which a civilizing process moves, as it were, on balance into 'reverse gear'" (1988, 243). That is one of the key problems to be clarified by further research.

The Permissive Society

For centuries, writers who have meditated on the causes of the down-fall of states and empires have dwelt on symptoms of moral decline as they saw it. In such cases as that of ancient Rome, modern histo-rians would at least want to ask whether their predecessors did not confuse cause and effect. But the matter has some contemporary res-onance because of popular (and sociological) discussions of the various tendencies that were collectively labelled "the permissive society" – the relaxation of controls, even "loosening of morals" as many saw it, and a pervasive informalization of social behaviour apparent in the 1960s and 1970s in many countries. I have described elsewhere (1989, 241–6) how sociologists in the Netherlands asked whether that meant that the civilizing process had gone into reverse. Since the increasing complex-ity of the web of social interdependencies in which people are caught up has manifestly not gone into reverse, does the emergence of the "permissive society" invalidate Elias's whole notion of the connection between structural development and the civilizing of behaviour? Might it, for example, suggest that the link between structural complexity and "civilizing controls" on people's behaviour is curvilinear – that perhaps beyond a certain point it generates pockets of metropolitan anonymity within which the external constraints on impulses (from the sexual to the violent), and in time also the effectiveness of pressures towards self-constraint, are diminished?

Elias was well aware of this question when he was writing in the 1930s. He discussed the apparent relaxation of morals that had taken place since the First World War (1994a, 153, 517). It was not, he pointed out, the first time that such apparent reversals of the civilizing process had occurred. In very long term perspective the overall trend was clear, especially among the upper classes, but on closer examina-tion there had always been criss-cross movements, shifts, and spurts in various directions. The informalization of the interwar years was probably just another such fluctuation.

On the other hand, he also pointed out that some of the symptoms of an apparent relaxation of the constraints imposed on the individual by social life actually took place within the framework of very high social standards of self-constraint – standards possibly higher even than formerly. He gave the example of bathing costumes and the relatively greater exposure of the body (especially the female body) in many modern sports. This development, Elias had already argued in 1939, could only take place "in a society in which a high degree of restraint is taken for granted, and in which women are, like men, absolutely sure that each individual is curbed by self-control and a strict code of etiquette" (1994b, 153).

From a debate between Brinkgreve, Wouters, and others sprang a good deal of research on contemporary trends in manners and morals (Brinkgreve and Korzec 1976, 1979; Wouters 1976, 1977, 1986, 1987; Kapteyn 1980, 1985). Wouters catalogued the manifestations of informalization processes in the increased use of the familiar second person (*tutoyer, duzen,* and so on in European languages other than English), the increasing use of first names (for example, by subordinates to superiors in offices and by children to their parents), the decreasing insistence upon titles, and the less-formal regulation of the written and spoken languages, of clothing, hairstyles, and of forms of music and dancing, in addition to the changes in the key fields of marriage, divorce, and sexual relationships. These last were the particular focus of Brinkgreve and Korzec's study of advice columns in a Dutch women's magazine between 1938 and 1978. Apart from the far more open discussion of problems of sexuality, they found that the expectation that teenagers submit unprotestingly to their parents' wishes, or wives to their husbands', diminished dramatically between the 1950s and 1970s, in consequence of more equal balances of power. For instance, when women did not have jobs of their own, their lack of financial leeway made them utterly dependent on their husbands and limited their alternatives. As this dependence diminished, the ideal of marriage came to be expressed less in terms of complete unity and harmony; the relationship was seen more in terms of competing interests, in which negotiations played a more decisive part than fixed roles. Blanket rules were no longer given for what was right and what was wrong. Brinkgreve and Korzec summed up the changes as a shift from "moralizing" to "psychologizing." It was less a matter of judging and censuring and more one of considering a situation from all angles.

The question was, though, how these changes were to be interpreted in relation to the theory of civilizing processes. Briefly, one can say that Brinkgreve initially thought that "permissiveness" did represent some reversal of the civilizing process, and that Wouters followed Elias in interpreting it as a "highly controlled decontrolling of emotional controls" and therefore in some respects a continuation of the main trend. Brinkgreve accused Wouters of trying to immunize Elias's theory from falsification. After much empirical research, however, the upshot was a measure of consensus, slightly in Wouters's favour. The demands of the "new freedom" are in fact quite high, and the level of "mutually expected self-restraint" has risen.

It emerges that some careful distinctions have to be drawn. Elias frequently stresses that the civilizing process is not a matter simply of more self-control. He speaks in terms of the changing balance between external and self-constraints and of the changing pattern of controls. In particular, he speaks of controls becoming "more even," "more automatic," and "more all-round," as well as of a movement towards "diminishing contrasts and increasing varieties." By "more even" and "more automatic" self-constraints, Elias means psychological changes: individuals' oscillations of mood become less extreme, and the controls over emotional expression become more reliable or calculable. "More all-round" ("more all-embracing" would be a better translation) refers to a decline in the differences between various spheres of life, such as contrasts between what is allowed in public and in private, between conduct in relation to one category of people as against another, or between normal behaviour and that permissible on special occasions such as carnivals which are seen as exceptions to the rules. Finally, "diminishing contrasts, increasing varieties" refers to social contrasts – reduced inequalities between social groups but a wider choice of permissible models of behaviour.

Bearing these distinctions in mind, we can see that the informalization processes in general represent a definite continuation of the latter two components – diminishing contrasts, increasing varieties – and more "all-roundedness." What is more ambiguous is whether they also represent a movement towards more evenness and greater automaticity. Because they involve a less tyrannical form of conscience formation and more conscious deliberation, it is easy to overlook how far the new, more liberal standards presuppose an extremely reliable capacity for controlling one's impulses and a still greater level of mutual identification. They do not, in general, appear to involve a switch backwards in the balance from *Selbstzwänge* towards *Fremdszwänge*, and so seem not to be "true decivilizing processes."

One concluding point on the permissive society, however: if it is so difficult to make these subtle distinctions from the abundant historical evidence of recent decades, how much more difficult are they to draw from the evidence of the more distant past?

DECIVILIZING PROCESSES OVER SEVERAL GENERATIONS

The first three areas of dispute about possible decivilizing processes all concerned relatively short-term trends. There are good reasons to think that decivilizing spurts may operate more quickly and dramatically than civilizing processes. As we have seen, rising levels of danger and incalculability in social life quite quickly render people more susceptible to fears and fantasies. In addition, it must be remembered that, though standards change from generation to generation in the course of a social learning process extending over many lifetimes, the prevalent standards of controls at any point in the process have to be acquired – or not acquired – by every individual in every generation through an individual learning process that is, by definition, no longer than an individual lifetime. Abrupt changes in social circumstances may seriously disrupt the continuity of socialization.

Yet because *The Civilizing Process* was a study of trends over a period of several centuries, it is interesting to ask whether there have also been long-term decivilizing processes extending over several generations. When civilizing pressures are dominant, the direction of change is towards the formation of social standards that require a more demanding level of habitual self-constraint by people in each successive generation. Are there any well-documented cases of decivilizing pressures dominating in such a way that, rather than abrupt change in response to sudden events from one generation to the next, the social standards of habitual self-constraint become *less* demanding? (We have already seen that the case of the permissive society does not clearly fit this requirement.) To observe such a case, one would really need to observe changes over a minimum of three generations. Loïc Wacquant has suggested that the black ghettos of the United States in the twentieth century provide a clear instance of just such an intergenerational process.

On a larger scale, perhaps the most obvious place to look for signs of longer-term decivilizing processes would be in the context of examples of the more or less total collapse of complex societies. The instance best known and most discussed among Western historians and social scientists is the collapse of the Roman Empire. The archaeologist Joseph Tainter gives a surprisingly long list. They include the Western Zhou empire in China, the Mesopotamian empires, the Egyptian Old Kingdom, the Hittite empire, the Minoan civilization, and several of the pre-Columbian New World empires.

The most significant questions that may be asked about these longer-term decivilizing processes fall into two main groups, corresponding more or less to the questions uppermost, respectively, in the second and first volumes of Elias's original discussion of civilizing processes. Questions in the first group are structural: in what circumstances do the chains of interdependence in society begin to break, and thus why do levels of complexity, differentiation, and integration start to decline? The second group concerns the outcome of such processes of structural unravelling for people's experience: what are the cultural and psychological consequences and the impact on people's day-to-day conduct?[9]

Tainter provides a careful eleven-fold categorization and critique of earlier explanations of social collapse, of great interest to sociologists. His own favoured explanation is essentially economic. Collapse comes about because "investment in socio-political complexity often reaches a point of declining marginal returns" (1988, 118). By "returns" he means "benefits to people" – by implication mainly powerful elite groups – and "investment" covers expenditure on legitimation activities or, alternatively, the means of coercion, as well as on more narrowly economic infrastructure. The main weakness of Tainter's theory, however, is that he has difficulty in specifying the point at which diminishing returns set in – independently, that is, of collapse itself. The theory therefore has a somewhat *ex post facto* quality.

In fact, we seem to have no general theory of structural collapse, and perhaps it is not sensible to look for one. The precipitating circumstances are possibly too varied to be effectively subsumed under a higher-level abstraction such as "diminishing marginal returns." The chances of fruitful generalization may perhaps be greater in relation to my second group of questions, those concerning the cultural and psychological effects and the impact on people's conduct when "structural unravelling" occurs in various forms and degrees.

It seems probable that an increase in levels of danger and incalculability and a decline in the capacity of central monopoly apparatuses to enforce their authority will be associated with the re-emergence of free-rider problems. The consequence will be the onset of disinvestment in collective goods. Individual people and small groups simply find it less safe than it formerly was to depend on other people located at a great distance down social chains. Collective arrangements that ultimately rested on the capacity of authorities to enforce them can no longer be relied upon. In the space of a generation or two, smaller and less-dense webs of interdependence, entailing fewer pressures towards foresight in the coordination of activities, may, through the socialization process, result in diminution of these capacities. People need to practise them if they are to be able to call on them at will. Conversely, in situations of greater insecurity, learning aptitudes resting on a very different temperament may have greater survival value. As Goudsblom has written,

In order to survive in the ecological and social niches in which they find themselves, people have to acquire certain skills. A repertoire of such skills may be called a regime; civilizing processes then consist of the formation and acquisition of these regimes.

Regimes give rise to a mixture of aptitudes and inaptitudes. Out of the virtually unlimited range of forms of conduct, people everywhere learn to realize a few. The skills and habits which help them to survive in one niche, be it a royal court or a university, may be of no value or even detrimental in other niches. Thus civilizing processes generate trained incapacities as well as capacities. (1994)

Thus when social circumstances (or niches) change, even if civilized self-constraints are not lost rapidly, over a period of time we would expect a kind of social selection of a new range of aptitudes. These changes of regime may be in what we have defined as a decivilizing direction, as, for example, when the regime of the warrior once more becomes of greater survival value than that of the democratic politician.

In studying the psychological and cultural components of this process in historical contexts such as the decline of Rome, contemporary studies of the effects of increased levels of violence on adults and children in places such as Northern Ireland and Lebanon ought to be relevant (Cairns and Wilson 1985; Hosin 1987). Increased levels of danger ought to be associated with increased fear and anxiety and with a lessening of controls. As always, in practice it is not easy to make inferences from short-term studies to long-term trends. The increase in anxiety shows up in Northern Ireland but as realistic, not neurotic, anxiety. On the other hand, it may be thought that the relatively high level of intercommunal conflict in Northern Ireland over many generations is reflected in the rather high fantasy content of popular beliefs in the province (MacDonald 1983). But applying such insights to historical evidence is quite difficult, in part because periods of social disintegration are times when documentary evidence is likely to be less complete and clear.

CONCLUSION

In recent years, several of the main controversies about Elias's theory of civilizing processes have concerned the possibility of such processes "going into reverse." Some of the issues involved have been raised in this chapter in relation to research on four possible instances of decivilizing processes: the case of Nazi Germany and the Holocaust, the question of whether violence is increasing in contemporary Western societies, the so-called permissive society, and the consequences for social habitus of longer-term processes of decline in social complexity. The last, in particular, requires far more thorough research. On the whole, however, it can be concluded that the study of decivilizing processes leads, not to a refutation of Elias's theory, but to an appreciation of the great insights it contains and to further development and elaboration of the theory.

NOTES

The French version of this chapter appeared in Garrigou and Lacroix 1997, 213–36.

1 My interest in decivilizing processes in fact arises out of criticisms that have been made of Elias's theory of long-term civilizing processes. The four principal lines of criticism are (1) criticisms from the viewpoint of cultural relativism; (2) criticisms from the argument that there are "stateless civilizations"; (3) the argument from the "permissive society"; and (4) the "barbarization" argument. The first two lines of criticism emanate especially from anthropologists. I have dealt with them at length elsewhere (1989, 227–41). Here I want to concentrate on the third and fourth criticisms, which raise the most interesting questions in relation to the problem of direction. They have in common that they are both concerned with apparent reversals in the main trend of the process which Elias traces through European history and appear to cast doubt on the validity of his explanation of that process.

2 See Elias's discussion of "the problem of the 'inevitability' of social development" in chapter 6 of *What Is Sociology?* (1978c), and also Philip Abrams's appreciation of Elias's solution to the problem (1982, 145–6).

3 Elias also departs from Weber's line of thought in always speaking of the monopolization of the means of violence *and taxation*, pointing out that, especially in the early stages of state-formation processes, it is meaningless to think in terms of separate economic and political spheres.

4 Johan Goudsblom neatly juxtaposes strikingly similar descriptions of such treatment from the *Iliad* and from Winston Churchill's account (Churchill 1930) of his participation in British operations against the Afghans in the 1890s (Goudsblom 1996, 62).

5 Tocqueville cites Mme de Sévigné's jocular comments on people being broken on the wheel after the tax riots in Rennes in 1675 as an instance of the lack of feeling of members of one social class for the sufferings of members of another, and he speaks of the subsequent "softening of manners as social conditions become more equal" (Alexis de Tocqueville, quoted in Stone and Mennell 1983, 102–6).

6 Recently it has come to light that Elias was himself as a young man deeply involved in the Zionist movement (Hackeschmidt 1997). An early and hitherto unknown article by him on German anti-Semitism (1929) makes an interesting contrast with the less "involved" stance that he took in *The Germans* (1996) at the end of his life.

7 For a recent study that uses both Elias's writings to understand the social position of European Jewry over several centuries before the Holocaust and his own Jewish background to cast light upon his writings, see Russell 1996.

8 This paragraph needs to be understood in the context of Elias's theory of knowledge and of involvement and detachment; see Elias 1987b and Mennell 1989, 158–99.

9 A third set of questions should not be overlooked: whether the possible loss of certain learned psychological qualities and behavioural capacities – for example, any tilting of the balance back away from self-constraints, any associated decline in the general capacity for detour behaviour and the exercise of foresight, and any decline in the breadth of mutual identification – may contribute to structural decline once it has started.

3 The Integration of Classes and Sexes in the Twentieth Century: Etiquette Books and Emotion Management

CAS WOUTERS

This chapter constitutes a summary of the preliminary results of a larger comparative study of changes in twentieth-century American, Dutch, English, and German etiquette books. A central hypothesis is that major directional trends in dominant codes and ideals of behaviour and feeling, as reflected by changes in etiquette books, are closely connected with trends in power relationships and emotion management.

In the twentieth century an important common trend in all four countries has been the diminishing of differences in power between all social groups; workers and women have come to be represented in the centres of power, and national states have become welfare states. This expansion and further integration of interdependency networks has implied a diminishing of institutionalized, as well as internalized, power differences – that is, in social stratification and ranking. Inequalities, together with more extreme forms of social and psychic distance between people, have diminished without losing importance. In the course of the twentieth century, direct references to differences in class, status, and gender have diminished or even vanished from the codes and ideals of behaviour and feeling. Extremes in these codes and ideals, expressing large differences in power and respect, came to provoke moral indignation and were eliminated; within the subsequent narrower limits the codes allowed for increasing emotional and behavioural alternatives. This development implies that the codes have become more lenient, more differentiated, and more varied for a wider and more differentiated public: a process of informalization is afoot. The expanding and strengthening of interdependency networks, and the concomitant processes of social integration and informalization, ran in tandem with marked changes in the social habitus of the people involved: increasing numbers of them pressured each other towards more differentiated and flexible patterns of self-regulation in behaviour and emotion management.

To what extent can this overall twentieth-century trend be specified for the relationships between the classes and the sexes in the four countries under consideration? This has been the leading question in this study of etiquette books, which focuses on connections between changes in ranking and formality, especially with regard to classes and sexes, and changes in emotion management, particularly with regard to feelings of superiority and inferiority.

My reading and collecting of Dutch etiquette books began in the late 1960s, but for this international study I have had to develop an overview of the literature with the help of existing bibliographies, bringing them up to date where necessary.[1] I then selected my sample of etiquette books, the main criterion being whether a book had gained wider recognition, that is, whether it was reprinted. From these and other books[2] I compared what was written on relationships between people of different rank (or class) and sex. The central hypothesis of this chapter covers broad developments and general trends, which are demonstrated through national variations in those *common* patterns. I have provided a fuller description of *differences* between countries elsewhere (Wouters 1998a).

After a preliminary section on etiquette and etiquette books as a source of evidence, the first part of this chapter concentrates on the diminishing social and psychic distance between people of different class and rank, interpreted in terms of expanding social integration and identification processes. It presents examples of changes in what was written on the "dangers" of social mixing, familiarity, the use of first names, and "social kissing." Taken together, these examples indicate a process of significant directional change in the regimes of power and emotions, expressing social and inner conflicts that accompanied the rise of outsider groups to positions of social proximity in relation to established groups. In the first two examples – warnings against social mixing and familiarity – the tone is still set by established groups that attempt to maintain their superior social distance. In the latter two – the use of first names and social kissing – the tone is set by the now more established (former) outsider groups and their demand for, as well as their demonstration of, social acceptance and proximity. In this way the examples also present a historical sequence. Around the turn of the century, when groups with "new money" were expanding and rising, creating strong pressures on "old money" establishments toward democratization, the "dangers" of social mixing loomed large. Warnings against familiarity intensified and multiplied well into the 1930s, when the use of first names became an additional issue, particularly in the United States. And ever since the 1950s, when it was first raised by British authors, social kissing remained a topic for discussion. This trend as a whole is interpreted here as an increasing social constraint toward "unconstrained self-restraint."

The second part of the chapter concentrates on the diminishing social and psychic distance between the sexes, and on changes in the demands on emotion management in the process of women's social integration and emancipation. A sketch of the expansion of upper- and middle-class women's sources of power and identity – traditionally restricted to the home and (high) society (or its functional equivalent among other social strata) – focuses on aspects of this process, such as the decline of chaperonage and the development of codes of behaviour for new situations: public transport, public dances, dates, the workplace. The concluding section focuses on the intensified tug-of-war between old and new relational ideals and sources of power, and concomitant feelings of ambivalence in both women and men.

THE JANUS-HEAD OF ETIQUETTE

One of the functions of etiquette is to draw and maintain social dividing lines, to include new groups that have "the necessary qualifications" and to exclude the "rude," that is, all others lower down the social ladder. In this way, changes in etiquette convey changes in established-outsider relationships, that is, in power relationships. Another function of etiquette is, within an environment protected by exclusion, to develop forms of behaviour and feeling that are considered and experienced as "tactful," "kind," "considerate," and "civilized." The social definitions presented in etiquette books are dominated by the established, those who are "included." From expressions that exclude – "They are not nice people" – it is clear that both functions are highly interconnected. Etiquette is a weapon of defence as well as a weapon of attack. Rules of etiquette function to define the boundaries between those who belong and those who do not belong to the group; they function to hold outsiders at bay *and* to set standards of sensitivity and consideration that preserve the (feeling of) purity and integrity of the group, group identity, and group charisma. This paradoxical function of etiquette – as an instrument of exclusion or rejection, on the one hand, and on the other, as an instrument of inclusion or group charisma – I call the Janus-head of etiquette.[3]

Since etiquette symbolizes and reinforces social (and also sexual) dividing lines, as well as serving to protect and stress the sensibilities and composure of the established classes and sexes, changes in manners or etiquette are therefore indicative of changing regimes of power and of emotions (Wouters 1994b). The two are closely linked: "higher status requires for its maintenance higher resources of power as well as distinction of conduct and belief which can be handed on ... [C]ivilizing differentials can be an important factor in the making and perpetuation of power differentials" (Elias and Scotson 1995, 148–53). Although this connection – between changes in class, status, and power relationships, changes in mutual expectations within these relationships, and changes in demands on emotion management – may be well understood in everyday life, it has not attracted much attention from social scientists. Most studies of etiquette books[4] contain extensive descriptions of the class and status aspects of etiquette, but the question as to what these changes mean in terms of self-regulation and personality structure has received much less attention. Exceptions are to be found to a greater or lesser degree, but only in the work of Norbert Elias is the relationship between social structure and personality structure, or, with a slightly different emphasis, between social status and identity, a dominant theme. Following Elias, my own study of twentieth-century etiquette books focuses on changes in social hierarchy and emotion management, taking feelings and gestures of superiority and inferiority into special consideration. The connection between the two has become more embarrassing and difficult to discuss. A study of changes in the dominant code of behaviour and feeling, documented through changes in etiquette, may help in understanding this development more fully.

As etiquette books were never written for sociologists or social researchers, they are necessarily "unobtrusive measures." The codes expressed in these books may reveal a mixture of actual and ideal behaviour, but these ideals are "real"; that is, they are not constructed by social scientists. In the world of publishers and booksellers, these books are called ephemera, which means they soon become outdated: they very much exude the spirit of the times. Precisely for this reason, etiquette books are an extremely rich source for sociological research.

DIMINISHING SOCIAL AND PSYCHIC DISTANCE BETWEEN CLASSES: INCREASING SOCIAL INTEGRATION AND MUTUAL IDENTIFICATION

In the twentieth century almost every etiquette book has contained comments on the ongoing processes of democratization and social integration, in the course of which ideals of equality and feelings of embarrassment about inequalities have intensified and expanded. Here are some examples of how German comments on the fading social dividing lines have become more emphatic. The first is from the 1930s: "In recent times these differences [between the aristocracy and the bourgeoisie] have largely vanished ... and today everyone feels equally subject to the laws of propriety and morality" (Dietrich, quoted in Krumrey 1984, 710). Similar remarks are made in the 1960s: "The dividing lines between classes, still very much present a generation ago, have disappeared ... That, of course, requires relating face to face to completely different people from those with whom one earlier restricted oneself ... People of the most simple descent have, by a change in comparative wealth, been enabled to lead a life in which they are also forcefully confronted with more demanding codes of behaviour ... In this process, the groups willing to be attuned to the dominant behavioural codes have extended and become numerically stronger than ever before" (Meissner and Burkhard 1962, 26). And from a recent etiquette book: "Today good manners do not distinguish any longer between 'the best people' and 'other people'; they function to enhance the understanding between all people. Away with all phrases and platitudes!" (*Umgangsformen Heute* 1988, 18)

These examples are both indicative of a diminishing social and psychic distance, involving traditionally accepted avoidance behaviour becoming increasingly unacceptable, and an ongoing, more inclusive process of social integration: more people come to direct themselves to the same code of behaviour and feeling. A rather unexpected illustration of this interpretation is presented in the preface to *Debrett's Etiquette and Modern Manners*. The author says that in his youth he was told that "the good fairy Do-As-*You*-Would-Be-Done-By should be emulated," but that he later discovered that "the true spirit to emulate is that of Do-As-*They*-Would-Be-Done-By, whether one agrees with them or not" (1981, 7). This "discovery" would have been unthinkable at a time in which social and psychic distance was strongly emphasized and advocated, as in the next quotation: "Etiquette is the form or law of society enacted and upheld by the more refined classes as a protection and a shield against the intrusion of the vulgar and impertinent, who, having neither worth to recommend them nor discernment to discover their deficiencies, would, unless restrained by some barrier, be continually thrusting themselves into the society of those to whom their presence would be not only unwelcome, but, from difference of sentiment, manners, education, and habits, perfectly hateful and intolerable" (*Etiquette for Ladies*, quoted in Curtin 1987, 130). Even to think of the possibility to "Do-As-*They*-Would-Be-Done-By, whether one agrees with them or not," seems to presuppose a society in which social groups or classes are highly integrated and a correspondingly high level of self-restraint is taken for granted, or in other words, mutually expected.

In the nineteenth century, especially in cities and towards strangers in particular, keeping one's distance – that is, reserve – was a firm requirement, because, as Curtin comments, "Strangers might not only be demeaning social inferiors; their uncertain moral character – perhaps repulsive or, worse, tempting – was a danger to the respectable in a way that associations with social inferiors alone were not" (1987, 150).

The "Dangers" of Social Mixing

Attempts at keeping the ranks closed as much as possible can be found in descriptions of the "dangers" of social mixing. The dangers of crossing established social and psychic dividing lines – "letting the side down," "not knowing one's place," and thus becoming too informal and too close – were avoided with the help of various formal rules. Particularly in Britain but also in other countries, an elaborate and complicated system of introductions, leaving cards, calls, "at homes," and dinners served this function (Davidoff 1973). This code of avoidance behaviour displayed and maintained the social dividing lines and protected the sensibilities and composure of the established classes in the face of offences that endangered their self-control: such were the dangers of social mixing.

As some social mixing became less and less avoidable, these rules became less formal and rigid, while demands on self-constraint increased, particularly constraining expressions of superiority.[5] Particularly around the turn of the twentieth century, however, social dividing lines were "on the move": the social definition of the spectrum between the extremes of keeping too great a distance and coming too close was changing. More and more people from different social classes had become interdependent to the point where they could no longer avoid immediate contact with each other. Especially in the expanding cities, at work and on the streets, in public conveyances and entertainment facilities such as dance halls, cinemas, and ice-skating rinks, people who once used to avoid each other were now forced either to try to maintain or to recover social distance under conditions of rising physical, social, and psychic proximity, or to accommodate and become accustomed to more and more social mixing. At the turn of the century a new spurt in emancipation processes made the old avoidance behaviour and other expressions of superiority and inferiority so problematic that the issue was dealt with openly in American, Dutch, and German etiquette books and somewhat less openly in the English ones.[6] The importance of maintaining a distance and avoiding familiarity was emphasized more strongly, while at the same time the requirement to show mutual respect was also underlined more strongly – another symptom of the Janus-head of etiquette.

Writers of etiquette books advised showing more mutual respect, especially in face-to-face contacts, by strongly attacking old, traditional expressions of superiority. In 1908 an English author wrote: "Let us never assert our superiority obnoxiously before those who are not as well dowered by fortune as ourselves; they already know it but too well ... Do not let us look down on those who are just one set beneath us in the social scale. So many find it easier to act the Lady Bountiful than to fraternise with those whose income and family connections are but little separated from our own. We must also remember, in dealing with servants, to temper firmness with kindness" (Porter 1972, 72). In the same year a woman from New Zealand is reported to have said: "It is considered bad taste now to use the terms 'upper' and 'lower' classes or 'superior' and 'inferior'; but it is no offence against taste to keep up irreconcilable class separation, and to assume all the superiority that was once frankly claimed" (Porter 1972, 72–3).

Another significant example of the increasing pressure to curb expressions of superiority is the change in the meaning of the word "snob." "In the terminology of the 1860s a 'snob' was a businessman trying to become a gentleman ... Within two generations the meaning of 'snob' was completely inverted. A 'snob' was now any social superior who on 'false' basis of wealth *or* breeding rather than achievement or inherent human qualities, held himself to be better than those socially below him" (Davidoff 1973, 60).

The pressure to control expressions of superiority continued. Until the 1930s, whole groups or classes were outspokenly deemed unacceptable as people to associate with, and some etiquette books still contained separate sections on "good behaviour" toward social superiors and inferiors. Later these sections disappeared. Ideals about "good behaviour" developed in the direction of being totally unrelated to superior and inferior social position or rank. An example of this process is the change in the introduction to America's most famous etiquette book, the one authored by Emily Post. In the editions published from 1922 to 1937, this introduction still referred to superior groups of people and their advanced "cultivation." "Best Society abroad is always the oldest aristocracy ... those families and communities who have for the longest period of time known highest cultivation. Our own Best Society is represented by social groups which have had, since this is America, widest rather than longest association with old world cultivation. Cultivation is always the basic attribute of Best Society, much as we hear in this country of an 'Aristocracy of wealth'"

(1969, 1). This statement was deleted from the new edition of 1937. Now the reader was informed, "In the general picture of this modern day the smart and the near-smart, the distinguished and the merely conspicuous, the real and the sham, and the unknown general public are all mixed up together. The walls that used to enclose the world that was fashionable are all down … We've all heard the term 'nature's nobleman,' meaning a man of innately beautiful character who, never having even heard of the code, follows it by instinct. In other words, the code of a thoroughbred … is the code of instinctive decency, ethical integrity, self-respect and loyalty" (1937, xi, 2). (This revision does not prevent the author from writing lines that would grade the sensibility of an English audience, such as "The hall-mark of so-called 'vulgar people' is unrestricted display of uncontrolled emotions" [1969, 307].)

This kind of change is indicative of social integration and identification: increasing numbers of people directing their feelings and behaviour to the same national standard. Etiquette books were written for – and sold to – an expanding public, for a rising number of people experiencing both the expectations and responsibilities attached to their elevated positions and accumulated wealth. At the same time, as they gained access to the centres of power (through representatives) and differences in income between the classes on the whole diminished, aspects of their codes of behaviour and feeling "trickled up" and were incorporated into the dominant codes (Wilterdink 1993; Brenner et al. 1991). Thus in expanding networks of interdependency, more and more people pressured each other via these codes increasingly to draw dividing lines on the basis of certain kinds of behaviour, not certain kinds of people. Whereas people of inferior status were once avoided, today behaviour that betrays feelings of superiority and inferiority is avoided: avoidance behaviour has been internalized; tensions *between* people have become tensions *within* people (for a fuller description, see Wouters 1998b). This development implies that social superiors are less automatically taken to be better people: superior and inferior behaviour is increasingly thought to be found in all classes. In the early 1960s this view was made explicit: "Bad behaviour is prevalent in all walks of life from the highest to the lowest; it is not confined to one class of person nor to one section of the community" (Bolton 1961:8).

These examples may help to understand why, in increasingly egalitarian societies, Elias's theme of the importance of class position and social status for personality and identity has become more embarrassing and difficult to discuss: as subordinate social groups were emancipated, references to "better" and "inferior" kinds of people, to hierarchical group differences, were increasingly tabooed. In the 1950s the once-automatic equation of superior in power and superior as a human being had declined to the point of embarrassment, and the new sensitivity to this difference urged one social arbiter to write in the introduction: "In this book, there occasionally crop up the words 'superior' and 'inferior.' These words are not used in the social sense, in any way, but are used merely to indicate difference in rank. Thus, it may be assumed that an older person is 'superior' to a younger person; that a child is 'inferior' to its parents and so on. The words imply no slur on the character of the person concerned, whatsoever" (*Etiquette for Everyone* 1956).

To repeat the theoretical connection: as bonds of co-operation and competition between people expanded and intensified, and hierarchical differences between individuals and groups diminished, more people pressured each other to take more of each other into account more often. Thus the dynamics of increasing interdependencies in Western societies contained a strong pressure towards increased sensitivity towards each other's emotional life, allowing a wider social acceptance of all kinds of behaviour and emotions, with the exception of expressing feelings of superiority and inferiority. In this way, changes in the spectrum of accepted ways of keeping a distance and of becoming more intimate correspond to changes in dominant patterns of emotion management; in particular, to changes in the management of superiority and inferiority feelings such as shame, embarrassment, and repulsion.

Other changes in the spectrum of accepted ways of becoming more intimate and keeping a distance are also related to changes in dominant patterns of emotion management. In addition to direct attacks on traditional ways of keeping a distance (avoidance behaviour) as an expression of superiority, there were also attacks on being too open and becoming too close. I shall sketch the line of developments in this sphere by focusing on direct warnings against psychic proximity or familiarity, on the spread of using first names, and on the increase in social kissing.

Dangers of Familiarity: Direct Warnings

At the turn of the twentieth century, the danger of not keeping enough distance was often mentioned. It was described as endangering even relationships with friends and acquaintances. The following example comes from a book that appeared in both Germany and the Netherlands: "It quite often happens that befriended families become enemies after having spent some time together in a summer resort; or, if they succeed in avoiding enmity, that they lose some respect for each other because of having become too intimate. Indeed, 'No man is great in the eyes of his valet.' The Great Wall of China that every sensitive person should raise around himself and also around his house would be quite appropriate here: a certain reserved distinction that no one dares to touch" (Bruck-Auffenberg 1897, 226).

Here are two American examples: "Discretional civility does not in any way include familiarity. We doubt whether it is not the best of all armor against it. Familiarity is 'bad style'" (Hanson 1896, 70); "Friendship does not mean familiarity. Indeed familiarity is the greatest foe. When a young girl allows a young man to call her by her first name, unless engaged to him, she cheapens his regard for her by just so much" (Harland and Van de Water 1907, 143).

In England the necessity of maintaining a distance was not emphasized as strongly. At that time the Great Wall of "reserve" had already become more of an integral part of the social habitus of the English establishment; the dangers of familiarity had come to be taken much more for granted. In order to find references to these dangers that are comparably open and direct, one has to look to books that appeared a few decades earlier. For instance, this quotation from 1861: "Indiscriminate familiarity either offends your superiors, or else dubs you their dependent. It gives your inferiors just but troublesome and improper claims of equality" (*Etiquette for All*, quoted in Curtin 1987, 125). In nineteenth-century England, more than in the other countries studied, it had already become taken for granted that the "proud ... disdained all kinds of familiarity ... because they interpreted aloofness as a sign of strength, independence, and self-sufficiency ... The well-mannered individual was not 'familiar'; he did not intrude on others; he did not ask personal questions; he did not thrust information about himself onto others; he kept his knowledge of others to himself; he did not talk to strangers; he did not snoop or eavesdrop; and he did not stand closely to his interlocutor, talk loudly, or gesticulate wildly" (Curtin 1987, 126–7).

Reserve was a particular requirement in cities, and English society was very much London-oriented. Whereas the dangers of familiarity were still a major theme in the German and Dutch etiquette books until the 1960s, in England reserve was taken for granted, to the extent that emphasizing the need for both social and psychic distance, even with friends and relatives, would most probably have been embarrassing. In contrast, the best-known Dutch etiquette book between 1939 and the 1960s advised:

Under all conditions, we would do well to keep some distance. Keeping one's distance means avoiding excessive familiarity. We all know that this danger exists in dealing with subordinates, but ... is there such a thing as excessive familiarity with our friends and relatives?

Yes! ...

Anyone who gets too close to us sees too much, too much of the petty, too much of the not so nice side of us, and the glimpse that we thus give others into our innermost regions can be a surprisingly unpleasant one that can never ever be eradicated. (Groskamp-ten Have 1939, 26–7)

In present-day German books, in certain contexts, keeping a "healthy distance" is still advocated, whereas in the Dutch literature this advice has been succeeded by an emphasis on privacy (for a fuller description see Wouters 1987, 419ff).

Dangers of Familiarity: First Names

Another example of diminishing social and psychic distance, and a way of avoiding feelings of superiority and inferiority, is the spread of the use of first names. In 1937, in the revised edition of her book, Emily Post strongly advised against this practice: "Surely there is little to be said in favor of present-day familiarity in the use of first names – because those at the upper end of the social scale voluntarily choose to do the very thing by which those at the lower end of the social scale are hall-marked. The sole reason why so many men and women who work prefer jobs in factories or stores to those of domestic employ is that the latter carries the opprobrium of being addressed by one's first name. It will be interesting to see whether the reversal will be complete" (Post 1937, 32). And: "We know very well that there are countless people of middle age, and even older too, who seem to think that being called Tilly or Tommy by Dora Debutante and Sammy Freshman is to be presented with a cup of the elixir of youth" (Post 1937, 34).

In the light of Americans' reputedly informal ways of addressing each other, it may seem surprising that these quotations can also be found in the "completely revised" 1950 edition, and that in the 1965 edition of this book, revised by the author's daughter-in-law, the same stance is taken and even italicized: "*It is in flagrant violation of good manners for children to call their natural parents by their first names*" (Post 1965, 17). In the 1975 edition the italics were removed, but now the sentence continued: "and furthermore, it undermines the respect that every child should have for his mother and father" (1975, 18). However, italics did not help to halt the trend, nor did anything else. Increasingly informal adult manners and mentality did find their roots in more informal parent-child relationships and were, in turn, reinforced by them. As Letitia Baldridge had it in the 1970s: "The parent's own attitude toward people in authority determines the mind-set of their children ... Side by side with respect for those in authority should go respect for those who serve us ... Harping parents make harping children who grow into harping parents" (Vanderbilt 1978, 6–9). Although the debate about the issue continued throughout the century until the present day, with hindsight the direction of change is unmistakable: "The widespread use of first names, sports clothing, audio recreation, and other attributes of 'informality' in the work world has assisted in the illusion that no-one really needs to perform a service for anyone else" (Martin 1983, 417).

In England, etiquette books show less resistance to this trend. In 1939 Lady Troubridge clearly welcomed the new informality by calling a first chapter "The New Etiquette Is Informal" and a paragraph "Accept the New Spirit!" "Friendships are made far quicker now that the barrier of undue formality has been lifted, and Christian names follow swiftly on mutual liking in a way which would make old-fashioned people aghast. [The author advises her readers] ... to steer a course nicely blended between old-fashioned courtesy and new-fashioned informality, so that we shall always be right" (1939, 10–11).

After the 1960s and 1970s, comments tend towards matter-of-fact acceptance: "Once, using someone's first name was a sign of family links, acceptance or long acquaintance, a goal for the would-be suitor, a mark of best-friendship, let alone a social signal that you yourself came from the same or a superior rank. In closed societies where interdependence had to combine with hierarchy, nicknames achieved the necessary closeness without overstepping the bounds of proper formality ... Today, all such criteria are largely obsolete. The use of first names is no longer a benchmark of intimacy but the norm [especially among 'media folk']" (Courey 1985, 19). And from 1988: "Most people today are introduced by their christian and surnames, in very informal situations by christian names alone" (Gilgallon and Seddon 1988, 25).

In Germany this process of diminishing social and psychic distance has been lagging behind. *Duzen* (the use of the informal "you") and the use of first names have remained relatively restricted. Yet repeated complaints about too hastily crossing these important borderlines signify the presence of the informalizing trend. In 1993 a return to formality and *Siezen* (the formal "you") was reported: "Today the motto in addressing someone is again 'Distance and Difference'" (*Der Spiegel* 1993). A variety of subtle differentiations of proximity and distance still prevails, as the next remarks on social kissing may show: "The social kiss is not to be considered a step towards saying *Du* to each other ... Such little kisses on cheeks have no other significance than 'We like you and you are now recognized as one of our acquaintances!' In these cases one might use Christian names, but they are certainly no indication that one may automatically start to *duzen"* (*Umgangs-formen Heute* 1988, 94–5).

Dangers of Familiarity: Social Kissing

From this warning it follows that social kissing is accepted, even in Germany. In 1988, when it was first published, the warning was new, but the social kiss was not. In 1973, for instance, one could read: "In circles of artists this way of greeting each other is very popular – something one should know. If one doesn't, a thus tempestuously greeted person will stand there a little silly and shy" (Wachtel 1973, 47). In 1977, in a new edition of the same book, this passage is revised as follows: "In circles of artists this way of greeting each other *was* very popular. In the meantime this social kiss has also become endemic at the better kind of party. In general, there seems to be a wide disposition and willingness to kiss and be kissed. The stars on stage and television show how to do it, and even football players ... give their emotions free reign when they want to express their completely uninhibited joy. What once gave offence to the highest degree has for a long time already belonged among the things taken for granted in our 'permissive society'" (Schliff 1977, 41).

Social kissing has spread in all the countries studied. "In the Netherlands, too, men and women nowadays exchange more kisses than ever in a thousand years of civilization ... The custom originated in the world of fashion, went across to the theatre, was taken up by the world of television, and has established itself today in almost every layer of society ... The number of kisses is also on the way up: twenty years ago one kiss would do; ten years ago kissing twice was on its way up; and today it has become fashionable to kiss three times – a custom that spread from the south of the Netherlands. If the present inflation continues, it is hard to predict where this all will end" (Loon 1983, 75).

The origin of social kissing is invariably seen in what is called "the world of fashion" – among actors and other artists. These people were also the first to be accepted in Society, despite their lack of any "old family" connection or wealth. As Eileen Terry wrote in 1925, "Notice the easy way in which the Stage has joined with the Peerage – obviously because the essential Stage training teaches good manners, correct speech and social actions, and also a careful toilet and a graceful walk" (1925, 11).

The acceptance and success of the stage in Society depended mostly on what today may be called "personality," that is, actors' command of a "presentation of self" that is experienced as at least attractive and as irresistible as possible.[7] From this perspective, overcoming existing social and psychic distance depended upon developing an understanding of the kind of behaviour and composure that those in Society and other centres of power experienced as attractive, as well as upon developing the capacity to direct oneself accordingly. Therefore, in this world, competition in self-regulation, in aristocratic ease and confidence, has most probably been relatively fierce, and awareness of self-regulation may have been stronger. The continuation of this kind of competition makes it plausible that social kissing originated within these circles.

Comments upon social kissing can also be read as clear examples of an increasing pressure to avoid expressions of social and psychic distance. A quotation from 1859 in defence of kissing in public, apparently on its way out, will serve to introduce the subject: "As a general rule, this act of affection is excluded from public eyes in this country, and there are people who are ashamed even to kiss a brother or father on board the steamer which is to take him away for some ten or twenty years. But then there are people in England who are ashamed of showing any feeling, however natural, however pure" (*Habits of Good Society* 1859, 184).

In the 1950s, kissing in public had returned, but perhaps it had become less an act of affection than a demonstration of social and psychic equality: "Oddly enough, although the English are rather reticent about shaking hands, certain of them are growing tremendously keen on saying 'Hello' and 'Goodbye' with a social kiss. Affectionate though this is, the gesture we are speaking of is no more than a peck on the cheek" (Edwards and Beyfus 1956, 199). In the 1980s, social kissing was reported to be "now the rule rather than the exception ... In most major metropolitan centres, the kiss has virtually replaced the handshake as the social *ave atque vale* of our times ... Most favoured embrace today is the double kiss ... although in some circles it is already being replaced by the triple kiss. In Manhattan they kiss on the lips – turning the other cheek to a New Yorker could be interpreted as a snub" (Courey 1985, 21–2).

From the following quotations from English and American etiquette books, it seems clear that social kissing is only half-heartedly accepted, if at all. They show an ambivalence that can also be interpreted as a fear of snubbing: the fear of rejecting others by refusing them social and psychological proximity, that is, equality. From a chapter called "Lip Service": "Social kissing has arrived. It didn't have to wait for the Channel Tunnel to open[8] ... Nowadays few ask themselves 'Do we?' The question today is: 'One cheek or two?' ... In my youth unnecessary kissing suggested theatrical leanings, or a flaw in the Anglo-Saxon pedigree" (Graham 1989, 15). "Miss Manners heartily joins you in deploring the debasement of both the dignified American greeting of the handshake and the intimacy of the kiss" (Martin 1983, 65). "Q. What is the correct sound to emit when kissing a friend by way of greeting or farewell? ... A. It seems that 'Mwa!' has recently been superseded by 'Mwu!' 'Mmm!' is currently not acceptable" (Killen 1990, 50).

This mocking, half-hearted attitude towards social kissing may be contrasted with the positive attitude of a German author who took the ascent of social kissing as evidence for his view that "relationships between people are moulded in ways that are essentially more natural and less uptight" (Wolter 1990, 10). Notwithstanding the reported return to formality, this evaluation is in line with that of most other recent German authors, who sincerely invite their readers to do away with uptight formalities: "We are against empty formalities as a substitute for humane behaviour ... Let us learn to have conversations with each other without having to know who and what we are! This only requires trust in all possible participants in a conversation, all fellow men, whatever their occupation or education!" (*Umgangsformen Heute* 1988, 10, 19)

However, no matter how one evaluates this process, both English and German social arbiters seem to realize that more informal codes of behaviour and feeling cannot be equated with easier codes. German authors are particularly explicit on this point: "Every authoritarian abuse of power is evil. We loathe constraint and drill, and with endurance and patience we consciously choose the *difficult road*" (*Umgangsformen Heute* 1970, 24; italics added). "Today's manners include a freedom for all to proceed in various ways, as far as tactfulness allows. This risk of choosing is better than being fossilized in yesterday's formalities. Formality is inhibiting. Smooth manners require a sense of togetherness between the generations and an understanding of fellow human beings" (*Umgangsformen Heute* 1970, 16). Here it is stated explicitly that abolishing formalities does give rise to the "risk of choosing," and that the chances of making the wrong choice increase if a sense of togetherness is lacking, that is, when there is insufficient identification with others, regardless of age, sex, or class. Therefore, no matter how strongly one may "loathe constraint," the constraint to chose "the difficult road" has intensified.

INTERPRETATION ONE: THE CONSTRAINT TO BE UNCONSTRAINED

A similar paradox can be perceived both in the increase in the use of first names and in social kissing. Both can be taken as examples of intimate and private forms of behaviour "going public," of increasing confidentiality, openness, or familiarity, intimacy or "instant intimacy" – the choice of concept depends on one"s evaluation of this development.[9] Whether evaluated positively or negatively, the trend is compelling. No one is able completely to ignore this development or withdraw from its inherent constraints. On the other hand, many people may not even experience or recognize any constraint, since it is a constraint to be unconstrained. As status competition intensified and the art of obliging and being obliged became more important as a power resource, demonstrations of being intimately trustworthy while perfectly at ease also gained in importance. In this sense, processes of democratization, integration, and informalization ran parallel to an increasing constraint towards developing "smooth manners." Thus the rise in public or anonymous intimacy – part of increasing emotional and behavioural alternatives – ran in tandem with rising demands on emotion management. The expression "a constraint to be unconstrained" seems to capture this paradoxical development.

This expression resembles one used by Norbert Elias: the social constraint toward self-constraint. Indeed, the two constraints are closely related. A quotation from the German Christoph Höflinger, writing in 1885, may illustrate this point: "Beware not to clean your nose with anything else but a handkerchief ... Indeed, courage and mastery over oneself is demanded in order to be able to control oneself so constantly and persistently, but only in this way one accustoms oneself to an uninterrupted decent demeanour" (1885, 12).

From these lines it is clear that the constraint towards becoming accustomed to self-constraint is at the same time a constraint to be unconstrained, to be confident and at ease. Almost every etiquette book emphasizes the importance of tactful, rather than demonstrative, deference and of "natural," rather than mannered, behaviour. However, in processes of emancipation and informalization, some ways of behaving, experienced previously as tactful deference, came to be seen as too hierarchical and demonstrative, just as what was once defined and recommended as natural came to be experienced more or less as stiff and phony, and branded as mannered. It then became so obviously a "role" in which so many traces of constraint had been "discovered" that "playing it" provoked embarrassment. People who stuck to these old ways of relating were running the risk of being seen as bores, as lacking any talent for "the jazz of human exchange" (Hochschild 1983). Thus new forms of relaxed, "loose," and "natural" behaviour had been developed. Some writers of etiquette books seem to be at least vaguely aware of this process, if only because they took it for granted that "natural" behaviour had to be learned. Full awareness was prevented, however, most probably because of their "hodiecentrism" (Goudsblom

1977) – their glorification of the actual definition of tactful and natural behaviour as the ultimate outcome, the end of the history of learning to act naturally. An example from 1923: "It is essential to *learn* to appear just as much at ease in one's dress suit in the presence of Royalty as one does in one's crêpe de chine pajamas in one's dressing room in the presence of a Persian cat. And it is necessary to *learn* to walk as if in sandals and not as if in tight boots on soft corns. *Be natural.* Go to a good tailor, even though he may seem a little more expensive" (*Etiquette for Gentlemen* 1923, 21).

In all countries considered here, this emphasis on ease and easy-goingness has tempered the emphasis on reserve or avoidance of familiarity. In Britain both sides of this tension balance were highly developed. As was noted, "anything that smacked of effort, awkwardness, or forethought was itself bad manners: above all things, one must be self-confident and at ease" (Curtin 1987, 56–7). This demand is clearly derived from the aristocratic tradition. The Germans may have a lot of reserve, as is demonstrated, for example, in the dividing lines of *duzen*, but here it is hardly, if at all, tempered by aristocratic ease. According to Heinz Dietrich, Freiherr von Knigge's famous courtesy book (1788) was revolutionary because he did not restrict himself to the manners of the nobility, but also added those of the bourgeoisie. Dietrich commented, "Yet he considered it necessary to write down other rules for them than for the aristocracy" (1934, 6). Indeed, the aristocracy and the bourgeoisie in Germany had rather separate centres of power: the noble courts versus the universities. English society was more integrated, more London-oriented, and the English blend of a code of good manners and a code of morals shows, according to Elias, "the gradualness of the resolution of conflicts between upper and middle classes" (2000, 426). Lord Chesterfield referred to "ease" as "the last stage of perfection of politeness." At present, and not only in England but all over the Western world, this still remains the case, only more so.

INTERPRETATION TWO:
EASE AND AUTHENTICITY

As "ease" and "naturalness" gained in importance, increasing numbers of people pressured each other to develop more differentiated and flexible patterns of self-regulation, triggering further impetus towards higher levels of social knowledge and of self-knowledge and reflexivity (see Kilminster 1998, chap. 8). Pressure to develop a keen eye for "the latent meaning of apparently insignificant details," for instance, by examining "the most trivial details ... involuntary gestures, slips of the tongue" (Kasson 1990, 94–5), was also accompanied by heated discussions about the distinction between a "false self" and a "real self," or between "phony" and "natural" or "authentic" behaviour and feelings.[10] There is a whole body of literature, from physiognomy to its modern form of semiotics, from Freud, Simmel, Veblen, and Weber to Goffman and Foucault, demonstrating a growing awareness of (and pressure towards) impression management. Many interpreted this shift as a loss of "true self" and embarked upon the quest for an "enduring substance" in the self, for universal and eternal realities *behind* all these changing and changeable appearances, a quest as old as religion and metaphysics. Some came to take what might be called a zero-sum perspective on emotion management, a perspective that also has a long tradition; for instance, as outlined by Georg Simmel at the beginning of the twentieth century: "punctuality, calculability and exactness become part of modern personalities *to the exclusion* of those irrational, instinctive, sovereign traits and impulses which aim at determining the mode of life from within" (Simmel, quoted in Krieken 1990; italics added).

The mode of life was seen as more and more determined or even dictated from without. However, as the management of appearance has become increasingly important, *both* inward and outward signals and signs have become scrutinized more severely and in ways more sensitive to shades and nuances. From this perspective, the zero-sum view may be seen as an expression of a nostalgic kind of moral masochism which still blinds many people to the controlled intensification of both sides of this tension balance in social and psychic processes.

DIMINISHING SOCIAL AND PSYCHIC DISTANCE BETWEEN THE SEXES: INCREASING INTEGRATION AND MUTUAL IDENTIFICATION

From the late nineteenth century onward, chaperonage was declining in popularity, and this aspect of diminishing social segregation was often discussed in etiquette books. These books contain quite explicit and specific information regarding the relationship between the sexes, since the importance of manners to upward mobility was especially relevant for women. "Society will fraternize with the millionaire and ignore his misplaced *h's* and his absence of good breeding, while they drink his wines and assist him in various ways to spend his money; but the wives and daughters of these men will not visit his wife and daughters, nor receive them into their houses, if they lack refinement and culture" (Klickman, quoted in Curtin 1987, 211). Ever since the nineteenth century, as women not only came to run and organize the social sphere of Society but also functioned as its gatekeepers, the whole genre has been female-dominated and quite explicit on gender relationships. Therefore etiquette books are a particularly rich source for studying changes in the behavioural codes and ideals regarding the relationships between the sexes.

Michael Curtin distinguishes between the English eighteenth-century courtesy-book genre and the nineteenth-century etiquette-book genre. Authors of courtesy books, such as Chesterfield, were aristocrats, thus familiar with courts and the lifestyle cultivated and appreciated within them. The transition of the one genre to the other is characterized by a declining importance of aristocracy and patricians and their centres of power, that is, courts. Whereas the courtesy genre was dominated by men, the whole etiquette genre was (and is) dominated by women, both as authors and, most probably, as readers. This change reflects the widening sphere of opportunities that women enjoyed in the nineteenth century: the opportunities of the drawing room, not those of the wider society. "It was in the sociability of the 'lady' – that is, the woman who toiled neither in the home nor the marketplace – that the etiquette book found its characteristic, though not exclusive, subject matter" (Curtin 1987, 419). Leonore Davidoff has also pointed to the connection between the rising middle classes and rising opportunities for women: "Society in the nineteenth century, especially in England, did become formalized. One way of formalizing a social institution is to use specialized personnel to carry out its functions. In nineteenth century England upper- and middle-class women were used to maintain the fabric of Society, as semi-official leaders but also as arbiters of social acceptance or rejection" (Davidoff 1973, 16).

In the United States, a male etiquette writer referred to this very process as "the tyranny in large cities of what is known as the 'fashionable set,' formed of people willing to spend money ... this circle lives by snubbing" (Hanson 1896, 39). His choice of words may have been gender-related for it was women who organized and to a large extent controlled the domain of Society. The functioning of Society and etiquette was an important resource of power for them, which they controlled via a constant stream of praise gossip and blame gossip. Especially in nineteenth-century Society, etiquette was decisive in making friends and, through friends, in gaining influence and recognition. It also functioned as a means of winning a desirable spouse. However important as a source of power and identity, "respectable" women and young girls were at the same time confined to the domain of their home and Society. "The only 'safe' contacts they would have outside the home were with a few selected other girls, clergymen, or in the context of small-scale charity work, particularly teaching in

Sunday schools" (Davidoff 1973, 51). Towards the end of the nine-teenth century, in "all of social life, in fact there was beginning to be provision for respectable women to meet in public places outside their own homes. Cafés, the growth of tea rooms, the use of buses, even the provision of public lavatories for women, were as important in freeing middle class women from strict social ritual as the slow erosion of chaperonage. Contact by telephone and the later mobility that came with cars began to undermine the most formal parts of etiquette" (Davidoff 1973, 67).

The processes of social emancipation and accommodation, and their inherent pressure to control feelings of inferiority and superiority, are also revealed in subsequent advice on courtship, dancing, dating, engagement, and marriage. From the end of the nineteenth century onward, "Alternative models of femininity – the university woman or even the suffragette – offered 'careers' that competed with some suc-cess against fashionable Society" (Curtin 1987, 243–4). By the inter-war period, "the reduced scale of living for most of the middle class, the decline of chaperonage and new freedom for girls, meant that even the 'career' sequence of schoolgirl, deb (or provincial variant), daughter-at-home, matron and dowager wielding power in the social/political world, had ceased to have much cogency ... It was the time of the 'flapper,' the 'roaring twenties' (Davidoff 1973, 99).[11]

Escaping Home: Becoming Her Own Chaperone; "Fast Girls" or "New Women"?

In the early 1960s an author sighs, "Boy meets girl and girl meets boy in so many different ways that it would be quite impossible to enumer-ate them" (Bolton 1961, 15). This impossibility became taken for granted to the extent that in later years the thought is no longer expressed, whereas before that time, enumerating the various ways of meeting was quite normal procedure. This sentence therefore indicates an important moment, a point of no return, before which changes in ways and places of meeting often attracted special attention. Here is an example from a Dutch author, writing in the 1910s: "Fifteen years ago it would have been completely unnecessary to say anything about danc-ing in public. Ladies and young girls from good families did not dream of exhibiting their talents anywhere but at invitation balls. Public dance halls were for soldiers and servant girls" (Viroflay 1919, 54).

By the end of the nineteenth century, particularly the seaside and the watering places, known for their greater informality, were consid-ered to be dangerous and worth a warning: "Promiscuous intimacies at summer resorts are a great mistake" (Harland and van der Water

1907, 293). And in 1897 Mrs Humphry wrote in her *Manners for Men*: "Picking up promiscuous male acquaintances is a practice fraught with danger. It cannot be denied that girls of the lower middle classes are often prone to it; and there are thousands of young men who have no feminine acquaintances in the great towns and cities where they live, and who are found responsive to this undiscriminating mode of making acquaintances ... The seaside season is prolific in these chance acquaintances – 'flirtations,' as they may perhaps be called. Bicycling is well known to favor them" (quoted in Porter 1972:33).[12] Warnings like these show there was more toleration of sexual licence. Indeed, according to Davidoff, the saying "You can do anything that you please as long as you don't do it in the streets and frighten the horses" was a common one (1973, 66).

Women, especially young women, wanted to go out, and even chaperones were under the influence. In her *Manners for Girls*, Mrs Humphry in 1901 noted the arrival of the dancing, flirtatious chaperone, no longer keeping a "sharp eye on the movements" of the girl she was watching over. She complained, "The class of girl who likes the irresponsible, dancing, flirting chaperone is not as yet a very numerous one; but yet English Society is well aware of her" (quoted in Porter 1972, 85). Around 1910, chaperonage was on its way out: "Young ladies are now frequently asked to dinner-parties without a chaperon, a hostess constituting herself chaperon for the occasion" (*Manners and Rules of Good Society* 1955, 228). In the 1920s an English etiquette writer concluded, "An unmarried daughter is no longer socially her mother's pale shadow, kept closely under the elder lady's wing, never allowed to be alone, unless under her vigilant eyes, for she may now form her own social circle, entertain friends of both sexes, and be entertained at their homes" (*Etiquette up to Date* 1925, 230). Yet traditional restrictions on young people's freedom to negotiate the dynamics and borderlines of friendships were still quite strong, as becomes clear from the way in which this writer continues: "When any gentleman, newly introduced to a girl, has escorted her home from the scene of the introduction, it is not correct for her to ask him to call, or for him to seek the permission from her. Any such invitation must come from the girl's mother, or any friends with whom she may be staying, so if she wishes to see more of her cavalier, she should introduce him to her mother or hostess" (*Etiquette up to Date* 1925, 230).

The process may have been experienced as slow or fast, but the direction was undisputed; it was moving towards greater freedom to control the dynamics of one's own relationships, whether romantic or not, and to decide about the respectability of meeting places and conditions. There was growing appreciation of the "new woman" (who was often the "fast girl" in the eyes of others).[13] "The 'new woman,' by easing her demands for deference, allowed gentlemen to enjoy themselves in a relaxed fashion in her company – an advantage which lower-class women and prostitutes had always exploited" (Curtin 1987, 280). Greater freedom ran in tandem with greater intimacy and a chance of friendship or camaraderie between the sexes: "Very often a man will come into contact with a girl, through business affairs, at a dance or other function, or under even still less formal circumstances, and a friendship will spring up" (Devereux 1927, 119). "There was a time, not so long ago, when a marked reserve was required between men and women in public. But today, following upon the CAMARA-DERIE between the two sexes bred by the War, and with the advent of women into almost every profession, art, and business, this social barrier is disappearing and a more friendly relationship is springing up between the two. The former stiff formality has been replaced by friendliness and understanding" (Troubridge 1931, 311).

On the way from complete surveillance to greater freedom came new inventions such as boarding schools for girls' and ladies'" clubs, both welcomed for enlarging the possibilities of making contacts out-side the home: "to the business woman, the lonely woman, or the woman who is not comfortably or conveniently settled at home, the club has become one of the greatest of boons and a necessity to happiness" (*Etiquette for Ladies* 1923, 136). And "Boarding Schools for girls can be found all over England, whereas of old they were confined to those unfortunate creatures known in advertisements as 'refractory girls'" (Terry 1925, 69).

Escaping Home: Dancing and the Ambivalences in Becoming Her Own Chaperone

This last author shifts from praising boarding schools for helping to open up the world for young girls to a discussion of dancing. In this discussion she expresses the typical emancipation problem of new demands on behaviour and emotion management; the following pas-sage focuses, in fact, on this specific ambivalence between old and new sources of power and identity:

Yet the limited outlook instinct seems to have been ground into women so thoroughly in the Ages, that they are unable to escape from it even in their new freedom. Thousands of girls think of nothing but dance, dance, dance! A doctor friend suggested to me that the "one partner" idea was probably a subconscious attempt on the part of women to get away from wide possibilities, and get back to the old ingrained safety of the narrow outlook … In the old days the girl or woman saw nothing but husband and family in the ordinary way, so the varying partner at a dance came as a distinct relief. Now in her wider life, women come up so much unexpected variety that they turn instinctively to the one man limitation to which, as a sex, they have been so long accustomed. The "one partner" craze was a bad one, from every point of view, especially when it came to women paying a particular man to dance with her, or, as was often done, hiring a stranger from some enterprising firm. When we reached that stage, dancing was no longer an amusement, but an obsession, and a dangerous one too. After all, there is really much more enjoyment in the change of partners, if we can only bring ourselves to admit it, and it is pleasant to see that it is coming into its own once more. (Terry 1925, 69–70)

In another etiquette book, also published in 1925, a chapter on dancing opens as follows:

The last few years have seen not only a change in the actual style of ballroom dancing but also a tremendous expansion of the opportunities for indulging in this pastime, and all classes of society have taken to dancing practically anywhere and everywhere, on every possible occasion ... Many of the restrictions with which Mrs. Grundy once fettered the dance-loving maiden were gaily cast aside at much the same time as when old favorites, such as square dances, stately minuets, graceful cotillions and waltzes were succeeded by the one-step and fox-trot, while chaperons faded away like dim ghosts of the past during the war and programs became unnecessary as a means of recording dances promised, as the fashion came in for a couple to become recognized "dancing partners," who would dance together throughout the evening, probably during the London season, accompanying each other to two or three dances in the same evening, or early hours of the next day. Now the pendulum is in some respects swinging back again. Gradually the chaperon is reappearing, though not often do we find her the formidable, lynx-eyed dragoness of former days, who kept her young charge strictly to her side between dances – the modern maid's independent temperament would not submit to that – and the chaperon of today is often as keen upon dancing and having a good time as are the younger folks. Many hostesses, too, now clearly intimate their dislike of the one-partner practice, so that it is again usual for a lady to distribute her favors among a number of gentlemen during the evening. This is certainly a more sociable practice. The one-partner vogue was carried to selfish and sometimes most discourteous extremes. (*Etiquette up to Date* 1925, 108–10)

This one-partner craze was typically English. It was not mentioned in the American sources, for instance, where most authors wrote in favour of dancing and against puritanical critique; the following is from a paragraph called "A Plea for Dancing": "Lately there has been a great deal of unfavorable criticism directed against the modern dances. There have been newspaper articles condemning the 'latest dance fads' as immoral and degrading. There have been speeches and lectures against 'shaking and twisting of the body into weird, outlandish contortions.' There have been vigorous crusades against dance halls ... Dancing, even the shoulder-shaking, oscillating dancing of today, is really not intended to be vulgar or immoral at all, despite the crusade of anti-immorality dancing committees!" (Eichler 1923, 2:104–5) Another writer went as far as to advise, "So roll up the rugs, turn on a new dance record or roll, and practice your steps" (Richardson 1927, 41).

In the Netherlands at the beginning of the "roaring twenties," one social arbiter tried to raise sympathy for the "new fashion," branding as "old-fashioned" all mothers' objecting to their daughters' presence "on a dance floor open to everyone." She added, "The only rule one can urge to maintain rigorously is: do not dance with a stranger" (Viroflay 1919, 55). Later in the decade, however, even the Dutch government was sufficiently worried by the new freedom of dancing and dance halls to establish a government committee whose task it was to investigate the "problem of dancing." One of the recommendations in the committee's report (*Rapport* 1931) was a mandatory appointment of "dancing masters" in charge of surveillance in dance halls. The report displayed hardly any confidence in the self-surveillance of both sexes, and it was written in the implicit assumption that both men and women would give in to their sexual desires if social control was lacking. The emphasis in sexual control still rested on obedience, on social control rather than on individual control of emotions: "In the modern dances the danger of sexual titillation has reached a degree that was absent before ... And thus, every young girl who visits a public dancing hall runs the risk of being 'led' in a reprehensible way, unnoticed by the public, and against which she practically cannot defend herself. And then we still assume the favourable condition that the will to defend herself is present. But how many ... do not maintain the moral endurance here required and end up with the rendezvous" (*Rapport* 1931, 31).

In Germany I have not found any trace of this dancing issue in etiquette books. Here the dance euphoria ran in tandem with widespread social misery, and a conservative politician explicitly preferred "the people to amuse themselves with music and dance instead of organizing demonstrations" (quoted in Klein 1994, 168).

Escaping Home: To Pay or to Be Paid for?

As women were trying to do away with chaperones and replace them with gentlemen-escorts, the question of whether they were allowed to pay for themselves became an issue of greater concern. Chaperones used not only to watch over their charges but also pay their way. Curtin has summarized the problem: "money was a real asset not merely a ceremonial gesture ... Some ladies wished to make clear that the relations between themselves and their escorts were of a public and egalitarian nature, not romantic as between lovers or dependent as between father and daughter. Chivalric deference was not well suited to comradely relations ... In addition, those who paid the servants ... owned their allegiance ... To transfer this power from husbands and fathers ... to outsiders was obviously dangerous" (Curtin 1987, 272–3). Apparently, women who wanted to "escape" from the imprisonment of the "home" and get rid of the system of chaperonage had to put up with this interpretation of a "transfer of power over women to outsiders." Going out with relative strangers without the protection of a chaperone was considered dangerous enough in itself, but being financially dependent upon this "outsider" enlarged the danger considerably. Whenever her way was paid for by such a person, her father or husband was advised to immediately send him a postal money order (Humphry 1902, 174). However much this interpretation of a transfer of power may have waned, it has not disappeared altogether. Most authors of American books and paragraphs on dating warn girls not to "feel compelled to 'pay' for every date. There's no law that says you must kiss your escort at parting!" (Sweeney 1948, 27). In the 1980s an English etiquette book held that the "person who issues the invitation pays. Usually he pays for her. His payment is for the pleasure of her company – nothing more ... If he is courting her he should pay. One day she will become pregnant or give up work temporarily to look after their under-fives and she needs to know that he is able and willing to pay for two – even three" (Lansbury 1985, 77).

In the statement "His payment is for the pleasure of her company – nothing more," the danger of the "power transfer" is still recognizably present. If he thinks his payment is for more, or "worth more," the occasion may even end in a "date rape." On their way to gaining greater control over the dangers connected with this view of a power transfer, women had to establish the right of paying for themselves.

The issue is first dealt with in English etiquette books. In 1902, for instance, a social arbiter writes: "It is the man's place to pay for what refreshments are had, if the ladies do not insist on paying their share; and if he invites the ladies with him to go in somewhere and have some, then the case is simple enough. But if the lady expresses a wish to pay, and means it, – and there is but little difficulty in knowing when she does mean it, – it is only polite and kind on the part of the man to let her do so, and whatever his feelings may be he must give in" (*Etiquette for Women* 1902, 59). By the 1950s, as this rule for ladies of independent means had trickled down the social ladder, the transition had reached a remarkable stage: "The going has never been so good for a bachelor woman who has a paid job. She not only gets her pay packet and her independence but she is still able to enjoy the remnants of masculine gallantry. In many fields she is paid a salary that compares with a man's and she can still graciously lie low when it comes to standing her round of drinks when men are about" (Edwards and Beyfus 1956, 135).

In the German etiquette books the issue of women paying for themselves is dealt with much later than in England – around approximately 1930. In 1933, for instance, Meister wrote, "Until a few years ago, it was still taken for granted that a man paid the bill. Today a young lady has achieved independence and often earns as much as a man" (quoted in Krumrey 1984, 399). Up until the 1950s it was repeated that he should pay, but she might pay her share in advance or later. Then in 1951 we read: "In former times it was taken for granted that a man paid the bill. Today a woman wishes to be independent of men in this respect too" (Franken 1951, 367). For some time, disputes over this issue continued, but from the 1970s onward, all social arbiters suggest that it should be a woman's right to pay the bill whenever she wishes to do so.

In the Netherlands, only for a few decades has it been that the Dutch have been "going Dutch": the possibility of women paying for themselves was mentioned positively from the 1950s onward, and in the 1980s a woman who did not pay her share by buying her round of drinks every now and then was even called a parasite (for more details, see Wouters 1987).

In the United States, the tradition of men paying for women lingered on for a long time. In 1937 Emily Post was already complaining about this tradition: "In this modern day, when women are competing with men in politics, in business and in every profession, it is really senseless to cling to that one obsolete convention – no matter what the circumstances – that the man must buy the tickets, pay the check, pay the taxi, or else be branded a gigolo or parasite. The modern point of view has changed in every particular save this one!" (1937, 365) This may sound modern, indeed, but Post's solution to the problem reads like an anticlimax; she only allows for one exception – "On occasion, when agreed beforehand, girls as well as men pay their own checks" (1937, 369) – and for the rest she advises not to let him pay more than he can afford. Around 1960 women were allowed to invite a man to dine with them – "A situation that caused great embarrassment some years ago but is taken casually today" – but her paying for the dinner had to be hidden. Post notes, "If she has no charge account and has to pay the check before her guest, this will be embarrassing" (1960, 62). On first dates, "It is the man's responsibility to plan and to pay for everything they do that evening" (1960, 176). And again on any date, "It's not so much what you suggest as *that* you suggest. If it's a 'Let's go out. Where'll we go?' kind of invitation, a man has more or less given a woman carte blanche on his wallet" (Ostrander 1967, 52). Until well into the 1970s it was still taken for granted that he paid, and although the possibility of "going Dutch" is mentioned earlier, only from the 1970s onwards is it spoken of favourably. Even today, however, "going Dutch" is not considered normal: if she does not suggest it, in most cases he is still expected to pay for both. Here the Americans seem to lag behind.

Escaping Home: Going to Work

Of course, gaining "the right to pay" was only a small step on the way to overcoming this interpretation of "transferring power over women from husbands and fathers to outsiders." A more important step was "the right to earn," to enter the labour market and aim at financial independence. Going out into the workforce is another aspect of the development of women "escaping" from homes, where they were "kept" by fathers and husbands, and entering the wider society. In the words of the English Lady Troubridge, whose etiquette book was popular from the mid-1920s through the 1930s, "There was a time not very long ago when women's interests were confined chiefly to the home. For a woman to be actively engaged in some business or profession meant one of two things, either she was an old maid or she was 'queer,' but to-day a woman is a citizen and may use her talents and capabilities in any way in which she chooses ... It may take many years before she is regarded as the equal of man in business and professional life and politics, and until that time arrives it behooves every woman ... to do her share in building up the right attitude towards sex equality" (1926, 375).

For a long time, women at work were strongly confronted with the problems related to the interpretation of a power transfer and were trying to cope with them. There both men and women were, so to speak, put to the test: both had to unlearn their habitual out-of-business social expectations of each other. These centred on sexuality and marriage. At work, both women and men had to learn how to relate to each other more or less regardless of gender and sexual attraction. This change implied that women had to unlearn their old

Society roles and attitudes. Finding a paid job and gaining financial independence demanded a price: women had to give up much of their traditional sources of power and identity, derived from their functioning at home and in Society (or its equivalent further down the social ladder). Moreover, quite often and especially in the beginning, they could only derive a little power and identity from their functioning in society outside Society. Therefore many women would have experienced a tug-of-war between their old, nineteenth-century sources of power and identity and their newly gained, twentieth-century sources. At some times and in some respects, they stuck to traditional resources and to the connected patterns of superiority and inferiority feelings; here are two early examples of such a pattern from around 1900. "Let the new woman prate as much as she please about her independence of man, but she is the first, nevertheless, to rise up in indignation if any of the same old chivalry is omitted" (Hanson 1896, 362). "The true love of a good man is worth winning. It is not won by the girl who lowers herself to a man's level. To her might apply the time-worn toast of man to 'The New Woman, – once our superior, now our equal'" (Harland and van der Water 1905, 345). At other times, sometimes even at the same time, women had to embody a rather opposed and contradictory pattern, especially when claiming access to the more modern resources of power and identity. A quotation from the same 1905 book may illustrate this point: "The prejudice which so long existed among men against women in business relations was partly caused by the thought that they could never forget they were women, could never discuss work or business relations on impersonal and rational grounds. The first lesson a woman must learn in making her own way financially is to appreciate that ... her place of employment is no place for superfluous courtesies. The cultivation of a cool, matter-of-fact, unsentimental way of looking at the work in hand, is the only path to honorable achievement" (447).

In etiquette books the change in this tug-of-war or ambivalence can be followed in many ways. Here is a rather general formulation from the 1950s: "The new problem is ... how far she should carry the new equality into her social relationship with men, when she should assert her independence and when she should fall back on her femininity" (Edwards and Beyfus 1956, 135). Of course, one might point to many other barriers to women's emancipation, but without taking this ambivalence into account, it will be hard fully to understand or explain why women's present-day struggle against having to work a "second shift" (Hochschild with Machung 1989) has been so weak for so long. As early as 1905, at a time when their attempt to escape from the

boundaries of the home was still very controversial, the principal argument against this "second shift" was formulated: "They expect from
her a double duty and this is manifestly unfair ... Men are treated far
more considerately in this regard than women. Nothing is allowed to
interfere with the average business man's arrangements. To facilitate
these everything possible is done by his family. This may be because
men are more insistent, because they have a way of *demanding* their
rights. It would be well for women in business, well also for their
families, that they should 'look sharp' and pursue the same policy
(Harland and van der Water 1905, 451–2).

Today this view of the consequences of having a job for women's
tasks at home may seem a truism. At that time, however, it was exceptional. It was not repeated, for instance, by Emily Post, the first edition
of whose million-copy-selling etiquette book was published in 1922.
She did, however, strongly emphasize that women should behave
"impersonally" in offices: "At the very top of the list of women's
business shortcomings is the inability of most of them to achieve
impersonality. Mood, temper, jealousy, especially when induced by a
'crush' on her employer, is the chief flaw of the woman in business"
(1922, 551). However, she should not try to become "one of the
boys"; that would be classed as going over the top to the other
extreme. Instead, a woman should try to see herself as one member of
the corporation, and ensure that she was treated as such.

A quote from 1975 reflects the spirit of the times, the "sexual revolution": "a little mild flirting, and occasional 'mixed' lunch, preferably not as a two-some, help to lighten the inevitable boredom of day-
to-day business" (Post 1975, 749). Advice like this would have been
unthinkable in Germany or the Netherlands, where women's entrance
into the labour force lagged behind by comparison. In the same era
the ambivalence and resistance of German social arbiters towards the
sexual revolution and the women's movement is expressed in the statement that it is *unavoidable* that men and women work together in the
same room, often right next to each other. Nevertheless, the author
continues, a certain minimum distance should be guaranteed, meaning
no flirtations and no love affairs (Hailer, quoted in Krumrey 1984,
374). In the United States, this strict stand reappeared in the 1980s,
when the issue of sexual harassment, especially at work, would have
led to Elizabeth Post's remark about "a little mild flirting" being
branded as "politically incorrect." Her 1992 edition does, indeed,
contain a paragraph on sexual harassment, while one headed "Sex in
the Workplace" is written entirely in the tone of "Neither sex nor
sexual attraction belong in the office" (229–30)[14].

INTERPRETATION THREE:
PSYCHOLOGIZATION AND
THE TUG-OF-WAR BETWEEN
OLD AND NEW STANDARDS

One of the main conclusions seems to be that individuals in all four countries, whether (potential) partners or not, were increasingly expected to be able to protect and take care of themselves, both financially and emotionally. This trend was noted and expressed in 1937 by Emily Post: "Since the modern girl is to go without protection, she must herself develop expertness in meeting unprotected situations. She must be able to gauge the reactions of various types of persons – particularly men, of course – under varying circumstances" (1937, 354). And in 1960 Post added her view as to how "the modern girl" develops this ability: "Today, however, parental *training* has largely taken the place of the chaperon's *protection*" (1960, 168). Indeed, more and more parents taught their children the principles of proceeding in mutual consent, how to avoid invading the privacy or integrity of others. This training implied the formation of a pattern of a more or less automatic reaction of shame and guilt feelings in the personality of these children, whenever they were confronted with any threat of more direct and extreme ways of expressing superiority or inferiority. In this way these expressions have been banned bit by bit as transgressions and regressions, each step implying a rise in the level of mutually expected self-restraint. Thus twentieth-century social integration of both classes and sexes coincided with the spread of a standard of emotion management that demands a more even, stable, and all-round control, especially over the fear of losing control and giving in to more extreme emotions. At the same time it allowed for a further differentiation in this management: a collective, controlled decontrolling of controls over emotions, especially those that were earlier considered to be too dangerous and/or degrading to allow. All kinds of conflict or conflicting needs and interests, formerly a tabooed non-topic, came out into the open to be negotiated.

Intimate bonds are increasingly expected to be kept as "pure" as possible, that is, unaffected not only by the use of violence and money as a means to settle conflicts but also by any appeal to traditional superiority. In and outside intimate relationships, both the value of intimacy and the expectation of women to become and remain financially and emotionally independent, to be their own protectors, have risen dramatically. As welfare and welfare states developed, the ideal of an intimate relationship has been changing towards one involving a couple who are independent people, well matched, both sharing the tasks of providing care and earning an income. This ideal also means that intimate relationships have become more strongly dependent on the style of emotion management of the partners: how is one to love *and* negotiate the terms of the relationship as two captains of the same ship? As the demand increased to negotiate and to proceed through mutual consent, the demand to manage emotions in more flexible and subtle ways also increased, adding considerably to the importance of emotion management as a source of power and also as a source of respect and self-respect or identity. On the whole, men were under women's (and each other's) rising pressure to control further their traditional superiority feelings and corresponding behaviour, while women pressured each other and themselves to control traditional inferiority feelings – for instance, their inclination to be submissive and give in. In this way, changes in the importance of violence, money, and emotion management as power resources and means to settle conflicts are related, such that a particular sequence can be observed (Wouters 1990, 1992, and 1998c).

Enlarged opportunities for women to become and stay financially independent have strengthened the ideal of sharing the tasks of providing care and earning an income. As these more egalitarian rules take time to sink in, this shift in the traditional division of labour between husbands and wives has intensified the tug-of-war between old and new ideals (and power resources) and the related feelings of ambivalence in both men and women. Both sexes – that is, most men and women – seem to be egalitarian on the surface but traditional underneath. Women may sometimes *seem* to be more extreme because they are the ones who are putting their husbands and other men under pressure. Most men react in accordance to the dynamics of established-outsider relationships: they do not want to accommodate themselves and do not easily perceive the "civilized" pleasures of a more egalitarian relationship. They will therefore use the gender strategy of appealing to her *old* identity underneath, trying to bring it back on top, whereas most women will appeal to his *new* identity, trying to reinforce it and make it sink in. Recent discussions on issues such as sexual harassment, pornography, rape in marriage, and date rape can be understood as a common search for ways of becoming intimate that are acceptable to both women and men. Negotiations about these issues will probably continue to emphasize mutual consent as a necessary precondition in these matters, and for the rest, both sexes will have to rely on experience as well as experimentation as they search for new balances between ways and means of intimacy and distance, between the quest for attachment and the fear of it, while avoiding the extremes of emotional wildness and emotional numbness. Also, in the quest for an exciting and satisfying balance between sex and romance or love, the tension level has risen, if only because the increased demands on emotion management will have stimulated both the fantasies and the longing for (romantic) relationships characterized by greater intimacy, as well as the longing for easier (sexual) relationships in which the pressure of these demands is absent or negligible.

This prolonged, deep-rooted ambivalence, together with the strong need for a cautiously calculated emotion management as a more important resource of power and respect, is characteristic of processes of diminishing segregation and increasing integration – that is, in relationships between people of different class (or rank) and sex. The inherent tensions and conflicts may be interpreted as part of the price to be paid for this movement of civilization, the successive rise of larger and larger groups.

NOTES

This chapter integrates two articles, earlier published in the *Journal of Social History* (Wouters 1995a and 1995b). I am grateful to Jonathan Fletcher and Stephen Mennell for help with my English.

1 With regard to England, I have profited from a bibliography and a number of excerpts of nineteenth- and twentieth-century etiquette books compiled by Stephen Mennell, who very kindly supplied me with copies. The studies of etiquette books by Davidoff, Curtin, and Porter served as an introduction to the early period of research. In finding my way into the world of German etiquette books, the study by Horst-Volker Krumrey has been of great help. It reports changes in etiquette books between 1870 and 1970. When my research took me to Berlin, I also benefited from discussions with this scholar. On the American etiquette books of the twentieth century, Deborah Robertson Hodges has published an annotated bibliography. Both this book and conversations with its author have been helpful for studying the American sources. In addition, my research project and I owe much to Michael Schröter, Berlin; Jonathan Fletcher and Lisa Driver-Davidson, Cambridge; and Irwin and Verda Deutscher, Washington, DC. Not only as hosts but also as partners in discussing problems and data, they have been most helpful.

2 For instance, all etiquette books for sale in the main, large bookshops in Berlin, London, and Washington at the time of my visits.

3 The paradox of exclusion or rejection and consideration is not, of course, equally strong everywhere. In England, for example, this

Janus-head of etiquette is particularly marked. To the present day, England is often described as a class-ridden society, meaning that English society is still characterized by relatively sharp boundaries. At the same time, protected by these boundaries, the established classes in England have pressured each other to increasingly demanding levels of consideration and kindness, and in this respect, too, the English have a reputation (Wouters 1997).

4 Compared with many other fields, this body of literature is rather small. In particular, I made use of the following books and articles: Aresty 1970; Carsons 1966; Cavan 1970; Curtin 1987; Davidoff 1973; Elias 2000; Finkelstein 1989; Kasson 1990; Krumrey 1984; Martin 1985; Nicolson 1955; Porter 1972; Schlesinger 1946; Visser 1991; Winter-Uedelhoven 1991; and Wouters 1987 and 1998a.

5 This trend, a concomitant of democratization and integration processes, is observed in earlier periods; for instance, "Almost all books on manners in colonial America ... contain an emphasis on 'superiors' and 'inferiors' that would dramatically lessen in the course of the nineteenth and twentieth century" (Kasson 1990, 12).

6 In England at that time, equally open discussions of lower classes and "lower" impulses, including references to the body and hygiene, were already largely excluded and experienced as embarrassing.

7 "The only identity one can still have as a person is as a personality, which seems to be something less than a person blown up to look like more" (Martin 1985, 55).

8 The belief that social kissing originated on the Continent and came to England from there is quite common. In 1992, for instance, Drusilla Beyfus wrote, "Social kissing has made the leap over the Channel" (1992, 340). In the United States, Elizabeth Post believes that social kissing originated in Europe; she writes in 1992 about "the European custom of kissing (either in the air or with contact) both cheeks. Some people even utter 'kiss kiss' as they perform this rite" (Post 1992, 4).

9 The other side of this coin, immediate verbal aggression, especially in city traffic, may be called "instant enmity" or even "anonymous enmity." Both instant intimacy and instant enmity can be interpreted as expressions of an ongoing "emancipation of emotions" in the transient and volatile or anonymous contacts between strangers.

10 Although Kasson also writes in praise of the search for a "real self," it was not in this context that he used the words quoted here but in contrasting the demands of city life to those of smaller communities.

11 In the 1930s there was a turning inward to motherhood and domesticity, "partly caused by a decline in Society functions ... The woman is now seen as guardian of her family's health and happiness rather than of its social place" (Davidoff 1973, 99). This increased isolation of a

more tightly drawn nuclear family and the strengthening of the mother's bond with her children may also be interpreted as a "civilizing offensive" of wives, consciously or unconsciously aimed at "bringing up Father," thus limiting double standards and his display of superiority feelings. ("Bringing Up Father" is the title of a series of popular drawings by the American George McManus, presenting Father as a captive of Mother and of her longing for success in "good society.")

12   Holidays are still considered to be dangerous and worth a warning, today against the dangers of unsafe sex. For instance, in the summer of 1993 a government-subsidized leaflet entitled "Have Safe Sex, *Also* on Holidays" was distributed in a great number of public places. It contained, among others, sentences such as "Have you ever heard of AIDS?" "Do you have a condom with you?" and "I'll put on a condom, it's safer" in English, German, French, and Spanish.

13   "To some extent the 'modern girl' was still the popular heroine that she had become when working on munitions in factories. She was known as 'the flapper,' yet this was not a term of reproach. Flapper in the Nineties had meant a very young prostitute, scarcely past the age of consent, but the word had improved before the war to mean any girl in her teens with a boyish figure. The craze for the flapper ... reached England about 1912 ... 'Flapper' was now a term for a comradely, sporting, active young woman, who would ride pillion on the 'flapper-bracket' of a motor-cycle. It did not become a term of reproach again, with a connotation of complete irresponsibility, until 1927 ... The women who only a year or so earlier had been acclaimed as patriots, giving up easy lives at home to work for their Country in her hour of need, were now represented as vampires who deprived men of their rightful jobs" (Graves and Hodge 1941, 43–4).

14   Because more formality and greater social and psychic distance between the sexes at work could help protect women when and where they would be unable to protect themselves, in 1992 America's Miss Manners (Judith Martin) is against using first names (although she realizes that she goes against the grain in this respect; personal communication, August 1992).

4 Exploring Netiquette: Figurations and Reconfigurations in Cybernetic Space

JORGE ARDITI

The March 1997 issue of *Scientific American* contains a special section on the Internet called "Bringing Order from Chaos." The section includes eight articles written by leading professionals in the computer industry, people whose work it is to develop the new realities of the information society. Articles deal with, among other things, how to search the Internet (Lynch 1997), the kind of interfaces that are being developed to that end (Hearst 1997), the software aimed at insuring privacy (Resnick 1997), techniques for making information available in digital form (Lesk 1997), and last but not least, programs designed to preserve the Internet and turn it into a digital library capable of storing everything that ever goes on to the net (Kahle 1997). The idea, indeed, is to create "order" out of "chaos."

"Order" and its mirror image "chaos" are terms defined here from the perspective of the people who are actively engaged using the net. The chaos is a product of the massive amount of information that hits the net every day from thousands of different points, information about everything and anything, much of it of little or no value except for the person who posts it. Valuable information becomes lost in the maze. Search engines indiscriminately list anything that happens to contain the sequence of words that we asked them to search for. Moving from link to link takes us to places that we never imagined, and we often end up in places that have no connection with our original interest. We waste time and energy surfing the net to find that, ultimately, if we want to know, we have to pay. "Order" thus concerns the complex array of instruments that help to manage information in its multiple facets and give users a sense of direction within the maze. Anyone who has surfed the net can identify with this meaning of chaos and understands the need for order.

But order can, of course, be understood in an entirely different way, and it is with this other conception of order – one associated as much with Elias as with Foucault – that I am concerned in this chapter, for things in cyberspace come together in ways that are specific to it. They stand in relation to one another according to a specific pattern of relations. They are associated with certain things and differentiated from others and are woven together in a specific configuration, namely, a network of networks. To echo Foucault's formulations, "things" in cyberspace are arranged according to specific practices of ordering – practices that, as they are brought into operation, generate an "order of things."

Clearly, every order has to be navigated – or in the case of the Internet, surfed – and people, usually the same people who are instrumental in bringing that order into being, develop techniques to navigate it. These include formal techniques such as the ones discussed in the special section of *Scientific American* as well as informal methods, as we learn from Elias or, for that matter, Goffman (1963, 3–12), in the shape of a set of behavioural rules or etiquette. Chaos is in this sense a function of the relative absence of these techniques. It is a function of the absence of instruments capable of taking us to our desired goals, as well as the absence of a road map able to tell us how to get there. Chaos applies to the perspective of the insiders of an order – in our case, the people engaged in using the net, the people who experience cyberspace – for whom navigating becomes, to a very significant extent, indeed chaotic.

This chapter examines the growing literature on "netiquette," or "network etiquette," posted on the World Wide Web as a means of exploring the implications of two major aspects of the order of things that seems to be emerging in cyberspace: the very redefinition of space implied in the term "cyberspace" and the almost complete detachment of bodies that it entails.

I begin with an overview of Foucault's concept of an "order of things" as a way of specifying the type of phenomena that I suggest we pay attention to when we attempt to understand cyberspace. After a discussion of netiquette and etiquette in general, I will turn to the analysis of space as given expression to in the most prominent sites. If corporeal dimensions of space indeed disappear in the universe of the net, netiquette literature suggests that a new space defined by bandwidth emerges. This is a space best understood as "a space of flows," as Manuel Castells has recently suggested. It is a space whose geography indeed takes the form of a network of networks, of a web-like structure connecting everything with everything else, generating an order that ultimately undermines the very notion of differentiation that helps shape it. I shall then explore the detachment of bodies that seems to have achieved complete realization in cyberspace. The netiquette literature suggests that this new level of detachment fosters extremes of subjective perception, extending, so to speak, the boundaries of perception in "real life." Following Simmel's insights concerning the dual character of modern culture and the emergence of antipodean tendencies in perception, it would seem that the increased detachment fosters subjectivity in two opposite directions. On the one hand, we observe an emergence of extreme forms of objectification. On the other, we see an intensification of non-rational elements: in particular, aggression and, in complete opposition to the objectification just mentioned, intimacy. To conclude, I attempt to place these two developments (the formation of a new space and the transformations of perception) in the context of Elias's thesis of the civilizing process. I suggest that these developments cannot be properly understood either as a simple continuation of the processes of civilization or as decivilization. Rather, it would seem that we are engaged in a process of *recivilization* that takes the civilizing process in directions which entail as much continuity as discontinuity.

ORDER AS PRACTICES OF ASSOCIATION

Foucault formulates his concept of an "order of things" in the introduction to the book that carries that title, a concept that can be usefully contrasted to Durkheim's ideas on "categories of thought" and "systems of classification" as developed in *The Elementary Forms of the Religious Life* (1965, 21–5, 169–73, 479–87). The very first paragraph of *The Order of Things* brings to mind Durkheim, whom Foucault, through his well-known quotation of Borges, problematizes significantly. "This book," writes Foucault,

first arose out of a passage in Borges, out of the laughter that shattered, as I read the passage, all the familiar landmarks of my thought ... This passage quotes a "certain Chinese encyclopaedia" in which it is written that "animals are divided into: (a) belonging to the Emperor, (b) embalmed, (c) tame, (d) sucking pigs, (e) sirens, (f) fabulous, (g) stray dogs, (h) included in the present classification, (i) frenzied, (j) innumerable, (k) drawn with a very fine camelhair brush, (l) *et cetera*, (m) having just broken the water pitcher, (n) that from a long way off look like flies." In the wonderment of this taxonomy, the thing we apprehend in one great leap, the thing that, by means of the fable, is

demonstrated as the exotic charm of another system of thought, is the limitation of our own, the stark impossibility of thinking *that*. (1970, xv)

Foucault points out how the bestiary invented by Borges makes us
aware of the impossibility of thinking in certain ways, and he makes
it his task to identify the specific characteristics of classificatory systems that render certain thoughts thinkable and others unthinkable.

Foucault's question goes well beyond Durkheim's remarks regarding
the need for harmony among collective representations. In the conclusion to *The Elementary Forms*, Durkheim made reference to the fact
that even "true" concepts – concepts, that is, that are in accord with
"the nature of things" (1965, 486) – might not come to be thought.
He wrote: "If they are not in harmony with the other beliefs and
opinions, or, in a word, with the mass of the other collective representations, they will be denied; minds will be closed to them; consequently
it will be as though they did not exist" (1965, 486).

The idea reminds us, to an extent, of Kuhn's concept of a scientific
paradigm and of its closure to thoughts and observations that cannot be
given expression from within its theoretical and empirical frameworks.
Concepts that cannot be thought by the terms of the paradigm remain
unthought; observations that are not recognized by its concepts remain
unrecognized. Foucault's point is different, however, for to him, the limits
of the thinkable are not a result of the contents of thought, of their
harmony or structural closure, but as Borges's passage suggested to him,
of the logic in whose terms systems of classification are constructed.

Foucault transforms what Durkheim calls a "framework for the
intelligence" into a shifting, historically contingent ground, the
"episteme," on which the very principle used to associate one thing to
another changes with time. He does not question the existence of
"order" but raises the question of what constitutes an order to begin
with. To him, the thinkable and the unthinkable, what becomes an
"order of knowledge," are not a function of the lines according to
which we place things together and, by extension, differentiate them.
It is a function of the logic that we use in attributing similarity among
things, of the specific method that we apply to associate and differentiate, to order things.

Foucault shows, for example, how a system of classification
informed by a logic of resemblance produces a different "order of
knowledge" than, perhaps, a system grounded on a logic of signification (1970, 50–63). In a logic of resemblance, the type of logic that
Foucault sees as constitutive of European Renaissance thought, associations are made by identifying affinities among things – by establishing relations of sympathy among the character allegedly given to things

by God at the moment of creation. Thinking through resemblance therefore involves a continual and infinite act of searching for "some sort of kinship, attraction, or secretly shared nature" between things (Foucault 1970, 55). Knowledge takes the form of "drawing things together" (Foucault 1970, 55), of making lists of things whose characters are "in sympathy" with one another. A logic of signification, in turn, is informed by a principle of discrimination and comparison. Things are related to one another through a common unit or sign that allows us to measure and order these things in a hierarchical sequence. Thought in this case (which Foucault identifies with seventeenth-century classicism) consists in establishing relations of equality and inequality between things and in arranging differences "according to the smallest possible degrees" (1970, 53). The sign, the instrument of thought and organizing principle of knowledge, thus becomes a tool of analysis, a mark of identity and difference, and the basis for establishing taxonomies, the form taken by knowledge in classical thought.

READING ETIQUETTE: FIGURATIONS AS PRACTICES OF ASSOCIATIONS

It is a similar dimension of order, applied to practice rather than knowledge, that I suggest netiquette and etiquette in general make manifest. Here I follow Elias's lead to think in terms of figurations rather than systems of thought: I suggest that the spatial and temporal dimensions of cyberspace imply a specific logic of association that yields a most specific "order of figurations," one that grows as cyberspace itself grows and is unique to it.

The very transformation that Elias describes in *The Civilizing Process* can be seen as a metamorphosis of the practices of association between people in western Europe during the thirteenth to the eighteenth century. For the detachment of bodies and psyches that he details in his masterwork through the analysis of changing manners, consists precisely in the gradual development of new patterns of association, of new practices of relationality, of an entirely new use and experience of the body in relation both to oneself and to others. It consists of a transformation of space, personal and social, within which bodies and individuals relate with one another and the figurations that fashion the experiential grounds of their realities originate.

As it instructs about how to navigate an order, "netiquette," like any form of etiquette, includes advice about how to relate to others, how to recognize personal and social space, how to maximize one's and sometimes others' participation in that order, and so on. It also charts the specific configuration of social relations inherent in that order and, as people put the etiquette into practice – Elias shows this process beautifully – helps to bring the order into being. The advice given in etiquette books is not supposed to be strictly followed; sometimes it is not supposed to be followed at all. What etiquette books do is draw lines, both separating and linking people, both in their individuality as in their groupings. Whether or not one follows the books' advice is not the issue; one might opt to transgress boundaries, to take risks, to attempt to manipulate rather than follow the formations within which one operates. Clearly, when an order is part of one's habitus, one does not need to read an etiquette book to be able to navigate it. One simply "knows" the lines that form the social. But when the order is not part of one's habitus, etiquette books become useful tools in charting a territory of action and the practices that constitute it. For people who aspire to belong to an order yet do not, the most important aspect is not simply to learn the ways of insiders but also to master the logic instructing their ways. It is not just to know a set of rules, to know their manners, but to capture and come to possess the logic instructing those rules and be able to reproduce them in their own behaviour. As the Renaissance author Baldassare Castiglione put it, what is important is not just to learn how to behave but to do so in such a way that the manners appear like a natural disposition of the person: "like a singer who utters a single word ending in a group of four notes with a sweet cadence, and with such facility that he appears to do it quite by chance" (1959, 47). Or as in painting, like "a single line which is not labored, a single brush stroke made with ease and in such a manner that the hand seems of itself to complete the line desired by the painter, without being directed by care or skill of any kind" (Castiglione 1959, 47).

The body of netiquette that I analyze below was determined through a cyberspace variation of snowball sampling. An initial cluster of texts was established using the World Wide Web's Yahoo search engine. Under the category "Society and Culture: Cyberculture," Yahoo includes a subcategory "netiquette" with eighteen entries at the moment of this writing. I then followed the links in each of the eighteen entries to expand the sample to thirty-five. Many of the links actually refer to one another and many of the entries borrow from one another, sometimes literally. I focus for the most part on the rules that seem to be repeated the most – rules parsimoniously organized and summarized in Virginia Shea's "The Core Rules of Netiquette" (1996).

This study is by necessity partial. The constantly changing nature of cyberspace, in particular, its continuously emerging character, suggests that the rules that I analyze will most probably change in the near future. Cyberspace is a very new space, and netiquette writers are only beginning to mirror the practices of association that constitute it. But although partial, this study has the virtue of grounding its understanding of cyberspace on empirical evidence, however unstable this might be. Cyberspace has spurred an immense amount of writing, mostly of an anecdotal nature (Castells 1996). In following Elias's methods, a study of netiquette can indeed provide us with a grounding missing from much of the literature.

THE SPACE OF FLOWS

What, then, do we learn from netiquette? I should mention from the outset that much of netiquette is a direct extension of everyday propriety outside cyberspace. Rule 2 of Shea's "Core Rules" (the list includes ten) is most explicit; it states quite simply, "Adhere to the same standards of behavior online that you follow in real life." The rule is not meant only to reproduce politeness – saying "thank you" or "please" when appropriate – but to achieve the same objective for which etiquette developed in the first place. The rule seems pretty basic, Shea admits, "but many people have gone a little crazy online, reveling in the anonymity of the Internet. *Please* try to control yourself!"

The one intriguing element of this rule is the suggestion that life on-line is not "real life," a distinction that has become so accepted in current jargon that to many it is my comment that might appear odd. The suggestion fits the general sense that life on-line is not "real" but "virtual." Netiquette itself, however, suggests that "life online" is as real as life in "real life." Indeed, social relations in cyberspace have nothing virtual about them. They are certainly fashioned and give body to a different sense of time and space. But they are as real, and as embodied, as social relations in any other space; only that the principles ordering them are different from the ones ordering relations outside cyberspace.

The very concept of cyberspace, understood as existing only within people's imaginations or within computers, would seem to be problematic – at least when we think about it in terms, as I just suggested, of a space containing and giving shape to embodied social relations. William Gibson, who coined the concept in his novel *Neuromancer*, defines cyberspace as a "consensual hallucination experienced daily by billions of legitimate operators, in every nation, by children being taught mathematical concepts ... A graphical representation of data abstracted from the banks of every computer in the human system ... Lines of light ranged in the non-space of the mind, clusters and constellations of data" (1984). Z. Sardar and J.R. Ravetz (1995) define it as "the ether that lies inside and occupies the in-between of all computers." But the space mirrored in the netiquette literature is neither the product of hallucination nor an unlimited expanse made of ether. It is, rather, a space in which bodies have become fully detached from one another. It is a space with its own limits and its own topography which the netiquette literature teaches us how to use and, in particular, as more conventional etiquette (regarding, for example, the use of the knife and fork) has done for centuries already, how not to misuse it.

Rule 3 of the "Core Rules" states, "Know where you are in cyberspace." Rule 4 urges, "Respect other people's time and bandwidth." Indeed, these rules suggest that one occupies a point in a server and space in the server, and that both one's time and one's space on that server are, in effect, limited. Many of the rules in the great majority of netiquette literature are in fact concerned with these two issues. The first rule of "Network Conduct" cited in John Smith's "Network Etiquette (Netiquette)" reads quite simply, "Don't waste bandwidth." The satiric "Dear Emily Postnews" (Templeton 1996), a spoof of Emily Post's etiquette book, devotes much of its humour to lampooning wasteful practices and the people who, intentionally or unintentionally, engage in them. The text follows a question-and-answer format in the style of the "Dear Abby" column in American newspapers. The first query (from verbose@noisy) asks about the length of one's signature. I quote the beginning of the answer: "Dear Verbose: Please try and make your signature as long as you can. It's much more important than your article, of course, so try and have more lines of signature than actual text. Try and include a large graphic made of ASCII characters, plus lots of cute quotes and slogans." The parody is not only directed to the waste of space; it also derides the arrogance of many users. But the concern with the proper management of bandwidth is unmistakable – the reference to large graphics is telling. In effect, Shea gives three major pieces of advice on the management of space: "1. Don't quote back an entire mail or news article to just say 'me too,' 2. Don't spam or give useless information, 3. [Avoid] extraneous pictures, to conserve bandwidth."

The image of cyberspace that emerges is clear, and many other examples would substantiate it further. Its most prominent aspect is that it is a space with precise points and precise lines linking these points, the management of which is among the fundamental subjects of netiquette. It is a space made of the sites to which people link and where the information is stored, and of the flows through which they connect with one another. The configuration that emerges, however, defies the sense of ordering of our established ways of being. The order of things that manifests itself in cyberspace is one marked by dispersion and randomness, one in which anything can be directly associated with anything else. To paraphrase Foucault, it is one that breaks the ordered surfaces, that violates the boundaries with which we are "accustomed to tame the wild profusion of existing things" (Foucault 1970, xv). Ordering, indeed, seems to loose the internal logic by which things are not only associated but also differentiated from one another. It yields an order that, as I suggested in the introduction, ultimately undermines the very notion of differentiation that helps to shape it. Or as Ron Burnett has recently written, it is an order from which "the very notion of boundary and geography disappears" (1996, 82).

A quick look at the taken-for-granted in netiquette is in this respect instructive. The very injunction to know where one is in cyberspace is eloquent, for the rule is in itself founded on the sense that one can go anywhere at anytime, that one can arrive at any one point in the dispersed field at any moment. Shea is mainly concerned with the type of site that one is connected to, whether it is a listserv, a chatroom, or some other type of meeting place. But the rule calls our attention to the randomness and dispersion of cyberspace and reflects the chronic suspicion of being lost, the same concern addressed in the articles in *Scientific American*. The sense of randomness and dispersion becomes even more marked in the Emily Postnews spoof because the many confusions that become possible are another constant source of humour. Just post your messages everywhere you can; never mind their contents, the spoof instructs. You never know where they will reach and what reactions you might get. Spread yourself in the net. Relish the dispersion and the randomness. After all, Ms Postnews asserts, you are so important that everybody will be glad to hear what you have to say, even if they do not care at all about the subject.

Meaningful association of things no longer follows a practice that generates stable lines of association and separation between things and therefore provides a stable order to the dispersion. It is a function of shifting, non-linear, syncretic practices of contextual linkages according to which each site is multiply "linked with" other sites, each series of linkages depending on a context of meaning defined at the linking site. The juxtaposition of linkages that results often looks like Borges's Chinese encyclopedia, a classification without a common ground other than the multiple, idiosyncratic interests of the person making the links. Again, the injunction of knowing where one is, where one has arrived, by following thread after thread makes perfect sense.

UNLEASHING SUBJECTIVITY

But how do the properties of this new space shape the ways in which people relate to one another? What figurations among people, as opposed to configurations of sites, emerge in cyberspace?

Clearly, the situation that I have just described opens the door to arguments about the development of a schizophrenic subjectivity or the erasure and transgression of the boundaries of one's self. And indeed, discussions about transgressions of gender, race, and other elements of identity and the suggestion that, as a consequence, identities become fluid – genderless, raceless – abound in the literature on cyberspace (see Reid). Here, however, I analyze a very different dimension of the ways in which cyberspace shapes social relations, one that follows Elias's insights in *The Civilizing Process*: the detachment of bodies, not the disappearance of the body, that seems to have achieved complete realization in cyberspace.

With Elias, indeed, we come to realize how detachment became a central element of people's experiences. The advent of the word "civility" in the sixteenth century marked an unfolding of material and psychological boundaries between persons, a growing separation of bodies and psyches out of which emerged, two hundred years later, the modern, civilized individual. Reading his masterwork, we can almost sense how the boundaries that started to form between people provoked a changed experiencing of "other" and, by extension, of "self." With the fading of behaviours rooted in practices of touching, of corporeal familiarity, of spontaneous intimacy, it was not difficult to understand how people started to experience themselves as separate beings, each with his or her own body, each with his or her own personal space.

In this light, the absence of bodies in cyberspace can be seen as implying, not their removal and perhaps irrelevance, but their total separation. Bodies continue to exist and continue to be relevant, but their complete detachment reshapes social relations, establishes new terms of relationality, and transforms one's experience of self and other.

The first of Shea's "Core Rules," a rule that, like the injunction to know one's place in cyberspace, has multiple meanings and implications, states, "Remember the Human." The directive is eloquent – first, for the simple fact that we need to be reminded that we are still in a relationship with humans; but secondly, because what Shea has in mind is to remember the civilized, modern individual, a person with a certain subjectivity, with a specific psychological and emotional makeup. This individual, the rule suggests, no longer finds his or her natural conditions of being in the figurations that emerge in cyberspace. And indeed, even the most cursory analysis of netiquette makes patently clear that the total detachment of bodies which we observe in cyberspace has, for consequence, to intensify the subjective tendencies of modern individuals, violating the structure of sensibilities that constitute what they are.

The argument can be best elaborated by using Simmel's insights on the transformations of subjectivity that followed the rise of modernity (in particular, 1971; also 1978, part 2). Differences of conceptualization aside, Simmel, like Elias, developed an understanding of modern societies on the thesis of an increase of social detachment. One of the major marks of modernity, he contended (1978, part 2), lay in the growth of social distance between people, in a multiplication of cognitive and material boundaries that gradually withered away the immediacy of life characteristic of pre-modern societies. According to Simmel, this loss of immediacy and its replacement by an experience constantly mediated by concepts or other elements of objective culture transformed the subjectivity of the person in radical ways. Experience and subjectivity became increasingly objectified, and a process of individuation similar to the one described by Elias gradually shaped people's bodies and psyches.

The usefulness and beauty of Simmel's understanding of society lies in general in the particular heuristics on which it is grounded. Often referred to as "dialectic," his approach is indeed founded on a recognition of opposites, every condition of being engendering a set of contrary, if not contradictory, tendencies. It is not a dialectics in the conventional sense of the term, however, for neither does one of the opposites emerge as a negation of the other, nor do the two together, out of the process that follows their encounter, generate a new reality. Rather, the two opposites emerge together, simultaneously, out of the effect of a common ground, and they remain active as long as the ground continues to exist. Their encounter is part of the reality produced by the ground, and its experiencing is part of the condition of being generated by that common foundation.

Simmel sees the development of detachment – or rather, the reality of detachment that marks modernity – as a foundation of this sort, one that triggers feelings of freedom and intensifies emotional response, yet simultaneously transforms everything, including other people, into objects (see also Arditi 1996). As a consequence of the myriad concepts mediating emotions, each fashioning feeling into a different sensation, the experience of life becomes richer, more varied, and in many ways more intense. As a consequence of the transformation of everything into objects, a condition of alienation, an impossibility of establishing a meaningful relationship with anything sets in. As attachments weaken, autonomy and freedom increase.

The total detachment of bodies that we find in cyberspace, netiquette suggests, takes the polar tendencies described by Simmel to new extremes, constantly violating the boundaries of civility as we have come to know and experience them. The extreme objectification of others is neatly conveyed in one of Shea's comments to rule 1 – "Remember the Human" – even though, as I have already mentioned, the very fact of the rule's pointing in that direction shows that we tend to forget there is a person at the other side of the line. "You're talking to a person with real feelings," Shea writes, "not a demographic statistic." The demographic statistic – the image of the rational, bureaucratic society at its utmost extreme. Rule 3 of a list circulated in January 1997 by the Bucknell Computer Center repeats, "Never forget that a human being is on the other end." John Smith's "Network Etiquette" warns, "treat people on a network in the same way as you would treat them in person."

The injunction may seem unexceptional, yet traditional etiquette books never saw a need to remind us that the other person was a human. Of course, they mentioned not hurting people's feelings; "do not offend others" was the typical expression. But they never had to remind us that people had feelings, for the patterns of relationality that these books mirrored did not include the possibility. In spite of the process of individuation that marks the very evolution of etiquette, patterns of attachment continued to be integral to the figurations that etiquette helped to fashion. A reality capable of prompting behaviours that completely ignored the human simply did not exist. Such a reality could be found in the most bureaucratized spheres of social relations, not in the public sphere regulated by etiquette.

Now this radical detachment does not imply that attachments are impossible in cyberspace – quite the opposite. As Simmel suggests, it implies an increased freedom of action, a release from obligations and established patterns of practice that reduces social control and bolsters self-expression. The extreme objectification – and Simmel would add, objectivation – of others is indeed accompanied by a strengthening of non-rational aggression and, quite paradoxically, intimacy.

As far as aggression is concerned, the much-discussed phenomenon of "flame wars" represents only the tip of the iceberg. The netiquette literature is careful to warn people not to flame and not to engage in flame wars, two commands that, again, are in fact totally unremarkable: they can be seen as the exact equivalent of the injunction not to offend, common in etiquette literature. But once more, netiquette would seem to go a step further. A sense of urgency that suggests the readiness and speed with which flame wars escalate online permeates many of the postings. They urge people to keep flame wars under control: "avoid unnecessary bickering"; "don't flame just for the hell of it," urges Shea's rule 7, suggesting both that some bickering is normal and that flaming is sometimes done for fun. Don't let yourself go, Shea begs; maintain yourself within the boundaries of civility; don't let conflicts grow: they easily get out of hand. Some writers present an image of flame wars that brings to mind the brawls popular in older Westerns: "don't just jump into a flame war for fun, or because you are having a bad day," Shea urges, as if cyberspace had become a replica of a bar in a Wild West movie and each of us a cowboy out of control. "If you see a fight, join in, and enjoy," exhorts Ms Emily Postnews. Nothing, indeed, could be as foreign to the real Emily Post as having to tell people not to get into an ongoing fight.

The type of aggression that netiquette warns about and attempts to moderate is not limited to flame wars, though. Abuses of all sorts seem to lurk in cyberspace, especially in the less formalized spaces of social intercourse – chatrooms and other informal meeting places of the Internet, in which detachment unleashes feelings and dispositions ordinarily held at bay by the mechanisms of social and self-control that fashion the world of the "civilized individual." Clearly, the injunction "not to forget the human" applies here as much as it applies to its opposite, to treating the other in a purely objectified manner. In both cases, the boundaries of the civilized individual are equally violated, although indeed from opposite directions. Warnings about transgressing boundaries, about violating the spaces of another's self, lurk in netiquette and become explicit in other types of network advice. We have already seen Shea plead in rule 2, "many people have gone a little crazy online, reveling in the anonymity of the Internet. *Please* try to control yourself!" "Respect other people's privacy," reads Shea's rule 8. Popular advice on love abounds in the Internet, with warnings about impersonation and manipulation, obscenity, harassment, and the protection that anonymity provides to abusers (Offit; Pitman 1996; Hoole 1996). What is of note is that these warnings do not caution only against becoming a victim of abuse. They also urge us not to become the abusers. They alert us to the ease with which we can cross boundaries, infringe on others' privacy, and threaten others.

But the fragility of existing boundaries has still another side: we are prone to open ourselves to others far more easily than we seem to be able "offline." And here too the implications are twofold, for on the one hand, we open ourselves to the abuse that I have just described, yet on the other hand, we are able to establish relations of intimacy and attachment as we can rarely achieve in the public spheres of sociability offline (Hoole 1996). The literature on love in the Internet focuses precisely on this opening of the self and its positive, as much its negative, consequences. In netiquette, it is true, this dimension of subjectivity becomes invisible, perhaps because of the perception that netiquette, like etiquette, should confine itself to the more public dimensions of social intercourse. Accordingly, questions of intimacy are excluded. But advice on love, as on "cyber sex," treads on the fine line between abuse and intimacy produced by the porousness of personal boundaries in cyberspace. The stories that authors tell include tales of betrayal and self-realization, perversion and closeness, exploitation and generosity. The aims of the sites they discuss range from the overtly abusive – "How to Dump Your Mate Electronically" and "Love Letters: You Fill in the Blanks," for example – to the inspiring and caring. And their message seems to be, for the most part, that cyberspace is a dangerous place for the soul, but it is a trip most definitely worth the risks.

CONCLUSION

The phenomena that I have just sketched might well be interpreted as implying a movement of decivilization – a movement away from the process of civilization that Elias described. The phenomena involve, after all, a violation of the complex sensibilities that make up the civilized individual. They involve a violation of boundaries, a weakening of self-control, a shift away from moderation. From the perspective of the civilizing process, they indeed look like a reversal.

But how legitimate is it to see the transformations that are occurring in cyberspace as decivilization? It is evidently so when we maintain our perspective stabilized in a concept that we take to be stable to begin with. To Elias, both practices and concepts of good manners change constantly, however slow and processual the change may be. From any point in the history of manners, change is seen as a violation of the existing. The story of the Greek princess and her use of a fork in eleventh-century Venice, a story that Elias recounts precisely to show the historical relativism of practices of good behaviour and the sensibilities they help to fashion, is a paradigmatic example (1982, 55). The princess, who had the impudence to make use of such an uncommon instrument (although it was in common use in her country of origin), was seen, literally, as a sinner. When soon afterwards she was stricken with a vicious disease, her predicament was viewed as a punishment of God. And indeed, Elias argues, it is because the use of a fork bears the imprint of a sensibility alien to the people in early Venetian society that they saw the behaviour as objectionable, even immoral – as an act that, compared to their ways of being, is unquestionably "less civilized."

Instead of speaking in terms of civilization and decivilization, it would seem more accurate to speak of new processes of figuration and reconfiguration, at least insofar as cyberspace is concerned. Perhaps, as I have already suggested, we should speak of processes that take

civilization in directions that involve as much continuity as discontinuity (see also Arditi 1994). The transformation in the order of things
in cyberspace and the detachment of bodies that mark its figurations
bring a change in subjectivity. They bring new channels to express
subjectivity, new attitudes to one's emotions, perhaps even a new complex of emotions. The qualifier is necessary, for as I mentioned earlier,
the phenomena that I am discussing are too new and changing too
rapidly. Netiquette itself is bound to change in the near future. But the
line of development seems to be nonetheless there, and the changes,
however fluid, seem to be happening. Whatever forms the future will
take – and these are open to us to decide – their beginnings can be
identified in the realities of today. Perhaps from the point of view of
the sensibilities emerging in cyberspace, the "civilized individuals" of
the late twentieth century will look as the Venetians looked to the
Greek princess.

5 Unpacking the Civilizing Process: Interdependence and Shame

THOMAS J. SCHEFF

This chapter is an attempt to identify and elaborate basic concepts and method in the work of Norbert Elias. Needless to say, these remarks are not dicta but only reflections occasioned by my reading of his work, particularly the translations of *The Civilizing Process*, *The Established and the Outsiders*, *What Is Sociology?*, *Involvement and Detachment*, and *The Germans* and the valuable summaries by Mennell. I seek to connect Elias's basic themes with recent work in family systems and in the sociology of emotions.

I am writing this chapter in homage to Elias's work. Pericles, in his funeral oration for those who died defending Athens, said that their actions were great, not because of the shrines that were built to them, but because they had become woven into the stuff of the everyday lives of the living. I believe that Elias's most significant monument will be the way in which his work will benefit future scholarship and human-kind at large. Pericles said that the whole earth is the cenotaph of a great man. So be it with Norbert Elias.

I think that Elias was one of the two authentic geniuses in social science in the second half of the twentieth century, the other being Erving Goffman. Like Goffman, Elias had a viewpoint that translates the reader into a new way of looking at the world. I am most impressed with two of his core concepts – interdependence, on the one hand, and the advance of the shame threshold, on the other – as I will indicate below. Also as with Goffman, the main significance of Elias's work has not yet been sufficiently explicated and understood. Here I attempt to contribute to such an explication.

THE CIVILIZING PROCESS:
CONCEPT OR RUBRIC?

As the first step toward amplifying and elaborating Elias's work, I suggest that we might demote or at least focus less on one of his most frequently utilized phrases, the civilizing process. Can we downgrade this idea from the status of a concept to a lower rank, to that of a rubric? The arguments that have formed around this phrase seem to me to have been mostly unproductive and distracting. I think that the phrase is unwieldy because it is much too broad and vague and because of an ambiguity at its centre. The solution that I suggest below is to use the term only as a summary rubric for the more specific processes that undergird Elias's contributions: rationalization, psychologization-interdependence, and the advance of the shame threshold. (These three terms are derived from Mennell 1989.) A fourth process, increasing self-control, is also central, but first a critique of the concept itself.

As Mennell's discussion indicates, there are two quite divergent meanings to the phrase "the civilizing process": the "popular concept" and the "technical concept." Elias himself made it clear that the popular concept is heavily value-laden: civilized is good, and uncivilized is bad. The technical concept, on the other hand, is intended not to be value-laden; it refers to the processes of formation of modern societies, without judging these processes to be good or bad.

There are two key problems in considering the civilizing process as a concept. The first is that Elias himself and more recent discussions sometimes confound the technical and the popular meanings. The words "civilized" and "uncivilized" carry such a potent emotional load that even scholarly caution cannot divest them of it. An example is Mennell's attempt, following Goudsblom, to define the meaning of "civilizing" as an "advance" and "de-civilizing" as a "regression from earlier standards" (1989, 201). The ideas of advance and regression clearly carry normative judgments of good and bad respectively. The phrase encompasses a penumbra of intense emotions. Although we try to strip it of connotation, I think that this cannot be done. Contrary to the Red Queen in Lewis Carroll's, *Through the Looking-Glass* vernacular words do not mean simply what we want them to mean.

Even if the first ambiguity were absent, the technical concept of the civilizing process would still be so broad as to be a veritable miscellany of different ideas. Unlike the popular concept, which is manageably narrow even though value-laden, the technical concept is so broad as to encompass all aspects of modernization, if not all social and historical change. Again following Goudsblom, Mennell's discussion (1989, 200–1) of socio- and psychogenesis suggests that the phrase includes three levels:

1 the process that each human undergoes from birth onwards (encompassing such concepts as socialization, enculturation, and personality formation);

2 development of social standards and codes of acting, thinking, and feeling; and

3 the common human process of development or change which has involved humanity as a whole.

This attempt at definition encompasses three somewhat different ideas at the first level, standards and codes for three different aspects of human activity (either as few as three or as many as six different ideas) at the second level, and at the third level, perhaps only one idea. At the very least, the definition includes seven ideas. Although there is certainly some overlap among these, each idea is also somewhat different from the others. It seems problematic to string together such a miscellany under a single phrase.

INTERDEPENDENCE

It seems especially unnecessary to focus on the idea of the civilizing process since Elias himself did not. To be sure, there is a discussion of it in the early pages of *The Civilizing Process*, but in most of his work he concerned himself with certain parts of this very large whole. Three of the components that contain much of his scholarly efforts are those that Mennell describes as "aspects of increasing foresight" (1989, 101): psychologization and increasing mutual identification, rationalization, and advances in the threshold of shame and embarrassment. A fourth is increases in self-control (to be elaborated later; increases in self-control are correlated with, but perhaps not directly related to, advances in the shame threshhold).

It seems to me that of these four basic ideas, most of Elias's work deals with the first, third, and fourth. To be sure, he sometimes concerns himself with rationalization, but in a way that mostly follows, rather than elaborates on, Weber's treatment of rationality and routinization. Furthermore, his major trope, interdependence, is closely related to the first process. What is the relation between interdependence, on the one hand, and psychologization and increasing mutual identification, on the other?

The technical conception of interdependence may form the core concept in Elias's work. Before I elaborate, it is necessary to distinguish the technical from the ordinary meaning of the word. The popular conception of human interdependence is clear and straightforward. It is a very broad idea, referring to the fact that in any society the activities of its members are interrelated. Unlike the popular idea of what is civilized, this conception is broad, vague, and emotionally neutral, since it does not take up the question of the actual types of relationships, the figurations; it is not that specific. Elias, however, in his work often uses the term "interdependence" in a way that seems to be much more specific. In *What Is Sociology?* and *Involvement and Detachment*, he implicitly uses interdependence to contrast it with two different types of relationship: "independence," or a relationship characterized by detachment, and "dependence," a relationship so over-involved as to be suffocating to one or both parties.

This more specific use of interdependence is also implied in his discussion of the "I-we" balance in the preface to *Involvement and Detachment*. In this passage a balanced I-we relationship would seem to correspond to interdependence. A relationship that did not involve a balance between the "I" and the "we" would not be interdependent: if one or both parties maintained an "I-self," the relationship would be one of independence; if one or both parties maintained a "we-self," the relationship would be one of dependence. As I suggest below, this typology could be extremely useful for elaborating Elias's conception of human relationships.

He is not always consistent in his usage of the term "interdependence," however. Although I have not found the reference, I have been told that Elias has written that war between two nations can involve interdependence (personal communication from John Fletcher). If that is the case, he would have been using the term in its popular sense: in war between two countries, their actions are interrelated. In the technical sense a protracted or destructive war could only be interpreted as a relationship of independence, both countries maintaining only an I-self in relationship to each other. Neither is willing to accept the kind of foresight and compromise necessary to balance the self and the "we" made up by the joint interests of the two countries in avoiding mutual ruin.

This idea can be further elaborated. In a protracted, destructive war, just as the external relationship between the two parties can be seen as independent, to use Elias's term, the internal relationships within each country can be seen as dependent. As conflict between nations develops, the kind of problem-solving discourse that is a product of interdependence breaks down in the face of demands for patriotism, unthinking loyalty, and blind obedience. In an earlier work, I have called the condition within and between countries at war "bimodal alienation," isolation between countries, engulfment (or what Murray Bowen called fusion) within (Scheff 1994, 1997). I think that the technical concept of interdependence allows for a clearly articulated dissection of relationships within and between groups. In a personal communication, Johan Goudsblom suggested that we can consider the us-them balance between groups, just as Elias suggested a I-we balance within them.

The technical concept of interdependence is also closely related to the second element of increasing foresight in modernization: increases in psychologization and mutual identification. Psychologization is a move away from the engulfed (dependent) nature of relationships in traditional societies. It is highly correlated with the development of individualism in modern urban, industrial societies. In traditional societies the individual almost disappears beneath her or his social and kinship roles. Typically, the identity of the other is not carried by the given name but by the social position. For example, a woman is called "older sister" rather than Mai-lin. Such arrangements reflect dependence rather than interdependence: the individual's viewpoint and creativity is subordinated to loyalty to the relationship and, by implication, to the group. Even today the development of Chinese and other Asian societies is still retarded by dependency in its relationships.

However, as suggested by Elias's idea of the *homo clausus*, individualism is usually carried too far in modern societies, to the point of independence. The individual is divested not only of his or her heavy clothing of relational identity but of necessary consideration of others. This is the type of relationship that Durkheim called "egoism"; the individual is isolated from others, rather than being interdependent with them.

Finally, interdependence also encompasses the idea of mutual identification. To be able to arrive at an I-we balance, to integrate the I-self and the we-self, it is necessary not only to identify with the other but also to be able to take their role. Just as the I-self takes too little account of the identity and the viewpoint of the other and the we-self too much account, interdependence balances the two, taking account of both equally.

The technical concept of interdependence, as elaborated above, also may clarify the meaning of the basic sociological ideas of solidarity and alienation. As in Durkheim's study of suicide, the technical concept implies two kinds of alienation, what he called egoism (independence) and altruism (dependence): groups in which relationships are too much oriented towards ego (the I-self) or too much towards conformity to the group (the we-self). In this conception, interdependence corresponds to solidarity, a balanced I-we relationship that allows sufficient freedom for the individual to contribute his or her unique point of view to public discourse, but not such licence as to disregard or suppress the viewpoint of others.

This terminology might correct the tendency that social scientists have for conflating solidarity with engulfment, as in the work of Marcus and Kitiyama, who see Asian societies as possessing significantly more solidarity than Western ones. My elaboration of Elias's idea of interdependence could give rise to a usable theory of social integration, long absent from sociological discourse.

ELIAS'S DISCOVERY OF THE SOCIAL MEANING OF SHAME

Since I am student of the emotion of shame, I was profoundly impressed by Elias's treatment in his first approach to the subject in *The Civilizing Process*. Unlike most other shame scholars, he discovered it on his own, without guidance from earlier scholars. He detected the concept in the historical manuals of advice and etiquette that furnished the main data for his book. Although Elias was aware of Freud's work, it would have been no help for the study of shame. Freud simply dismissed shame as infantile and regressive, an emotion fit only for children, women, and savages. He thought that the proper emotions for adults were anxiety, guilt, grief, and anger. Until recently, most emotion research has also ignored shame.

In the English-speaking world, shame is a strange beast, to many a fearful monster. Although we sometimes use the word casually, as in the comment "What a shame!" it is usually serious business indeed. Shame is a crisis emotion in English, involving extreme emotional pain, on the one hand, and social disgrace, on the other. As it turns out, when we compare the concept in other languages, the English definition of shame is narrow and extreme. Since shame itself is taken to be shameful, it is a heavy and ominous emotion. Shame is an emotion to be avoided, and if that is not possible, ignored.

In the other European languages, shame is defined more broadly and less negatively. In French, as in all the other languages, there is a shame of crisis, *le honte*, whose meaning is similar to our "shame." But there is also an everyday shame, *pudeur*, which is not negative because it connotes modesty, shyness, or to use Schneider's 1977 phrase, "a sense of shame." In this latter meaning, everyday shame is an admirable quality. Shamelessness, the absence of a sense of shame, is a negative concept. In the languages of Asia and in traditional societies, shame is defined still more broadly, ranging over what would be considered in the West as a wide variety of feelings. Mandarin Chinese has an emotion lexicon much larger than English, and its shame lexicon is also much larger (Shaver et al. 1992).

The most detailed discussion of the shame lexicon of a traditional society is about the Maori concept of *whakamaa*. This term is frequently and readily used by the Maori in everyday conversation; it refers to feelings that are considered separate in Western languages: shy, embarrassed, uncertain, inadequate, incapable, afraid, hurt (in its emotional sense), depressed, or ashamed (Metge 1986, 28–9). As the informants' examples make clear, the feeling of fear is not danger to life or limb but social fear – the anticipation of embarrassment or shame. In Maori, *whakamaa* is also used to refer to certain kinds of social relationships, a practice that I recommend below. As I discuss later, the Maori recognize "shame-anger sequences" and the damage caused by shame that is hidden or not expressed.

The narrow and negative character of shame in English, and to a lesser extent in all the other European languages, suggests that in these societies there is either less shame than in Asian and traditional societies or it has gone underground. The first possibility, that there is less shame, is the gist of the proposition that in modern societies shame has been replaced by guilt. In Ruth Benedict's *The Chrysanthemum and the Sword* there is the thought that individuals in industrial societies are socialized to feel guilt, a highly individuated emotion, rather than shame, an emotion with strong social components. Benedict's thesis is that in traditional societies social control is externalized; one conforms to avoid public shame. In modern societies it is internalized; one conforms to avoid private guilt. Her idea has wide currency, even though it is supported only by anecdotal evidence.

Benedict's formulation is the social application of Freud's treatment of shame, which he thought of as an infantile, regressive emotion. In current orthodox psychoanalytic theory, guilt is the adult emotion of self- and social control. Both Freud's and Benedict's formulations demote shame to a minor emotion in modern societies. However, the counter-position – that there has been no decrease in shame but, rather, an increase in undercover shame – seems to me to be more credible. Indeed, it is the thesis of Norbert Elias's *The Civilizing Process*. Here he examines etiquette manuals from the thirteenth to the nineteenth century. The large number of excerpts that he quotes suggests that the overall amount of shame has grown in European societies rather than diminished, but it has simply gone underground, such that it is usually ignored or denied.

Elias's treatment does not merely suggest that shame is one of the major emotions but promotes it to the role of the *master emotion* in all societies, both traditional and modern. Both Lewis (1971) and Tomkins (1963) have emphasized the psychology of shame, but they only imply its sociology. Since Elias's approach is the broadest of the three and gives full scope to the social dimensions of shame, I will briefly review his study to illustrate the view of shame that counters Freud and Benedict.

Elias shows that many of the principal sources of shame in modern societies – the body functions, one's appearance, and one's emotions (especially anger and shame) – produced little or no shame in European societies from the beginning of the thirteenth to nearly the end of the eighteenth century. For example, Erasmus, perhaps the foremost European scholar of the sixteenth century and a man of great repute and dignity, showed no embarrassment in writing about the most intimate personal details in his manual of advice to young people. He spoke as straightforwardly about sexuality – how a young man should make sexual approaches both to a prostitute and to a virtuous girl – as he did about table manners and personal hygiene.

Erasmus and his fellow writers in the Middle Ages were explicit in a way that no modern writer would even consider. For example, he describes in detail courteous and discourteous ways to blow one's nose. He advises that one is to use a handkerchief rather than one's sleeve, the tablecloth, or the ground. One should turn one's head away, blow as quietly as possible, and not examine one's handkerchief afterwards, as if looking for treasure. These matters are not only taken for granted by modern teachers of manners; silence is also a matter of embarrassment and decorum. Silence implies that a well-brought-up person should know without being told; this has a shaming implication in and of itself. Until the nineteenth century, the use of shame to teach children the rules of hygiene, etiquette, deference, and demeanour was not yet a routine fact of life.

Shame signals serve not only to help us keep the right distance from others but also to establish a moral direction for our behaviour. What is called "conscience" is constituted not only by cognition but also by emotion. Feelings or anticipations of shame in considering an action serve as an automatic moral gyroscope, somewhat independent of moral reasoning about consequences. Apparently we thus feel morality in a way similar to that in which a chess champion feels the meaning of chess moves.

Unlike Elias, I did not discover the social significance of shame on my own but was guided to it by the work of the psychologist-psychoanalyst Helen B. Lewis. In her magnum opus, *Shame and Guilt in Neurosis* (1971), she used hundreds of transcripts of psychotherapy sessions to show that shame was a pervasive presence in these sessions. Again, unlike Elias, she did not discover shame on her own. Rather, she was confronted with it in her transcripts because of the coding device she used. Seeking to systematically detect all emotional expressions, she followed a coding procedure devised by Gottschalk and Gleser (1969) which involved consulting long lists of words reflecting fear, grief, anxiety, shame, and anger.

Although Lewis found indications of anxiety, grief, and anger in her transcripts, the emotion that clearly predominated was shame, and also embarrassment, which she treated, following Darwin, Gottschalk and Gleser, and others, as a shame variant. Unlike the other emotions, indications of shame were found in every transcript, and in many of them with repetitions so frequent as to be alarming. However, as Lewis reported, shame was almost never mentioned explicitly by either the patient or the therapist. Instead, it was manifested by words and manner in a particular context, one where the patient seemed to feel rejected, inadequate, or inferior. Because of her discovery of vast amounts of unmentioned shame in psychotherapy, Lewis called the emotion she found to dominate sessions "*unacknowledged* shame." Goffman's purely theoretical essay on embarrassment (1967) reaches a parallel conclusion – that all human contact, not only psychotherapy, is pervaded with embarrassment, either actual or anticipated.

In his study of the history of manners, Elias made the same discovery, based entirely on inferences from the texts of advice and etiquette manuals, but seemingly without help or guidance. It is important to note that his analysis of shame in this work is explicit: "No less characteristic of a civilizing process than 'rationalization' is the peculiar moulding of the drive economy that we call 'shame' and 'repugnance' or 'embarrassment'" (1994b, 492). With respect to explicitness about shame as a central concept, Elias was far bolder than in his later study *The Germans*.

In *The Civilizing Process*, shame provides one of the key concepts for the entire study: it is mentioned early and frequently, and occurs also in section headings and in the index. Although he seldom used the term, Elias outlined a theory of modernity. By examining instance after instance of advice concerning table manners, body functions, sexuality, and anger, he suggested that a key aspect of modernity involved a veritable explosion of shame. Elias argues that decreasing shame thresholds at the time of the breakup of rural communities and decreasing acknowledgment of shame had powerful consequences on levels of awareness and self-control.

The flavour of Elias's treatment of shame can be clearly seen in his analysis of a lengthy excerpt from von Raumer's nineteenth-century work *The Education of Girls*, which advises mothers how to answer the sexual questions their daughters ask:

Children should be left for as long as is at all possible in the belief that an angel brings the mother her little children. This legend, customary in some regions, is far better than the story of the stork common elsewhere. Children, if they really grow up under their mother's eyes, will seldom ask questions on this point ... not even if the mother is prevented by a childbirth from having them about her ... If girls should later ask how little children really come into the world, they should be told that the good Lord gives the mother her child, who has a guardian angel in heaven who certainly played an invisible part in bringing us this great joy. "You do not need to know nor could you understand how God gives children." Girls must be satisfied with such answers in a hundred cases, and it is the mother's task to occupy her daughters' thoughts so incessantly with the good and beautiful that they are left no time to brood on such matters ... A mother ... ought only once to say seriously: "It would not be good for you to know such a thing, and you should take care not to listen to anything said about it." A truly well-brought-up girl will from then on feel shame at hearing things of this kind spoken of. (Quoted in 1994b, 147–8)

Elias's commentary on this excerpt is masterful, interpreting the repression of sexuality in terms of unacknowledged shame. His interpretation implies several significant questions: Why is the author, von Raumer, offering the mother such absurd advice? Why does the mother follow such advice (as most did and still do)? Why do the daughters also (as most did and still do)?

Modern feminists would respond quickly to the first question that von Raumer's advice arises from his social position as a male authority: he sought to continue male supremacy by advising mothers to act in a way that is consonant with the role of women as subordinate to men. The woman's traditional role is *Kinder, Küche*, and *Kirche* (children, kitchen, and church). Keeping women ignorant of sexuality and reproduction helps to continue the system.

This formulation answers the first question in part, but not the other two. Why do mothers and daughters comply with male-oriented advice? Elias's analysis implies answers to all three questions without contradicting the feminist answer. Each of these three principals, the man and the two women, is too embarrassed about sexuality to think clearly about it. Their minds have been silenced on this issue. It is true that von Raumer's advice is partly derived from his male chauvinist position, but it is also true that he is too embarrassed to understand his own advice.

The thoughts, feelings, and actions that produce gender inequality are partly conscious and intentional, but most of them are probably unconscious. Gender inequality may be partly a product of men wanting power, but it is probably also driven by a desire for prestige and status, which involves a shame dynamic. Those men who have authentic pride in themselves would not need women to be subordinate in status to them. It is only those men who have false pride, whose actions are driven by attempts to avoid shame and inferiority, who propagate the domination of women.

Elias's analysis implies a central causal chain in modernity – denial of the emotion of shame – and of the threatened social bonds which cause and reflect the denial. His study suggests a way of understanding the social transmission of the taboo on shame and the social bond. The adult, the author von Raumer in this case, is not only ashamed of sex, but he also is ashamed of being ashamed and probably ashamed of the shame that he will arouse in his reader. The reader, in turn, will probably react in a similar way, being ashamed, being ashamed of being ashamed, and being ashamed of causing further shame in the daughter. Von Raumer's advice is part of a social system in which attempts at civilized delicacy result in an endless chain reaction of unacknowledged shame. The chain reaction is both within persons and between them, what I have called in a "triple spiral" (1990).

Certainly, Elias understood the significance of the denial of shame: it goes underground, leading to behaviour that is outside awareness and compulsive. In his discussion of von Raumer's advice to mothers about their daughters' sexual questions, he notes: "The primary concern is the necessity of instilling 'modesty' (i.e., feelings of shame, fear, embarrassment, and guilt) or, more precisely, behavior conforming to the social standard. And one feels how infinitely difficult is for [von Raumer] himself to overcome the resistance of the shame and embarrassment which surround this sphere for him" (1994b, 148).

Elias's analysis suggests some of the negative – indeed, destructive – effects of secrets and secrecy in a way that directly contradicts Simmel's famous essay of 1960. I believe that understanding the dynamics of unacknowledged shame will lead to exact models of repression and precise and reliable methods of understanding behaviour that is unconsciously motivated and compulsive. In his demonstration of the change of mood concerning manners, Elias followed advice manuals from the Middle Ages to the present, showing an extraordinary change in the content and manner of advice about matters that would be now considered too tasteless (or embarrassing) to write about.

In the fifteenth and sixteenth centuries, advice on courtesy and politeness, personal grooming, and the like was almost entirely a matter of adult-to-adult discourse, which was frank and, by modern standards, blushingly explicit. In this era the advice was usually justified in no uncertain terms as showing respect for other persons. Erasmus and the other counsellors felt no shame in talking about matters that are today considered too shameful to speak about. Virtually none of the matters that were openly discussed in these earlier books are even mentioned in current books on etiquette. In part, these matters are now taken for granted. But most perhaps involve delicacy and tact about embarrassment and the silence of shame. These matters can still be discussed, but only in privacy between intimates and in allusions by the more radical comedians. Erasmus did not hesitate to instruct *his* reader that after blowing one's nose in a handkerchief, one should not examine the contents "as if looking for pearls." Note that I have led up to this detail by first alluding to it earlier, hoping in this way to avoid abruptness and the consequent embarrassment to my reader. In our current alienated state, all are caught in a net of denial, denial of denial, and so on.

In the late seventeenth and early eighteenth century, a change began occurring in advice on manners. What was said openly and directly earlier begins only to be hinted at or left unsaid entirely. Moreover, open justifications are offered less and less. One is mannerly because it is the *right* thing to do. Any decent person will be courteous; the intimation is that bad manners are not only wrong but also unspeakable. It is the beginning of repression.

The change that Elias documents is gradual but relentless; by a continuing succession of small decrements, the manuals fall silent about the reliance of manners, style, and identity on respect, honour, and pride and the avoidance of shame and embarrassment. By the end of the eighteenth century, the social basis of decorum and decency had become virtually unspeakable. Unlike Freud or anyone else, Elias documents *step by step* the sequence of events that led to the repression of emotions in modern civilization.

He proposes that, by the nineteenth century, manners are no longer inculcated by way of adult-to-adult verbal discourse in which justifications are offered. Socialization shifts from slow and conscious changes by adults over centuries to swift and silent indoctrination of children in their earliest years. No justification is offered to most children; courtesy has become absolute. Moreover, any really decent person would not have to be told, as suggested in the text interpreted above. In modern societies, socialization of most children *automatically* inculcates and represses shame.

TOWARDS A CONCEPT OF SHAME

Although Elias made it clear in *The Civilizing Process* that shame analysis is a key element in his argument, it figures much less clearly in his study with John Scotson, *The Established and the Outsiders*. In this work, shame is not the central concern, but it is indirectly present in the idea that outsiders are stigmatized. In his study *The Germans*, though again not made completely explicit, shame plays a much larger role. Although the word "shame" and its variants (embarrassment, humiliation, low self-esteem, lack of self-confidence, and the like) occur literally hundreds of times in the book, Elias does not ever make explicit that shame is a key concept, as he did in *The Civilizing Process*. For reasons that are not immediately obvious, in the later two books, shame was demoted from a concept to a vernacular word.

Elias's argument in the more recent book is that the Germans, both as people and as a nation, have historically been unable to respond to humiliation in any other way than by fighting. His argument is quite similar to my analysis in *Bloody Revenge* of the humiliated fury that arose in the three Franco-German wars of 1870–1945. I proposed that because of the French defeat in 1871, unacknowledged shame was a key element on the French side leading to the First World War, and following their defeat in 1918, on the German side leading to the Second World War. In this study and earlier ones published by Retzinger and me, we define "shame" and "shame/anger loops" as technical concepts in order to document their occurrence in verbatim texts, such as the telegrams exchanged between heads of state just prior to the First World War.

Following his success in analyzing shame in *The Civilizing Process*, why did Elias not develop a technical conception of shame, just as he moved towards a technical conception of interdependence? There is no sure way of answering this question, but one possibility concerns the response of the audience to that book. Unless I am mistaken, there was virtually no response to his shame analysis, even though it plays a central role in his overall thesis. The only mention I have been able to find is by Sennett, who recognized the applicability of Elias's shame analysis to the problem of social control; Sennett argued that shame and social-economic dependence are intertwined (1980, 45–9) and that shame plays a central role as a tool of discipline of workers by management (1980, 92–7). However, just as there was virtually no response to Elias's shame analysis, so there was none to Sennett's. Just as Elias failed to develop a technical concept of shame, so too this emotion disappeared from Sennett's later work. It might not be stretching a point to conclude that both Elias and Sennett were shamed into silence by the silence of their audiences.

My explanation is that Elias's uncanny ability and insight led him to an analysis of the underlying process in our civilization that was too advanced for his audience. In Western societies, as he pointed out, the threshold for shame has been advancing for hundreds of years, but at the same time awareness of this emotion has been declining. As his own analysis could have predicted, in our era the level of awareness of shame is so low that only those trained to detect unacknowledged shame could understand the point that he was making. Only because Retzinger and I were guided by Lewis's work were we able to understand Elias's shame analysis.

We have developed a technical concept of shame and a method that allows one to detect it in texts even when it is hidden or disguised (Scheff 1990; Retzinger 1991; Scheff and Retzinger 1991; Scheff 1994). We define shame as a broad family of emotions with many cognates and variants, some of which are not negative.[1] We also trace the way in which shame regulates and amplifies other emotions, as in the "shame-rage loop" of humiliated fury. To our surprise, we later found that our technical concept of shame is very similar to the conception of shame in many traditional societies.[2] In Maori and Mandarin the emotion lexicon is much larger than in European languages and much more central. Shame and shame/rage are familiar ideas in these languages and constantly alluded to in ordinary discourse. Especially in Maori, the destructive effects of unacknowledged shame are clear, as in Elias and the Scheff and Retzinger formulations.

METHOD IN *THE CIVILIZING PROCESS*

Elias says very little about his research methods in *The Civilizing Process* or anywhere else. Yet if elaborated and made explicit, his analysis of the advice excerpts might lay the foundation for a powerful micro-macro theory and method in the human sciences. I will address this issue briefly here because it is related to the issue of the development of technical concepts discussed above. In my *Emotions, Social Bonds, and Human Reality: Part/Whole Analysis* (1997), a fuller treatment can be found.

The use that Elias made of the advice excerpts exemplifies what I call "part/whole analysis." The first step in this method is to closely examine one or more individual specimens, even though each specimen has a unique content. This step involves a consideration of what Spinoza called the "least parts." As elaborated by Sackstetter, Spinoza proposed that human understanding requires relating the "least parts to the greatest wholes." In botany the least parts would be the specimen plant itself and the details of its construction and dynamics. In human science the least parts are usually the verbal and non-verbal parts of discourse, words and gestures. This method is similar to what in botany is called individual morphology. A great deal can be learned from a single plant specimen by microanalysis about the internal system of the plant, even if little is known about other specimens of the same plant. How does a plant or a passage of advice work as a system?

The second step is to compare specimens with each other, looking for similarities of pattern, even though the particular content of each specimen is unique. This is the step Elias took when he recognized that the historically later excerpts were shame-ridden. The next part of this sequence involved his comparison of the latter excerpts with earlier ones, which suggested a second pattern: an advancing threshold of shame along with a decreasing awareness of it. This latter step involves a larger whole than the first step, since Elias proposed a pattern of change made up from the excerpts: an advance in the shame threshold and a decrease in awareness of shame.

The third and final step in part/whole analysis is interpreting the patterns that have been discovered in the parts in terms of the largest possible wholes: the biographical, historical, and cultural contexts in which the parts are embedded. Elias, unlike most microanalysts of verbatim texts, also took this step. He interpreted his findings in terms of large wholes – changes in population density and changes in key social institutions, such as the distribution of power and the means of violence.

The morphological method that Elias used with his advice excerpts in *The History of Manners* goes much deeper than Goffman's frequent use of examples in *Interaction Ritual*, which were usually from clippings from newspaper and magazine stories. Both authors employ what at first seems to be vernacular language in their writing, and both frequently use verbatim excerpts. The way in which these two authors illustrate almost all their abstract argument with concrete episodes, in this way evoking human faces and voices, brings to their work a clarity and a force usually missing in most social-science writing.

In most social scientific work, theory is too abstract to evoke actual human beings; it deals only with large and abstract wholes. Both quantitative and qualitative research, on the other hand, contain very little abstract theory, but deal almost entirely with parts. By using abstract concepts to interpret concrete episodes, the method that Elias and Goffman employed was akin to part/whole analysis: microanalysis of the parts that is interpreted in the context of ever-larger wholes.

Unlike Elias, however, Goffman was always content to interpret a single example to make his point. Elias's method of dealing with the advice excerpts is much more sophisticated. First, his analysis of key excerpts is much more microscopic than any of Goffman's. The way he teases the shame dynamics out of the von Raumer excerpt (discussed above) goes deep into the shame dynamics of both the individuals and the relationships involved. By comparison, Goffman's finely wrought essay on embarrassment (1967) is entirely abstract and theoretical.

Furthermore, Elias does not stop with a single example but takes the next step in what I call "the morphological study of discourse": he compares a series of similar excerpts on advice concerning sexual and other types of behaviour (table manners) to establish whether or not the same pattern that he found in one instance occurs in all of them. He finds little evidence of shame in the historically early instances of advice but much shame in the historically later ones.

The third step in the part/whole method is to interpret the microanalyses of the parts in the context of ever-larger wholes, concepts at the level of relationships, social institutions, and whole societies. As already indicated, Elias interpreted the patterns he found – advance in the shame threshold, and decreasing awareness of shame – in the context of larger wholes – increasing social density, rationalization, and state monopoly over the means of violence. Unlike Elias, Goffman seldom located his concepts and propositions within larger wholes. His analysis of the micro-world is largely ahistorical and not connected with social institutions and large-scale social systems.

The last step in the part/whole method is to generate an explicit micro-macro theory on the basis of the findings and an explicit method for testing the theory. Although Elias came close to taking this step in his analysis in *The Civilizing Process*, he did not formulate his findings in the kind of explicit propositions that are needed for a formal theory, nor did he explicitly delineate the actual procedures that made up his method. I believe that his failure to take this last step is a limitation of this work. Even so, because of the explicitness of his analyses of the advice excerpts, he came much closer to taking the last step of part/whole analysis than Goffman.

Since both Goffman and Elias used vernacular language and many examples, their studies of concrete excerpts give readers the feeling that they have understood the main arguments and their implications. I believe the readers' feeling of understanding is largely an illusion, however. The analyses in these studies are quite complex and have implications that would be difficult to understand without considerable preparation, especially in Elias's study.

The combination of genius and the part/whole method lead Elias and Goffman to assessments of social relationships that are complex and profound. So much so, in fact, that their analyses break through the wall of custom, the point of view of the everyday world, in Schuetz's terminology. In modern societies the nature of interdependence and of shame – in my view, the two key concepts in Elias's work – are both denied and repressed. The cult of individualism in Western societies suppresses the reality of human interdependence, as Elias argued with his idea of *homo clausus*, and as his findings on the advance of the shame threshold and the decreasing awareness of shame suggest, modern societies repress the emotion of shame.

The concept of habitus, the thoughts, feelings, and actions in a culture that are so frequent as to be unconscious, can be understood in this way. The habitus of Western societies involves not only individual but also collective representations. In the current Western representation of reality, there is no room for Elias's technical conception of interdependence nor for his findings on shame. If contemporary scholarship is to benefit from them, we must conduct studies that are directly concerned with actual social relationships and their degrees of integration and with individual and collective emotions. Arguments about the civilizing process are so abstract that they can easily fit into the current status quo. If we are to benefit from Elias's profundity, we should recapture the human faces and voices that can be found in his study of the advice excerpts.

NOTES

1 As in French word *pudeur* (shyness, modesty, and in classical Greek, awe).
2 For the case of Mandarin Chinese, see Shaver et al. 1992; for the Maori shame lexicon, see Metge 1986.

6 On the Relationship between Literature and Sociology in the Work of Norbert Elias

HELMUT KUZMICS

THE PROBLEM AND FIRST CONSIDERATIONS

There are few great sociologists whose work reminds one of literature as strongly as does that of Norbert Elias. This observation seems to be true in more than one respect, for reading *The Loneliness of the Dying*, a book written in old age and after severe illness, generates a nearly cathartic effect stimulated by an unpretentious language that does not deny fear, grief, or sadness. But at the same time, one listens to a human being who, being aware of the *conditio humana*, is nonetheless able to find courage and meaning in it. Avoiding the technical and formalized "new-speak" of sociology, which exhausts one through the creation of "variables," Elias's empirical work contains numerous literary examples that produce a vivid impression, seldom reached by most sociological studies. Last but not least, Elias was also a poet and translator of poetry, although this activity was in strict separation from his work as a sociologist.

The style of Elias's writing throughout all his publications is demonstrative of a quality that might be called "literary." He adopted this approach as an aspect of his strategy of "concept avoidance," a methodology of writing aimed always at overcoming the barriers of rigid stereotypes in thinking. Thus it is obvious that we should deal with the literary quality of Elias's writing and thinking without using only stereotyped formulae such as "the literary style of the author." Is this quality more or less accidental, neutral to the sociological substance of the theory of civilizing processes? Or is it something belonging to the very essence of his sociology, without which we would be unable to understand that sociology in a profound way? Or is this literary element rather annoying, an impurity in science, muddying the clear waters of sociological research? I want to place this discussion in a broader context. In the social sciences of today, it is still very unclear if and how far they should or could follow the line of the more successful natural sciences in respect to their intellectual power and method. Ideas of a possible growing maturity of the social sciences are opposed by conceptions that regard them as a sequence of forms of "discourse," without any cumulative growth of knowledge. Is not, after all, "high literature" a better kind of sociology, referring to the function of the literati in providing appropriate precepts for life in industrial society?[1] On the other hand, have not novelists and literary critics alike always stressed the point that the very essence of fiction is to be fictitious? Nabokov expressed this view quite drastically when he said, "Literature is fiction. Fiction is fiction. To call a story a true story is an insult to both art and truth" (1980, 5). Nonetheless, we may read many sociological books and essays in an attempt to understand a certain piece of social reality, and very often we gain the impression that we are no wiser than before. How is it possible that it is often a novel or a piece of journalism which teaches us more about the world than masses of sociological prose?[2] Elias's prose is certainly different. Can his sociology help us to answer this general question too?

A solution to this problem demands some conceptual clarification. First, it is evident that all forms of "high" literature (fiction, poetry, and drama) have to fulfill at least two functions: they have to entertain, to move, to keep the audience in suspense, to give advice, to accuse, and generally to do those kinds of things with words which Searle has called "performative speech-acts." Second, if it is to be of sociological value, the novel (we will concentrate on this genre) does not only have to tell a "good story." Among the criteria of what can be seen as a "good story" must be included those that hold good as criteria for sociology as well. If we may call the former function predominantly *non-cognitive*, we can regard the latter as *cognitive-descriptive* with respect to improving our knowledge about the social world. It is important to see that this distinction is, both for literature *and* for sociology, a gradual one. A single example that justifies this point of view in the case of sociology is the enduring importance of style, a criterion that can be neglected in the sphere of the natural sciences, as book reviews regularly show.

Another important dimension that serves to characterize the relationship between literature and sociology is that *of competition versus complementarity*. In so far as both branches of human imagination are intended to improve our understanding of the complex modern world, they can be seen as being in a kind of competition – what Lepenies (1988) calls a *Deutungskonkurrenz*, a competition in interpreting modernity or industrial society for the quite pragmatic purpose of individual orientation, the search for meaning, and a guide to conduct in life. He describes the relationship between sociology and literature as a history of reciprocal influences and demarcations for a period stretching from the beginning of the nineteenth century to the first third of the twentieth.

However, the offering of an "orientation to life" (*Lebensorientierung*) is only one of several possible functions of the social sciences. In spite of this restriction – which, nevertheless, still leaves room for the image of the sociologist as a "hunter" or "destroyer" of myths (Elias 1970b, 51–74) – Lepenies's book deals in an original and fruitful way with one stage in the long process that sociology has needed in order to become a respected, autonomous discipline.

During this stage, sociology establishes itself as a science, but it oscillates permanently between scientism (following the model of the natural sciences) and hermeneutics (following the model of the literal interpretation of texts). According to Lepenies, it does so through a partial process of differentiation of the literary mode of production from a scientific mode. At the same time, the separation of sociology from a literary style of reasoning coincides with the important conflict between reason and sentiment, a conflict typical of the developing bourgeois society. Lepenies's manifold examples, from French, English, and German, are proof of the existence of both competition and complementarity in the relations between sociology and literature. He is thus able to show that Thomas Mann can claim priority over Max Weber as a discoverer of the "Protestant work ethic" in his *Buddenbrooks*. Indeed, Marx frankly admitted his debt to Balzac as the most authentic chronicler of the bourgeois world.

To use fiction sociologically can have two meanings. A rather conventional approach sees it as a "source" or a "document" providing evidence for sociology. The other would be to give literature the status of a serious contribution to sociology itself. Very few would argue against the former usage, especially in the weak form of the argument, where every cultural product can serve as an expression or indirect representation of underlying social processes and structures. But our question goes deeper and asks whether literature is not only able to but sometimes even privileged to offer "true" representations or mappings of the social world.

Which kind is Elias's sociology? How does it deal with literature, and how does it deal with "science"? Where is its exact position on a scale reaching from explanations *more physico* to the idea of the whole world as *text*? Does it treat literature as a "source" or as capable of being "sociology" itself, in the sense of providing good descriptions or even theories? Today there exists a widespread conception that every discourse in literature or in science is not a "representation" but a "construction" of reality. What is Elias's position in respect to this general proposition?

In order to answer these questions, I shall follow a simple scheme. In the first part Elias's method of using literature will be shown through two examples, and its difference from a naturalistic under-standing of sociology outlined. In the second section I discuss two positions from different origins that coincide in their skeptical attitude towards the validity and credibility of literary evidence; one descends from the spirit of measurement-oriented empiricism, the other from the tradition of disbelieving literary criticism. I shall then balance these ideas off with a concluding discussion.

TWO EXAMPLES OF THE USE OF LITERATURE IN ELIAS'S WORK AND THE CONTRAST WITH THE "NATURALISTIC" SELF-CONCEPTION IN SOCIOLOGY

Throughout his work, Elias makes extensive use of fiction. Caroline von Wolzogen's German novel *Agnes von Lilien* was published in Schiller's journal *Die Horen* at the end of the eighteenth century. It pursues a specific tradition; from the point of view of a German middle-class culture and intelligentsia (consisting of well-educated offi-cials, clergymen, and professors) the courtly-aristocratic "civilization" is put under a massive, moralizing critique. Embedded in an often-romantic plot, quite detailed portraits of courtly life are drawn. The heroine of this novel says of herself: "I knew but little of conventional life and the language of worldly people. My simple principles found many things paradoxical to which a mind made pliable by habit is reconciled without effort. To me it was as natural as that night follows day to lament the deceived girl and hate the deceiver, to prefer virtue to honor and honor to one's own advantage. In the judgment of this society I saw all these notions overturned" (quoted in Elias 1978a, 21). Here the author, Caroline von Wolzogen, expresses her ideals and moral principles, and they are directed against the dynamics of an aristocratic society regulated by the struggle for prestige and honour. Her estrangement from this society makes her experience courtly conventions as producing "paradoxical effects." But in this quotation, her language is still rather abstract. It becomes much more concrete in the following passage, as she delivers a detailed picture of the prince:

The prince was between sixty and seventy, and oppressive to himself and others with the stiff, old French etiquette which the sons of German princes had learned at the court of the French king and transplanted to their own soil, admittedly in somewhat reduced dimensions. The prince had learned through age and habit to move almost naturally under this heavy armor of ceremony. Toward women he observed the elegant, exaggerated courtesy of the bygone age of chivalry, so that his person was not unpleasant to them, but he could not leave the sphere of fine manners for an instant without becoming insufferable. His children ... saw in their father only the despot.

The caricatures among the courtly people seemed to me now ridiculous, now pitiable. The reverence that they were able, on the appearance of the lord, to summon instantly from their hearts to their hands and feet, the gracious or angry glance that passed through their bodies like an electric shock ... the immediate compliance of their opinions to the most recent utterance from the princely lips, all this I found incomprehensible. I seemed to be watching a puppet theater. (Quoted in Elias 1978a, 21)

The text that Elias reproduces here is realistic within certain limits. It mirrors a considerable complexity of social perception on the part of the author. She has many insights which we may call today "sociological." They are indeed predominantly about regularities of courtly life, but we find in them also psychological considerations of a more general nature. To these belongs the realization that habits can become a person's (second) "nature." Certainly, the prince's etiquette appears to be "natural," and we might note that Elias's notion of "habitus" as "second nature" expresses the same idea.[3] The image of the "armor of ceremony" is well chosen and informative in this section, and Elias accordingly takes the author seriously; her knowledge and her observations are meaningful for his own interpretation. Her reflexivity forms an indispensable part of his own theory.

Things are different in the tradition of the behavioural sciences, which we can call "scientific" or "naturalistic" (as opposed to the "hermeneutical" or *verstehende* conception of sociology). Its main intention was to overcome the German *Geisteswissenschaften* by seeing the social sciences as natural sciences, with the criteria of explicit and exact formulation and empirical verification at every single point

(Bernstein 1979, 36). Banned should be all logical, folkloristic, and anthropomorphic considerations. Hull expresses the hope of a "Copernican turn," which was to occur if these postulates were met. R. Bernstein calls this position – exact measurement in the sphere of observation; clear and general laws in the sphere of theory – that of "empirical theory." He reconstructs it from the strangely harmonious methodological utterances of its otherwise often differing representatives, such as Merton, Parsons, and Homans. In this understanding, theory is separated from empirical evidence, "theoretical terms" are rather strictly distinguished from everyday language, and where measurement is important, it follows the line of "operational definitions" and prefers visible, observable indicators to the unclear and somewhat mystical "inner" states of human consciousness and emotions.[4] The applications of these principles did not help much in bridging the gap between a micro and a macro level of analysis, for psychological reductionism and systems theory were both built on them.

Elias's sociology deviates from these postulates in some decisive ways. It is open to everyday language, and it does not postulate an opposition between theory and empirical reality. By using fiction, he completes von Wolzogen's interpretation through a *synthesis* by adding elements that were not available to her. There is, for example, knowledge about her social background, the German *Bildungsbürgertum*, in its opposition to the aristocracy and their manners, which are stigmatized as "superficial." The novel is part of a larger movement. To it, knowledge about German *Kleinstaaterei* (particularism) is added – the many small courts, princelings, and petty states, with their narrowness and the seclusion of their circles of social intercourse – all of which can also be inferred from other sources. And Elias knows about the sharp, specifically German line of demarcation between *Kultur* (education), *Innerlichkeit* (inwardness), and *Zivilisation*, (politics, society, and manners). Their meaning, though, can be deduced from his familiarity with the peculiarity of German social development, which differs from the French and English civilizing processes in their forms of shaping affects – of "modelling the affects" – in many respects.

Similarly, Elias draws on Goethe's *Die Leiden des jungen Werther* in order to make visible the feelings of inferiority that vexed members of the German bourgeoisie in the face of aristocrats, the social cleavage between them, and the compensatory strategies of the former when humiliated and excluded from social intercourse with their superiors.[5] These strategies refer largely to *Bildung* (education) as a source of pride. In the same context, Elias lets Sophie de la Roche have her say in her then widely read novel *Das Fräulein von Sternheim*, which tells the story of a heroine of bourgeois and petty-aristocratic origin deceived by a courtly nobleman. Here above all, it is Elias's concern to elucidate the emotions of middle-class individuals, in particular, their sentimentality: the girl swings from fear of the socially stronger seducer, for whom the marriage would be a misalliance, to a certain fascination in face of the evil in the courtly way of life. Finally, she saves her virtue and moral superiority through her own death. Contemporary readers gourmandize on a curious emotional cocktail – one loves the pain and idealizes the virtue to the point of a voluptuous feeling of being deceived. A culture of sensitivity and sentimentality arises, behind which Elias localizes the social distance between the strata. This culture owes much to its shaping by the preaching clergyman and the teaching professor at the university. The broader context of these examples is Elias's attempt to explain the sociogenesis of the concepts of *Kultur* and *Zivilisation* which express the opposition between the bourgeois and the courtly-aristocratic conceptions of good behaviour. This opposition leads directly to the difference in national character between the courtly-shaped French and the more middle-class oriented Germans. Insofar as the endangered Western civilization of the 1930s can be also seen as a starting point for Elias's interest in the long-term changes of "affect economies," the examples mentioned form important pillars for the analysis of the European courtly civilizing process that follows.[6]

Let us provisionally summarize the argument so far. In contrast to the naturalistic perspective in the social sciences, Elias uses literary examples in order to solve a widely stretched problem of explanation. He needs them, first, for making visible emotional structures that can scarcely be recognized in other sources. Secondly, he reconstructs these feelings, not like a behaviourist (only in their expression), but by gaining access to the inner experience of contemporaries who report on their sensations. Thirdly, in these quotations, ways of acting, perception, and reflections can be seen which could scarcely be otherwise so reconstructed; without referring to them, it would be impossible to develop sociological explanations oriented towards actions *and* the entanglements of actions and actors. Further, the literary observations and interpretations quoted by Elias indicate even more – they overthrow the restrictions regarding "sources" and take on the character of quite intelligent sociological remarks themselves. And finally, he also pays heed to the sociology-of-knowledge dimension of the relation between text, author, and audience and its effect on a "realist" interpretation. With all that, he differs from the *more physico* model. He gives exceptional space to the important detail, the historically particular, which derives its meaning from the broader social context. Concept formation is not technical or restricted by its being embedded in law-like generalizations, although there is room for the more general too.

Another impressive example was given by Elias in his book *The Germans*. Here the problem was to explain how it was possible that the peaceful, backward people of *Dichter und Denker* adapted themselves to a more aggressive canon which was soon to become part of a German national habitus. In a chapter dealing with the formation of a "good society" in the newly erected German Kaiserreich, we find several quotations from a university novel by Walter Bloem, *Der krasse Fuchs*. The first gives a picture of the social structure of a German university town around 1900:

Marburg's citizens were divided into two castes: society, and those who did not belong to society. Whether a particular person or family was to be counted as belonging to the one or other class was decided by a very simple distinguishing mark: the members of the "Museum Association" formed society; anyone who did not belong to this circle was an inferior form of life. Members of the civil service, of the university, the municipal corporation, the officer corps of the rifle battalion, as well as all members of the graduate professions and the wealthy merchants belonged to the association. For a modest amount, the students could acquire associate membership, and thus all members of the corps, the fraternities, the associations of students from the various regions of Germany, and the university gymnastic clubs were without exception eligible for museum membership.

Within this society, however, there were numerous more exclusive circles, which, even if they were rivals in certain particulars, nevertheless by and large formed another inner social hierarchy with rungs which were at first very wide apart and then slowly narrowing.

That the young corps students had to stick only to certain precisely defined topmost rungs of this hierarchy was impressed on them at every initiation ceremony for junior members by the "fox major." Werner thus already knew very well when he went to his first Museum Ball that he could by no means dance with every girl he might take a fancy to; that instead, before he let himself be introduced, he had to inquire every time from a senior corps member whether the particular lady belonged to the circle in which the corps moved.

But he knew too little of life to feel particularly hemmed in by the narrow limits within which he was allowed to seek pleasure and stimulation. Bit by bit, he had become so much a Cimber that he found it quite natural to dance only with "Cimber ladies." For his blue-red-white feelings, the other ladies came as little into question as the women of those foreign peoples with whom there was no *commercium et connubium* would have been regarded by a citizen of ancient Rome. (Quoted in Elias 1996a, 47)

In this quotation, it becomes visible that the novel itself is unequivocally based on observations and interpretations that we tend to see as sociological ones. Up to the sentence beginning "Werner thus already knew ...," we would not be able to detect a difference from the sociological interpretation that follows without knowing that it is a quotation from literature.[7] Indeed, Elias modifies the text in only a few points: "As in probably every German town, large or small, in Marburg there was a group, 'good society,' which stood out from the rest of the city's population" (1996a, 47). He thus generalizes here. Consequently, he interprets the local stratification hierarchy as an expression of a broader social power distribution in Wilhelmine Germany. The representatives of the state occupy the top positions, while the economic bourgeoisie is inferior in power and status, and Elias considers how difficult it must have been for outsiders in this society: "A young corps student would have had to break through a number of barriers and, probably face the full force of his comrades' anger if he had preferred a pretty little merchant's daughter to a lady, from the circle 'in which the corps moved'" (1996a, 48). If we let the quotation from Bloem's novel pass, we may detect that here the stress is laid less on individual experience than on the so-called objective characterization of a social microcosm with its institutions. This focus changes if we move forward in the novel.

The "crass fox" Werner Aschenbach, a still quite subordinate figure in the fraternity, visits one of his older colleagues, who is in serious trouble. This young man had not fulfilled the criteria of his fraternity brothers in a fencing match, and they have supposed that his failure was the result of his engagement to a girl, which had taken place the previous evening. As a result, the student is dismissed in disgrace, and he sits quite severely wounded in his room. Between the visiting Aschenbach and the injured and ashamed Klauser (the student), the following dialogue develops:

"Well, look here, for us corps students, fencing is not a simple sport, a game with weapons, but a ... means of upbringing. That is, the corps student is supposed to prove in fencing that bodily pain, disfigurement, even severe wounds and death ... that all that is a matter of indifference to him ... When you have been in the corps longer, you will learn to understand all this better. In the corps over the last few years the standards of fencing competitions ... have become a bit exaggerated. Things ... are demanded, which ... well, which not everyone can perform. And some can achieve them today, but then not again tomorrow. Mood plays a big part ... health ... one's nervous condition."

"Well really, my God – so you are being punished in this way because you ... you got engaged the previous evening –?!"

"Yes – to speak bluntly – that's right."

"That is crazy. It's crazy."

"Mmm, look – you really shouldn't ever forget ... those are people who are judging us ... young devils like you and me ... naturally they are not perfect. The C.C. thought that my fencing was poor, and so it was poor. It is just like being in front of a jury. Sometimes even an innocent person takes the rap. That is just tough luck."

"Tough luck?! I think that is terribly severe, a horrible shortcoming of the corps!! – Oh, Klauser ... The whole thing with the corps!! – ... I'm really almost at my wit's end!! – And what about you? You must be in a similar state! You are really and truly feeling the blessings of this wonderful institution with your own flesh and your own blood ... at this very moment!"

"With my own flesh and my own blood! Yes, I am ... As I sit here, the corps has debarred me from my fifteenth fencing match, has taken my office away from me, and I don't even know if I'll be readmitted Saturday week or whether I'll be thrown out permanently. Yes, believe you me, I'm not really in the mood to paint a rosy picture and hush things up. Yes, a great deal is not very nice in the corps. A lot could be different – gentler, more humane, less in the same old way. But ... if I were a 'crass fox' again ... I would nevertheless still be a corps student!!"

"Really, again? In spite of all this?"

"Yes – in spite of all this! I don't know: my feelings tell me that things must be so. That it is all just so, so that we shall become useful for what is to come later ... So that we learn to grit our teeth – so that we become men!" (Bloem, quoted in Elias 1996a, 109)

This passage differs from the previous one in a significant way. Here dialogues are mapped, emotions are described, and the inner life of a very particular institution is exhibited in a way which would be impossible to reproduce from outside. At the same time, a key institution is shown here which had for a certain time a large share in the formation of a typically German habitus, and it is Elias's synthesizing, theoretical achievement to have worked this out. The focus is on the membership in the new German "establishment," just formed from older and newer elements. Let us see how Elias interprets this passage theoretically.

There is, first, the so-called *Bestimmungsmensur*, the ritual fencing match of the male student youth. Such events differed from the ancient duel in more than one respect: they were organized by the fraternities and so were not spontaneous activities; rather, they had the function of a "means of education." Together with drinking rituals, they formed part of a deliberate reanimation of student customs in the spirit of the common, ancient European warrior code. Elias points out that these duels can be seen as *rites de passage*, being neither bloodier nor more cruel than similar tests of courage in many simpler societies of the world. The corresponding code gets its special meaning in the context of the formation of a German nation-state. The peaceful German *Bildungsbürgertum* of the eighteenth century, far from politics and the sphere of power, became "militarized" under the aegis of the Prussian Junkers. A new personality structure was then modelled and repro-duced itself through several generations. "And indeed, in a society where a tradition of conduct in which life is seen as a struggle of all against all has gained dominance, and where there are institutions directed towards bringing up people with an appropriate personality structure, this type of social life may have such deep roots that, with-out far-reaching upheavals in the entire social structure, it will continue to reproduce itself" (Elias 1996a, 108). The fraternities here have the function of a linking structure between the microsphere of everyday life in the interior of a pacified state-society and the macrosphere of the state, the class structure, and the cobweb of European competition between nation-states. Again, as in the earlier example, Elias differs from the more physicalist understanding of sociology by including – via literature – emotions, perceptions, and cultural interpretations and definitions of the situation. His analysis of the German process of state formation, which is often seen as a process of modernization, is far from the nomothetic claim of a variables sociology. The quotation illustrates the weight and emotional meaning of membership in a stu-dent "corporation." It shows the degree of severity with which frus-trations steered behaviour in this specific national context.

Bloem's novel highlights the social constraints of competition that exist among the members of the corps and also their loyalty to it, their esprit de corps. Elias's interpretation shows the importance of a char-acter training that stresses rigour and ruthlessness as elements of an ancient, untamed warrior ethos which is revitalized by the ascendancy of (partly) bourgeois groups. For him, this is an attitude that is not restricted to the narrow sphere of its origination but – and this is decisive – spreads out to other domains and social relations where people do not fight with rapier in hand. The tendency of members of the new German leading strata to hit hard and without mercy whenever one shows weakness can also be seen elsewhere. Identification with others and compassion give way to *schadenfreude*, the delight of seeing others lose. Furthermore, the quoted passage offers Elias evidence of the human capacity to gain (dubious) meaning from suffering severe frustrations: the blindness of unintentional social constraints sees a personal reinterpretation as "meaningful." To become "hard" and "smooth" turns into a personal goal. Yet it is the (almost accidentally) victorious war that provides the opportunity for a warrior code to gain ground: aristocratic groups owe their hegemonic position to the wars against Austria and France. Indeed, by not accepting the attitude that "we must grit our teeth in order to become men," he who does not take part is punished with a stigmatization and exclusion that endangers his entire later career. The "modelling of affects" towards a bourgeoisified warrior ideal is only possible since it is enforced on pain of expulsion from the highest-ranking stratum. The literary example helps to make clear how much this treatment hurts: in such experiences, one's sense of meaning and self-esteem is threatened. An almost Hobbesian image of the human being in a struggle of all against all is the unplanned result, such that mental and physical toughness as well as honour become dominant traits in German national character, as all the time, moral questions gradually seem correspondingly to lose importance. Elias goes on to show how this unplanned process is mirrored further in Nietzsche's ethos of discipline and mercilessness.

Nonetheless, from both of the literary examples presented here, we can infer how Elias's usage of fiction deviates from the naturalistic canon. We find here neither the well-known "hard" data – statistical frequency rates of "attitudes" gained with the help of surveys – nor a slavish orientation to "laws" that are as general as possible. Rather, decisive stress is laid on emotions, be they conscious or unconscious. It is precisely here that literature, predominantly the novel, provides relevant information. How people act is reconstructed as an outcome of constraints and is thereby made intelligible.

However, Elias's usage of fiction does not correspond to the physicalistic notion of observation as "measurement." Nor does it deal with fiction in the sense of a "source" that has to be evaluated in order to confirm or reject a ready-made theory. Instead, literature itself receives the status of a sociological theory about the people involved, and how they assess their social situation becomes for Elias a constitutive part of the sociological description and explanation itself. As a result, the sociologist is someone who depends in this enterprise on the novelist or other intelligent witnesses. They help the sociologist to make observations and to interpret these observations conceptually; thus the novelist shares responsibility for the accuracy of theories to social reality. Here a ready-made theory is not compared to a ready-made "world of data"; instead, both enterprises are inseparably linked.

A CRITIQUE OF REALIST INTERPRETATIONS OF LITERATURE IN THE SOCIAL SCIENCES AND LITERARY CRITICISM

For the success of melding the sociological with the fictional perspective, it is necessary to treat literature as "realist" in at least those cases where we use it. However, at the same time such a supposition is now contested by two mighty strands of contemporary human science, one from the social sciences and the other from the tradition of literary criticism.

An example of the former comes from quantitatively oriented social history – more particularly, from the history of the family, shaped by the spirit of English empiricism. Peter Laslett published his essay on the relationship between literature and science under the heading "The Wrong Way through the Telescope." Written against tendencies in his field, such as were prevalent in French histories of childhood, dying, and sexuality, to employ "soft" methods (such as the interpretation of literary sources), his article pleads for a return to the hard data of demography. With such terminology he has in mind the frequencies of birth and deaths, family size, age at marriage, and the like. His main proposition is contained in the title: those who use fiction simply resemble the spectator who wants to see nature but stares into the diminished eye of another spectator instead. Reading Shakespeare to gain information on the past, we would arrive at seeing with Shakespeare's eye, and all we would really have then is what he wants us to see or is willing to allow us see. Following Laslett, we need to find a positive answer to these questions:

1 Since novels also have non-descriptive functions (to entertain, to accuse), do they not distort reality by putting emphasis on these interests?
2 Could the author not have invented what he describes?
3 Can literary evidence be confirmed by further, perhaps non-fictional, evidence?
4 Could the author have been in a position to know the social phenomena from first-hand experience?
5 Fiction normally contains only vague, if any, statements of frequency (of events, properties, etc.). Are the proportions accurate reflections of reality?
6 A sociology of literary expression is needed which deals with the problem as to what kind of audience was being addressed by the message. Since exaggeration, colourization, suppression, and invention are common elements of literature – "poetic truth" is different from "plain truth" – the social scientist must have a theory of, or at least a suspicion about, the intentions of authors and their effects on the subject: how their positions are related to the interests, attitudes, and expectations shared by members of those strata in which they suppose their readers to be. Not only are the conscious intentions of the artist important, but also the many unconscious traits of the socially shaped person of the literary author.

The empiricist skepticism of Laslett thus scarcely allows us to use fiction sociologically, although he shows a possible way out, consisting of a patient sociology-of-knowledge reconstruction of the complex communication process in which literature is produced.

Skepticism about realist interpretations of texts is nearly as old as literary criticism itself. Nabokov's comments have already been mentioned. Literary theory, though, has developed in a powerful way within recent decades under the influence of Marxism, structuralism, hermeneutics, phenomenology, psychoanalysis, post-structuralism, and postmodernism. What has been the effect of these contributions and attacks on the old understanding of reading and literary criticism? At one end of this development, so-called deconstruction arose, where the claim of literature being capable of representing reality was denounced out of hand as ridiculous.

I do not want to deal here with the most radical solipsists but, rather, with an attempt to bridge the gap between the various conceptions in a kind of synthesis. Robert Hodge's *Literature as Discourse* is an interesting work since he explicitly wants to reconcile literary criticism with literary history. He pleads for a revision of the "traditional criticism" of F.R. Leavis, whom he accuses of presupposing aesthetic standards as self-evident, of regarding language as not needing further analytical elaboration, and of naively assuming the meaning and "truth" of a literary product as given. Against that position, Hodge mobilizes the whole arsenal of "social semiotics," a theory of the sign that has the function of reconstructing semiotics as a social process generating meaning. This theory strongly resembles interpretative forms of sociology, such as symbolic interactionism or ethnomethodology. Every text refers – as "signifier" – also to the "semiotic" context, the condition of its production and reception. Authors/speakers meet readers/listeners; in principle, this concept resembles Laslett's sociology-of-knowledge perspective quite closely. Differing from Laslett, though, Hodge places the text in the foreground, as used to be the case in "classical" literary criticism. At last everything concentrates on the necessity of making literature understandable to the reader and student: here there is no difference from the arch-skeptic Nabokov. The only difference consists in Nabokov's general hostility to sociology and the kind of psychoanalysis that uses social history only in order to let the fertile imagination of the author shine in an ever-brighter light.

The restricted credibility on which literary texts can count is, in Hodge's language, a low degree of "modality." Between "true" and "semiotic" reality there lies a fractured relation of representation: different genres, domains, production regimes, and reception regimes imply different values (high or low) of the "modality" of a text. This "modality" (of the detective novel, pornography, poetry) refers to context and usage, and it cannot be seen simply as a relation between the text and reality. The mimetic content of poetry, fiction, and drama differs: the former has a lower modality value than the latter two. Signs are understood as "motivated" (intended) or "arbitrary" or "conventional." Otherwise they often possess – following linguistic structuralism – a merry life of their own, and their meaning can only be deciphered by a mystical process of detecting reciprocal reference. "Domains" are types of context that generate – a way similar to the phenomenological sociology of Schütz – provinces of knowledge which can be discovered by patient reconstruction. One must know the rules of a past genre rather well in order to correctly estimate their reality content.

Reality becomes a "reality factor" that can only be guessed if one recognizes "characters," "plots," "settings," or "speeches" as constructed and thus reconstructs them. "All literary texts play a complex game with modality. They use markers of unreality to allow contact with their truths and construct illusory realities to enhance their power, giving rise to the contradictory and unstable modality-characteristics of literature that have caused such puzzlement since the days of Plato" (Hodge 1990, 170).

What is the application of this analysis? It is stupefying to realize that nearly all the literary examples Hodge discusses orient themselves more towards the literary text which has to be made intelligible and less to the explanation of society itself. Thus he is considering the problems of realism in a way not dissimilar to that of the old-fashioned literary criticism of the past. Also, the literary products dealt with nearly always belong to genres of "low modality value." Hodge thus discusses Ionesco, the dramatist of the absurd who scarcely ever thought of portraying a recognizable realistic social world. In the case of Jane Austen's *Emma*, the question of credibility does not refer to the social milieu, to social regularities and types, but to the narrative itself. Bob Dylan's anti-war poetry may perhaps mirror the mood of the 1960s, but it certainly does not contain an analysis. One can say the same about Sylvia Plath's poems. *Star Trek* and Benjamin Franklin's advice on the right usage of time and money are not pieces of analysis but belong to the categories of entertainment and instruction.

One of the examples given by Hodge that leaves itself relatively open to sociological interpretation is Emily Brontë's *Wuthering Heights*. It contains a passage that has been taken by Philippe Ariès as evidence for the modern way of romanticizing death. In this instance, Hodge is able to demonstrate that Ariès does not fully understand the genre of the Gothic novel (and at the same time, underrates Emily Brontë as an observer of burials). The structuralist and semiotic interpretation unveils a narrative structure that embeds both the fictitious narrator and Heathcliff. At the outer end of the bracket, Emily Brontë, who has chosen the male pseudonym Ellis Bell, herself appears. Without elaborate fiction, "the distinct personas would collapse into a single ambiguous persona, oscillating between male and female, middle-class and working-class, oral and literary, though its primary form is female, middle-class and literary" (Hodge 1990, 55). Hodge thus interprets Emily Brontë's description of Heathcliff's morbid desires as the invention of an anti-ritual juxtaposed to traditional conventions and frozen in a so-called logonomic regime by powerful forces. Among them he finds a suppressed sexuality with regard to the author's gender role and the inadequacies that she might have felt regarding the puritan attitude towards death.

The argument is thus half sociology of knowledge, although highly speculative, and half structuralist, but not very fruitful. The mixture of the two arguments, however, does not double the utility of such an approach. Later Hodge goes on to deal with Defoe's *Moll Flanders*, which can be seen as the expression simultaneously of a new commercial spirit and possibly of an ironically reflected style. Above all, the focus of the analysis here is on text and narrative and not on society itself. At the centre of attention is the detail and not the comprehensive sociological description and explanation of the area of interest. Decisions about what can be seen as needing an explanation are not taken with the perspective of systematic research interests but, rather, the caprices and contingencies of the business of literary criticism.

In some respects there is a stupefying mutuality between Laslett's measurement-oriented critique and Hodge's literary criticism. Both stress the strategic detail whose meaning should be reconstructed from a sociology-of-knowledge perspective. Both also point out the pragmatic functions of literature that damage the realism of the representation; they direct the attention to genres that indeed scarcely aim at realistic observation, but they also ignore or downplay the possibilities of a holistic, contextual interpretation of social reality with the help of literature. They fail to take into account the irreducibly double character of the novel: not only to entertain but also to inform.

How does this analysis apply to Elias's method of using literature? Three main points of difference can be outlined. The first relates to the treatment of literature (mainly fiction or drama) as "source" or "sociology." Laslett refers, rather, to those passages in literature that can verify or falsify hypotheses about the nature of social reality at crucial, strategic points. He thus rejects Shakespeare's *Romeo und Juliet* as a realist picture of society since in this play Juliet's age at marriage is given as thirteen against the well-documented fact that

English women in the sixteenth century married much later, normally in their early twenties. But Elias's usage of fiction does not focus on such a narrow detail (by the way, Shakespeare's Juliet was Italian), but refers to novels that paint a whole picture of the society in question – those in which we have a whole web of data, interpretations, metaphors, and even theories that can be judged like sociological data themselves. At every point it is possible to validate or refute the information through a comparison with other sources and interpretations, and with plausible everyday assumptions regarding acting and behaving taken from the implicit knowledge of the sociologist. Thus neither von Wolzogen's nor Bloem's novel poses any serious problem. They both create whole structures of data and interpretations that can be evaluated from the background of numerous other authors and sources. The examples given differ only in one respect. They concentrate more either on the "exterior," outer world (Marburg's social structure) or on the inner world (the emotions and perceptions of the bourgeois heroine and the members of the fraternity). In the latter case the interpretations are riskier but even more valuable.

The second point refers to the argument that the pragmatic and poetic functions of literature distort reality without providing any chance of correcting it. Elias, too, knows that "genre" and "domain" can influence interpretation. In the de la Roche example he recognizes the paradoxical element contained in the speech of a courtly villain who characterizes himself in the same words as a preacher might choose to condemn his vicious, idle frivolity: "You know that I have never granted love any other power than over my senses, whose most delicate and lively pleasure it affords ... All classes of beauty have pandered to me ... I grew sated with them ... The moralists ... may have their say on the fine nets and snares in which I have captured the virtue and pride, the wisdom and the frigidity, the coquetry and even the piety of the whole feminine world" (quoted in Elias 1978a, 20). The whole reflexivity of the villain flies in the face of the truth of this self-characterization. Here and in other cases Elias distinguishes carefully between the construction of the narrative and those realistic moments where the gaze penetrates the typical and sociologically relevant – where we can "borrow" the novelist's eye in order to notice things that are otherwise left unnoticed.

The third point regards the tendency in modern literary studies to use and adapt a structuralist and relativist vocabulary in the interpretation of texts. In the extreme (which is not reached by Hodge) this tendency turns into a radically constructivist attitude where everything is "constructed" and nothing is real. Elias has expressed in manifold methodological remarks his profound disbelief in the value of half-philosophical modish labels such as phenomenological sociology and structuralism. In the former he sees the powerful ancient philosophical tradition of the lonesome, isolated mind which is unable to communicate to others – the famous *homo clausus* critique. In the latter he perceives processes reduced to unchanging structures. In the case of linguistic structuralism, Elias sees both traditions at work: symbols of human language cannot be understood as if they were used "by monads without windows," unrelated to group experiences, tradition, emotions, and cognitions which are always intrinsically linked to behaviour in human groups (Elias 1991b, 20). All three examples discussed show his conviction that literary symbols must be made understandable by a theoretical synopsis that follows these lines.

BALANCING THE DISCUSSION: ELIAS'S SOCIOLOGY AS BETWEEN "NATURALISM" AND "RELATIVISM"

This chapter started with a comparison of Elias's model of an interpretative sociology and the naturalistic program in the social sciences. First, we summarized his critique of explanations *more physico* and passed in review the examples where he uses fiction in a sociological way.

Elias sees behind the sociological orientation of the model of the natural sciences a thorough conceptual misunderstanding, one essentially based in the tendency of European languages to use nouns for processual phenomena that receive the status of "things" at "rest," whereby these "things" are isolated artificially. "Individual" and "society" also belong in this context, and so does the idea of reducing all changeable and movable aspects of the physical, biological, and social worlds to something unchangeable and immovable, namely, to eternal "laws of nature." The whole parlance of "causes" (in German, *Ursache* – *Ur-Sachen*, things without an origin) is an expression of that tendency. Relations are often reduced to simple properties (the "power" of persons) of objects; the normality of movement is transformed into an artificial state of rest which receives, additionally, the exceptional state of movement. According to Elias, sociological analysis also separates "variables" or "factors" in thought without much intellectual effort being spent on the comprehensive relations between those isolated aspects (1970b, 124).

This criticism applies to survey research on communities where the relationships between the various members of these communities are ignored, but also principally to the concept of "individual action," which simply does not exist. Behind this concept Elias sees the idea of a separated and lonely adult who has, as *homo clausus*, never experienced any learning process or social modelling; in Kant's philosophy, it means the a priori of universal categories of thought. Against this tendency of philosophical nominalism, which still shows even in a sociology operating with "variables," Elias always stressed the central role of language in the understanding of genuinely human communication. In his empirical-theoretical analyses, examples of the assessments, emotions, and perceptions of actors play a central role. Every use of language refers to a "group language," and contextuality of meaning mirrors this origin of all human-made symbols in group behaviour. The two more extensively discussed examples of fiction reveal that emphasis. But differing from much of interpretative sociology, Elias also develops theoretical models of the so-called macrosphere and the personality of its psychic organization. The linkage between the refinement of manners, growing inhibition, and pacification – the now-famous elements of civilizing processes – and psychic structures and state formation are examples of his more general insight: that the relations between human beings are not given circumstances from outside. Instead, what is involved is changing consciousness and emotionality within human beings. The most important macro-process here is the organization of societies as states that acquire the monopoly on the legitimate use of physical violence and on taxation. During the development of states, the anatomy and functions of the most important institutions that shape and model affects slowly change in a largely unintentional but structured way. Human experience and the change of human institutions need for their explanation a theoretical synthesis – the ability to detect patterns and formulate them in process models. This is something we simply can not gain from literature, although the sociological enterprise is not different in kind but, rather, in degree from that of fiction.

Interpretative approaches to sociology and "sociologies of everyday life" that focus on *understanding* resemble realist fiction in their particular emphasis on the micro-aspects of society. Elias's position tries to integrate the macro-aspect, and this is where it can also be distinguished from some approaches in literary criticism:

Currently, it is common practice to use the concept of the "everyday life-world" in observing and investigating such more or less private forms of behavior and experience. Unfortunately, as used today by some philosophical-sociological sects, it is a rather useless research tool. That can be seen here. Dueling by the upper classes, like brawling among the lower, can be assigned to the "everyday life-world" of phenomenology, ethnomethodology and other philosophoidal branches of the fragmented sociology of our day. But the spineless use of this concept paralyses any understanding of structures in human beings' lives together, especially power structures. It leads to single situations being analysed in isolation, as if they existed in a social vacuum, and to losing oneself in endless arbitrary interpretations. One is then drifting without a compass in an episodic sea. How can one hope as a social scientist to bring to life such everyday experiences as dueling by the upper classes or brawls among the lower without attempting at the same time to find theoretical models of the social structures which embrace them both? (Elias 1996a, 67)

Sociological explanation is a synthesizing enterprise; it links elements of seemingly unrelated areas and has an active, constructive character. Even a concept such as time – the synchronization of human periodic processes with those occurring in nature – is an effort of linkage, not of abstraction; and in everyday life, as in sociological theorizing, human beings are capable of such achievements in synthesis. But against a sociology of everyday life that lacks orientation and takes every problem as equally important, it is necessary to develop a strategy of concept formation that is able to extract the relevant sections from the abundance and detailed complexity of social reality. In this context, Weber wrote about *Kulturbedeutung*, the cultural meaning of social phenomena whose historical uniqueness should be treated with justice on the basis of explicitly stated *Wertbeziehungen*, or value relations (1973, 261). But certainly they can scarcely be discussed without referring to the experience and emotions of human groups, not of the isolated individual but always of human beings in their membership in groups.

The critique that Elias has expressed against an "understanding" sociology of philosophical origin can be extended to those descendants in literary studies that refer to the same dualistic philosophy. Texts, signs, and symbols represent only one side of social communication; the social figurations of socially shaped individuals who understand social symbols represent the other. As there are no structures without processes, so there are also no signs without the feelings and relations of their users. The "understanding" of texts or individuals can be an extremely difficult process, but only in the world of phenomenological or structuralistic human sciences has it been made so mysterious that one *homo clausus* no longer understands another. A realist sociology that does not shun reality is as possible as a realist literature aimed at an understanding of society. Neither differs very much from the other in some of its aspects; in others, they can complement each other in a way that needs neither to disquiet the researcher nor to betray the poet. Elias's sociology is an example of this relationship.

NOTES

I wish to thank Eric Dunning, of the University of Leicester, for his generous help in improving my written English and Gerald Mozectic, of the University of Graz, for a close reading of this text.

1 One can refer here to Lepenies's *Drei Kulturen: Soziologie zwischen Literatur und Wissenschaft* (1988).
2 One might look at Foucault's rhetorical question: how it comes about that his horizon narrows rather than broadens through his reading of sociological treatments of prisons or immigrants (reported in Sennett 1994:61).
3 Reference here is to Dunning and Mennell in the preface to Elias's *The Germans* (1996a, viii–xvi, ix).
4 Of course, there is substantial divergence between Parsons's theory of action and Hull's behaviourism.
5 Here one should refer to Scheff's treatment of this novel from a "sociology of emotions" perspective (Scheff and Retzinger 1991, 103–22).
6 Elias makes cautious comments about this factor in *Über sich selbst* (1990, 75).
7 Elias sees this himself when he states: "The social divisions of a small German university town around 1900, seen from the perspective of the upper class, are vividly evident in this description. If used critically, novels can help reconstruct a past society and its power structure for us" (1996a, 47).

7 The Trials of *Homo Clausus*: Elias, Weber, and Goethe on the Sociogenesis of the Modern Self

THOMAS M. KEMPLE

In spite of differences in style, method, and even empirical focus, the sociological projects of Weber and Elias can be understood to converge on a single question: through what processes of social and political control has the modern self been put on trial? Though they may appear to disagree over the exact date of birth of European modernity – of its characteristic economic and political institutions and its distinctive modes of social and personal experience – they nevertheless share a concern with explaining why the emergence of new forms of social regulation is accompanied by techniques for subduing the natural world and disciplines for intensifying one's relationship to oneself. Rather than simply narrating in very broad terms the principal historical shifts involved, such as the transformation from a feudal to a capitalist social order, they immerse themselves in the empirical details of the various situations and sequences involved. In particular, their concern is to trace relationships between the salient cultural phenomena or key historical configurations that define the unique character of the West, such as the ecclesiastic integration of Christian culture in the Middle Ages, the urban organization of trade, and the Protestant concept of the calling (in Weber) or the political and economic dynamics of feudalization, the monarchical monopolization of power, and the courtly concept of civility (in Elias). For them, the task is not simply to identify objectively the various social types that predominate in the period or society under study – the monk, the burgher, and the penitent, on the one hand, for example, or the lady, the nobleman, and the courtier, on the other – but also to examine the subjective meaning of these transformations for the individuals caught up in them.

It cannot be my task here to produce even a superficial comparative sketch of the historical and sociological projects of Weber and Elias, notwithstanding the occasional attempts of the latter to do just that (Elias 1978c, 117, 120; 1994b, 204, 207).[1] Rather, I think that the interesting complementarity of their work and the productive contradictions between them can be usefully approached by introducing a third figure, who can serve to mark the ground between them. In particular, I shall show how Goethe's classic literary treatment of the birth of the modern age in *Faust* has some important resonances and dissonances with the work of his successors in social science. Further, this affinity is not just a result of their intimate familiarity with and frequent references to this work, but it is also because Goethe's fictional constructions provide both an uncanny illumination of what Weber and Elias have in common and an amplification of how they diverge. While my use of this text is based on a method I have developed elsewhere (Kemple 1995, esp. part 1), my main concern here is more generally with how a certain literary approach to a sociological theme – that is, to what I am calling here the sociogenesis of the modern self as *homo clausus*, or "man enclosed" – suggests some new directions for studying the cultural and psychological dimensions of the institutional process or trial (*Prozess*) of civilization.

As a convenient starting point for identifying the issues involved, consider the parallel formulations of the two "exordia" to Weber's famous speeches "Science as a Vocation" and "Politics as a Vocation":[2] "I shall, according to your wish, speak about 'Science as a Vocation'; now we political economists have a certain pedantic custom, which I should like to follow, of always beginning with the external conditions" (1958, 129; translation modified). "This lecture, which I give according to your wish, will necessarily disappoint you in a number of ways: you will naturally expect me to take a position on actual [political] questions of the day, but that will only be the case in a purely formal way and toward the end" (1958, 77; translation modified). In a manner that is unique in the history of the social sciences, Weber directly addresses the wishes and expectations of his audience, situating his own discourse not within the rhetorical context of persuasion and conviction but as itself (already) the artifact of a distinctively disciplinary – that is, scientific and academic – enterprise. The promise of a formal and external treatment of issues which are nevertheless of immediate and passionate concern to his listeners, who in this case are mostly the young radical members of the Free Students Association of the University of Munich, is thereby designed not just to instruct and inform but even further to dash the hopes and desires that might otherwise be expected on such an occasion. At the same time, Weber's cold "pedantry" intentionally marks a clear generational difference between the impatience of his youthful listeners and the mature fortitude of his own detailed and dispassionate analysis. Without entering into the complexities of the methodological problems to which these contrasts give rise (which Weber treats at length in *The Methodology of the Social Sciences*), we should note that certain general historical questions – namely, the precise character of the cultural "vocations" of modern society – are here articulated with reference to the locally determined and topical concerns which characterize a specific generational conflict. At the same time, a broad civilizational project is individualized in its expression as an academic, if not a civic, calling.

It is not surprising then to find Weber exhorting his younger audience throughout these speeches by reviling their desire to search for "sensation" and "experience" at the expense of "understanding" and "study." Significantly, in his concluding remarks (or "perorations") to both discourses, a sobering appeal is made to recognize the harsh social and cultural realities of the age, which make the personal decision to pursue either science or politics as one's vocation such a difficult one. As if to displace some responsibility for his own discourse into another domain, he does not speak here in his own voice but in the words of Mephistopheles, himself uncharacteristically interrupting his monologue to address the younger audience members directly, as indicated in the stage direction of Goethe's play: "Consider now, the Devil's old; To understand him, grow old also! This does not mean age in the sense of the birth certificate. It means that if one wishes to settle with this devil, one must not take flight before him as so many like to do nowadays. First of all, one has to see the devil's ways to the end in order to realize his power and his limitations" ("Science as a Vocation" in Weber 1958, 152). "The sentence [above] ... does not refer to age in terms of chronological years. I have never permitted myself to lose out in a discussion through a reference to a date registered on a birth certificate; but the mere fact that someone is twenty years of age and that I am over fifty is no cause for me to think that this alone is an achievement before which I am overawed. Age is not decisive; what is decisive is the trained relentlessness in viewing the realities of life, and the ability to face such realities and measure up to them inwardly" ("Politics as a Vocation" in Weber 1958, 126–7).[3]

What interests me in Weber's parallel commentaries on the passage from Goethe's *Faust* is not only the way that the thematic continuities between them provide a kind of frame for these speeches considered together and as a whole (and which might themselves be treated as the frame for the entirety of Weber's work, a conception of the "vocation" of rational capitalism at its centre) but also the *rhetorical form* through which these themes are expressed. That is, Weber's relationship to his audience (and by extension, his readers) is here dramatically enacted and simulated through a citation that is itself a dramatic simulation and enactment of the central relationship in the play from which it has been taken, namely, that between Mephistopheles and Faust in Goethe's tragedy. To take a keyword from Elias's work while giving it a literary and an active sense, the institutional networks of knowledge and power are here allegorically *figured* as a cultural conflict between generations and as a problematic relationship to oneself. In what follows, I try to examine what is at stake in the dialogic interplay of these discourses for our understanding not just of Goethe's play but also of the social and intellectual history which it dramatizes and which Weber and Elias are concerned to analyze.

THE PROBLEM OF GENERATIONS

Weber's choice of these lines in both speeches has at first the ironic effect of casting him in the role of Mephistopheles, who delivers them in the first scene of act 2 of the second part of Goethe's *Faust*. In the context of the first speech, Weber's manifest intention is to affirm his personal conviction of the value of science as a vocation, though science cannot itself provide the foundation for this conviction. Although he shares his audience's hate for "intellectualism as the worst devil," science is obviously incapable of exorcising it. In the second context, he wishes to convince his listeners that the one who pursues politics as a vocation inexorably meets with "diabolical forces," which "enter the play" however much they may remain unknown to or out of the control of the actor (Weber 1958, 152 and 126). Ultimately, then, Weber's aim is to address the more general problem of the self in its relations with others – including the impersonal forces of good and evil – and with oneself, notwithstanding one's own contradictory desires and personal demons. In this sense, then, Weber's plea for "understanding" ("so werdet alt, ihn zu verstehen") differs from Mephistopheles's in the way that it displaces the focus from the speaker to the larger world which he shares with his listeners, as well as to the inner "daemon" which holds the fibers of every being.

Although Weber's specific concern here is to articulate the conditions necessary for choosing between these two important cultural vocations, at issue is also his own broader conception of the tasks of an interpretive sociology (*verstehende Soziologie*). Implied is the methodological innovation of Weber's that I think provided the keynote for the tradition of sociological investigation to which Schutz, Mannheim, Elias, and even Habermas are among the most important contributors. In this context, what interests me is how later writers took up as an explicit theme Weber's general sense of the temporality of social and sociological understanding as a particular problem concerning the (mis)understandings and power struggles *between generations*. Thus Schutz's argument – that "*Verstehen* is, thus, primarily not a method used by the social scientist, but the particular experiential form in which common sense thinking takes cognizance of the social cultural world" – expands the implications of this method beyond its formulation as an epistemological and disciplinary problem or as a technique of introspection and empathy (1962, 56). The social scientists' "understanding" is conceived as an abstraction from the social and historical world they inhabit along with any other member of society, a world that is thus temporally populated by contemporaries (both absent and present, who act with varying degrees of identity and anonymity), predecessors (who themselves may provide the personal motives or general conditions for present actions), and successors (who remain ultimately indeterminate and indeterminable) (Schutz 1967, 176–214). This social time-consciousness is thus the very matrix for what it means to share a world in common, as Elias argues. "What shapes and binds the individual within this human cosmos, and what gives him the whole scope of his life, is not the reflexes of his animal nature but the ineradicable connection between his desires and behavior and those of other people, of the living, the dead, and even, in a certain sense, the unborn – in a word, the function of others for him and his function for others" (1991a, 30).

Schutz and Elias break open the conventional and intellectualistic constructions of *Verstehen* by reformulating the problem of scientific objectivity and detachment as a question concerning their "reference," "adequacy," or "accountability" to the subjective meanings and common-sense understandings of the everyday actions of human beings who experience a world whose present dimensions intersect with the remembrance of times past and the anticipation of a future (see also Garfinkel 1967). For his part, Mannheim puts the matter in more specific terms as a problem for the sociologist who wishes to find a middle way between the excesses of an objectivist law of history's vitalistic rhythms and an subjectivist intuition of spiritual time-consciousness. His solution is to rethink the notion of *age* in terms that do not reduce it to a biological entity, a psychological entelechy, or a sociological *Zeitgeist*, but conceive of it as a process of *generation* through which changes in life cycle, geographical location, social status, and the like can also be understood as patterns of perceiving and anticipating, remembering and forgetting. "One is old primarily insofar as he comes to live with a specific, individually acquired framework of useable past experience, so that every new experience has its form and its place marked out for it in advance. In youth, on the other hand, where life is new, formative forces are just coming into being and basic attitudes in the process of development can take advantage of the moulding power of new situations. Thus a human race living on forever would need to learn to forget to compensate for the lack of new generations" (Mannheim 1952, 298). Mannheim's largely unnoticed and untested thesis is an attempt to explore an aspect of human life that is usually left unquestioned as a natural, psychological, and sociological fact of life, that is, to subject it to the kind of cultural and historical interpretation that may also be applied to the concepts of "race" and "sex." Patterns of change and continuity, networks of interdependence and transformation, and structures of meaning and motivation are not uniformly given and universally accessible to everyone; rather, they are taken up in different ways by each person according to his or her own location (*Lagerung*) in time and circumstance.

Mannheim's reflections are partly a response to the generational conflicts of his own age in the years following the Second World War, which he characterized in general terms as a strain between the "up-to-dateness" of a younger generation dramatically aware of its place in a process of destabilization and an older generation desperately clinging to the reorientation that had been the drama of *its* youth (1952, 300–1). In the 1960s Habermas described a later stage of these conflicts in terms of his own generational rebellion against some of the more cynical attitudes of his teachers towards the revolutionary potential of the new student movements in Germany. Speaking in 1967 to an American audience already schooled in countercultural theatrics, he distinguished the fundamentally new dimension of protest among the students of his own country. He claimed that these students' lack of personal experience with political terror and economic crisis had motivated both their critique of the alienating and reckless system of which they were themselves the product and their demand for the fulfillment of this system's unkept promises and the realization of its undeveloped possibilities. These students, he said,

are the first generation that no longer understands why, despite the high level of technological development, the life of the individual is still determined by the ethic of competition, the pressure of status-seeking, and the values of possessive individualism and socially dispensed substitute-gratifications. They do not understand why the institutionalized struggle for existence, the discipline of alienated labor, or the eradication of sensuality and aesthetic gratification should be perpetuated – why, in short, the mode of life of an economy of poverty is preserved under conditions of an economy of abundance. On the basis of a *fundamental* lack of sympathy with the senseless reproduction of now superfluous virtues and sacrifices, the rising generation has developed a particular sensitivity to the untruth of prevailing legitimations. (Habermas 1970, 24–5)

A similar assessment of how a lack of understanding and sympathy can have radical consequences and delegitimizing effects seems to inform Weber's address to the youth of his day, who were caught in the drama of the final years of the First World War. Like Habermas after him, he seems to worry that these students may have inherited the confidence of Cartesian certitude while forgetting its roots in philosophical skepticism, and without questioning the ruses of the "evil geniuses" of history and politics, if not of art and science. His concession that the physical process of aging as measured on a birth certificate is no guarantee of political or intellectual maturity is perhaps implicitly informed by his sobering sense of how this process of registering social membership, even before the active exercise of citizenship rights, already absorbs us within the modern state's machineries of "mass individualization."

Weber's warnings against youthful naïveté here ironically recall the generational rebellion of the young Weber against the conservative Prussian liberalism of his father's contemporaries (see Roth 1971). And in the scene from *Faust* from which he quotes, a similar play is scripted by Goethe almost a hundred years earlier when he satirizes the iconoclastic idealism and philosophical neodoxy of the student societies (*Burschenschaften*) that formed in Germany after the Wars of Liberation. As Williams notes, the scene is commanded by Mephistopheles, who returns here to "the narrow, high-arched, gothic chamber" of Faust's famous study, now masquerading in his protegé's dusty and moth-ridden scholastic robes while the latter lies unconscious and unseen behind a curtain, and while the Baccalaureus – who had appeared in the first part of the drama as "the Freshman" – provides its comical centrepiece (1987, 141–3). The Baccalaureus's send-up of the scholastic traditionalism and orthodox self-righteousness of academic authority (itself an echo of Faust's exasperation with scholastic pedantries in the opening lines of the drama) is in turn parodied by Mephistopheles's (and thus Goethe's) caricature of the young student's egoistic arrogance and naive forgetfulness:

> This is Youth's noblest calling and most fit!
> The world was not, ere I created it ...

Who, save myself, to your deliverance brought
From commonplaces of restricted thought?
I, proud and free, even as dictates my mind,
Follow with joy the inward light I find,
And speed along, in mine own ecstasy,
Darkness behind, the Glory leading me!

(Goethe 1967, 74)[4]

As a contrast to the return of our heroes to the primal scene of their diabolical pact in the study, and to their eventual descent into the abysses of time (as they prepare to travel into the mythical past of the classical Walpurgis night and the imaginary world of Helen of Troy), the Baccalaureus announces his new-found noble vocation (*Beruf*) to deliver others from "the Philistinism of confining ideas" into a world of his own making, himself called by nothing more than his own inner voice. In spite of the medieval setting, with its dark and oppressive enclosure left unchanged from its earlier appearance in the play, the boasting of the Baccalaureus – an ironic repetition of Faust's denunciation of his "outgrown academic rods of old" and anticipation of the diabolical powers of a new world in the first part – resonates through Goethe's time, through Weber's, and into our own.

THE TRIALS OF *HOMO CLAUSUS*

In a very literal sense, this scene also resonates with another act of *Faust* which miraculously unfolds at the same time: that is, while the Baccalaureus and Mephistopheles argue in the "high-arched, narrow, gothic chamber," Mephistopheles is also somehow able to assist Wagner (Faust's hapless assistant from the first act) in his experiments to create the first human-made man, the Homunculus. The simultaneity of these scenes is indicated by the fact that the bell which Mephistopheles tolls to summon the old Famulus near the beginning of the second study scene is also ringing at the start of the scene in Wagner's laboratory. Its resonating sounds, in fact, are shaped as if to repeat the divine creation of human language, as Mephistopheles exclaims, "Hark! as the ringing tones expand / They form a voice, result in speech" (Goethe 1967, 77). Hamlin notes that the significance of this bell, which rocks the foundations of the edifice of scholarship, making halls tremble, doors fly open, stairs shake, and walls rattle, and which announces the creation of a new being, is indeed "epochal": it marks the propitious moment (*Sternenstunde*) in which the self finds its "liberation from the imprisonment of the self in its own knowledge," and it thereby signifies the tocsin of classical culture and its renewal in the scientific learning of the Renaissance (1976, 331). In a way that Goethe could only depict fantastically as the product of "an extensive, ponderous apparatus" (Hamlin 1976, 75), and that Weber could perhaps only guess at, if he could glimpse it at all, the peculiarly Western invention of the pure knowing self, abstracted from time and place, is dramatized here as the scientific creation of rationalized power.

A consideration of this scene moves us beyond the parameters of Weber's more narrow concerns with the follies of youth and into the contiguous domain of another scene (*ein anderer Schauplatz*, as Freud might put it), in which the modern experiment to conquer time and transitoriness with sheer will and intelligence is underway. Of course, the Homunculus is still a figure of generational rebellion, an expression for intellectual precociousness coupled with physical immaturity, and for the arrogance of things new in their disregard for origins. Nevertheless, as Binswanger points out, this artificial man – *filius philosophorum in vitro* – is represented as the highest achievement of human intelligence, as the sheer energy and restless spirit that precede the experience of embodiment and exceed the vicissitudes of history (1994, 61–72). The foundation for this being is not the "I am" of Descartes by the fireside, or even the "I act" of Faust in his study (as echoed by Goethe's own romantic and philosophical contemporaries), but the mere fact of existence: "Since I exist, then I must active be" (Goethe 1967, 77). While the precedent for this magnum opus seems to stem from the time of the Egyptian alchemist Zosimus in the third century AD and Paracelsus in the sixteenth century, the distinctively modern and futuristic character of Goethe's image lies in the conception of a being without nature or historical development, a parthenogenic creation of intellect out of intellect, of pure active existence, which nevertheless seeks completion in a body.

Wagner's search for "crystallized humanity," but from "a purer, loftier origin," made "without enamored pair" in the "old, senseless mode" and without the "mutual irritation" of body and soul "wedded and blended" (Goethe 1967, 75–7), thus provides us with a perfected image of the modern quest for self as an unchanging, stable, and singular being. In contrast to the natural macrocosmos that Faust had first conjured up in his study in the opening scene of the play, this artificial world encapsulates all within itself and is thereby divided and separated from the outer world of objective and social reality. As such, it provides us with the perfect image of the pure self-consciousness, the "personal essence," and the "we-less I" closed in on itself which, as Elias reminds us in his 1968 introduction to *The Civilizing Process*, is a distinctively modern project and Western product. "The conception of the individual as *homo clausus*, as a little world in himself who ultimately exists quite independently of the great world outside, determines the image of man in general. Every other human being is likewise seen as a *homo clausus*; his core, his being, his true self appears likewise as something divided within him by an invisible wall from everything outside, including every other human being" (1994b, 204). Elias's insight, which I am arguing is dramatically figured in the character of Goethe's Homunculus, invites us to consider the degree to which psychical processes are themselves sociogenically shaped – how the perception of self at the zero point of individuation is already a mediating link in the network of sociation. Like the Homunculus, the individual at the threshold of the modern age is ultimately conceived as a disembodied subject existing alone, dependent on nobody, and never having been a child; indeed, "this preconceived image of *homo clausus* commands the stage not only in society at large, but also in the human sciences" (1994b, 204).

It is not surprising, then, that in the wake of the Enlightenment and on the verge of the birth of the human sciences, Goethe's medieval image should illuminate the techniques by which the human being would become an object of knowledge and power in a new project of self-regulation and social control. In this sense, the scientist's construction of an "ideal actor gifted with consciousness" to explain certain patterns of observed behaviour within the relevancies of scientific investigation and political control is an invention no less artificial than the experiments of Wagner. Again, it is the Weberian methodological innovation to which we may appeal to recall that the abstractions of scientific detachment themselves have their source in the lived reality of the social world. The social scientist "thus ascribes to this fictitious consciousness a set of typical notions, purposes, goals, which are assumed to be invariant in the specious consciousness of the imaginary actor-model. This homunculus or puppet is supposed to be interrelated in interaction patterns to other homunculi or puppets constructed in a similar way. Among these homunculi with which the social scientist postulates his model of the social world of everyday life, a set of motives, goals, roles – in general, systems of relevances – are distributed in such a way as the scientific problems under scrutiny require" (Schutz 1967, 64).

In the construction of "models of motivation" that impute springs of action to individuals involved in an ongoing social process, the cultural and historical world is itself imagined to be the creation of a scientific consciousness. From this perspective the task of the social scientist appears to be the reformulation of the self as a closed system acting and reacting within the constraints and controls of similarly operating entities. In other words, in the scientific reduction the process of civilization is lost in the trials of *homo clausus*. "And so long as we see the individual human being as by nature a closed container with an outer shell and a core concealed within it, we cannot comprehend how a civilizing process embracing many generations is possible, in the course of which the personality structure of the human being changes without the nature of human beings changing" (Elias 1994b, 212).

Perhaps this is the intuition that led Goethe to depict the episode of the Homunculus in the aftermath of Mephistopheles's and Faust's disastrous exploits in the imperial court (in act 1 of the second part) and just before their descent into the imaginary world of ancient Greece (in acts 2, 3, and 4), where the Homunculus himself meets his end without succeeding in his quest for corporeality: the medieval scholasticism of Faust cannot be superseded by the proto-modern experiments of Wagner because the social and economic institutions that could sustain them and give them their sense have not yet come into being. Thus, in contrast to the triumph of Faust's spiritual trans- figuration and eternal redemption in the high mountain gorges of heaven in the final scene of act 5, Wagner's Homunculus is doomed to the same fate as Gretchen's baby and Helena's Euphorion. And yet, ironically, the Homunculus himself provides the catalyst for the devel- opment of the rest of the drama by diagnosing the source of Faust's unconsciousness and prescribing his cure. That he does so in a proto- psychoanalytic way by somehow "interpreting" Faust's dream of Helena's conception in the primal scene of the rape of Leda by the swan and that his "therapy" involves a return to the classical age of the primal mothers are further indications of Goethe's prescience in anticipating the birth of the human sciences in a fictional realm. As if to echo the wry comments about the departing Baccalaureus as quoted by Weber, Mephistopheles again concludes the scene by directly addressing the audience, this time with reference to the sorrows of Wagner, who has been rudely abandoned by the Homunculus: "Upon the creatures we have made / We are, ourselves, at last dependent" (Goethe 1967, 81). In his inability to control his own creation or even to comprehend its wishes, Wagner prefigures the new age of science with its brave new world of human experimentation and engineering.

In its historical orientation and sociological profundity, the Webe- rian tradition, which finds its literary source in Goethe and its fullest expression in the writings of Elias, provides us with both a vivid picture of our own self-imposed techniques of confinement and an image for their transformation. In contrast to a conception of the human being enclosed in the contemplative darkness of the study or trapped in the translucent light of science's glass tubes, it envisions the notion of the "open personality" who exercises a greater or lesser degree of autonomy with respect to others (though never absolutely) and who is always oriented towards and dependent on others: beyond the imaginary figure of *homo clausus*, with his controlled and contained impulses, we may anticipate the figurational reality of *homines aperti*, of open emotional valencies and mutual interdependencies (Elias 1978c, 125, 135; 1994b, 215). At stake in these personal trials and social processes is nothing less than our own humanity.

NOTES

1 See Arnason 1987. Elias's critique of Weber's supposed "axiomatic belief in 'the absolute individual' as the true social reality" will not be explicitly addressed here, though my own disagreement with this assessment should be evident from what follows.

2 The revised texts of both speeches were first published as essays in 1919, although "Science as a Vocation" was probably actually delivered in 1917. See Schluchter 1996, 46–7.

3 In both cases, Weber quotes the same line from Goethe's *Faust*, which I have modified slightly from Taylor's translation (Goethe 1967, 74). The German text reads as follows:
Bedenkt: der Teufel, der ist alt,
So werdet alt, ihn zu verstehen!
        (Goethe 1986, lines 6817–18).
Dies ist der Jugend edelster Beruf!
Die Welt, sie War nicht, eh ich sie erschuf ...
Wer, ausser mir, entband euch aller Schranken
Philisterhaft einklemmender Gedanken?
Ich aber, frei wie mir's im Geiste spricht
Verfolge froh mein innerliches Licht,
Und wandle rasch, im eigensten Entzücken,
Das Helle vor mir, Finsternis im Rücken.
        (Goethe 1986, lines 6793–4, 6801–6)

4 This speech echoes the one that Faust delivers in part 1 as he prepares to leave his study with Mephistopheles to begin his magnificent "career" (Goethe 1986, lines 1086–9), the same one that Weber quotes in the conclusion of his early essay "Objectivity" when he tries to express how science must prepare "to change its standpoint and analytical apparatus" in order to view the streams of new cultural problems "from the heights of thought" (1949, 112).

8 Civilizing Sexuality: Marie de France's Lay with Two Names

STEPHEN GUY-BRAY

At the end of the epilogue to her *Fables*, Marie de France does something relatively unusual: "At the end of this text, which I have recited in French, I shall name myself so that you remember: Marie is my name; I am from France. It may be that many scholars will take my labour for themselves; I do not want anyone to do this" (1991, lines 11–17).[1] Of course, saying that your name is Marie and that you are from France is not particularly helpful, but the very presence of a woman's name in a literary text is significant. In any case, Marie's name is important not merely as a referent to an individual woman but as the origin of the works ascribed to her and, increasingly, as a figure for the writing woman in the Middle Ages. It is not easy to say what this distinction means. How can we tell that a literary work was written by a woman? How can we say that a text is feminine rather than masculine? In a recent essay on Marie, Sharon Kinoshita suggests that we can locate "the 'woman's voice' less at the stylistic or thematic level than in Marie's radical challenge to the structure of feudal society through her canny manipulation of literary codes" (1993–94, 268).

My concern in this essay is with Marie's highlighting of the literary code that governs the naming of texts. Names play an important part in the lays of Marie de France, as they do in much of medieval narrative verse. Often, for example, the narrator will withhold the main character's name until the point in the story where the character begins to be heroic. Sometimes the narrator will give the title of the story in more than one language, as Marie herself does in two of her lays. What I am interested in here is her decision to give a lay two titles, one connected to a feminine interpretation of the lay and the other to a masculine interpretation. Marie does this in two of her lays: *Eliduc*, which is the most famous of all her works, and *Le Chaitivel*. I want to look at *Le Chaitivel* because what is at issue in this lay is not only the outcome of a romantic intrigue but also the status of women and of the role they play in an increasingly complex social organization. In this context, many of Norbert Elias's insights in *The Civilizing Process* are relevant. While most of this work is concerned with the later Middle Ages and with the centuries that followed them, he bases his work on his analysis of the consolidation of feudal power in the eleventh and twelfth centuries, or, in other words, on the time in which Marie wrote. Before going on to discuss *Le Chaitivel* itself, though, I shall briefly mention the points at which my and Elias's analyses overlap.

Elias does not devote much space in *The Civilizing Process* to the condition of women or the state of literature, but the few comments he does make on these subjects are instructive. He suggests that "the great feudal courts of the twelfth century ... offered women special opportunities to overcome male dominance and attain equal status with men" (1994b, 326) and that "in this human situation what we call 'lyric poetry' evolves as a social and not merely as an individual event" (1994b, 327–8). Elias's concerns here are Marie's as well. Throughout her lays, she displays a keen interest in the connection between gender relations and issues of power and control within the society of the poems as a whole. At several points in her lays, she raises the possibility of female autonomy, either in the real world or in some sort of feminine realm, such as a convent or an otherworldly kingdom. The opportunities for women that Elias describes are especially important to *Le Chaitivel*, in which the heroine turns out to be the author of the poem and the choice between titles becomes to some extent a question of who will own it. The lay demonstrates that women are subject to male control not only in their own persons but also in the products of their bodies.

We can approach the question of male control over women by invoking Elias's concept of monopolization: "a society with numerous power and property units of relatively equal size, tends under strong competitive pressures towards an enlargement of a few units and finally towards monopoly" (1994b, 341). In his analysis the monopoly takes the form of the gradual absorption of a formerly independent knightly class into the service of a few territorial magnates. This at least is how monopoly works in relations between men; in relations between men and women the term can describe the process by which a woman becomes the property of an individual knight. These two meanings come together in the world presented in *Le Chaitivel*, in which women seem to have replaced land as the objects over which a knight is expected to demonstrate his control and mastery.

Elias says that one of the necessary conditions for the development of the feudal system is a change in population which ensures "the formation of a human surplus ... among the nobility" (1994b, 329). Although a surplus of knights may be advantageous to a feudal lord in his struggles with other lords, it may well give rise to problems in times of peace. Marie explores the consequences of this surplus in *Le Chaitivel*, which tells the story of a beautiful and courtly woman with whom all men are in love. This is, of course, a familiar situation, but Marie complicates the cliché by having the Lady loved by four knights and having her love them all in return. "They were all so precious that she could not choose the best. She did not want to lose three for one" (1991, lines 53–5).[2] The knights appear in the poem as a surplus because it is impossible for either the Lady or the reader to choose among them. "This group, which has in its number – that of the four seasons, the four winds, the four elements of the cosmos and of the human body – the sign of universality, constitutes a perfect group; but none of its members can have a distinct and individual life" (Mora-Lebrun 1986, 24).[3] The knights are introduced as a group: "In Brittany there were four barons, but I do not know their names" (1991, lines 33–4).[4] Although the female protagonist is not named either, it is remarkable that Marie draws attention to the fact that she does not know the knights' names. Furthermore, the knights are all equally wonderful: "they were very beautiful and valiant and brave knights, frank, courteous, and generous" (1991, lines 36–8).[5] There is no suggestion, here or elsewhere in *Le Chaitivel*, that one knight is better than the others.

This idea of surplus has a particular relevance to Marie's own work. In the prologue to her collection of lays, she speaks of the ideal readers of difficult classical texts as those "who can gloss the letter and give the surplus of the meaning" (1991, lines 15–16).[6] Most obviously, the surplus refers to the implications and significations that are not apparent at a first reading, but the word has its own hidden implications. Citing line 533 of Marie's lay *Guigemar*, Alexandre Leupin points out that "the word 'surplus' has a particular emphasis: it can denote sexual pleasure" (1991, 230). In my reading of *Le Chaitivel* the text that the Lady glosses is the social text which restricts female sexuality to one object. The Lady adds the surplus (in this case, more men and more pleasure than women are normally allowed) which, in Marie's theory of reading, is necessary to the proper understanding of a text. Furthermore, in transforming this text, the Lady does what Marie herself claims to do with the material she cites as her source for the lays: "In

Chaitivel, Marie de France ... presents a narrative example of her own double, the female creator of lays" (Faust 1988, 19). The Lady's glossing of the social text is the first movement towards her emergence as a writer.

The resulting surplus – the simultaneous possession of four highly impressive lovers – may not appear to present a serious problem, and in fact, Marie does not present it as one so far as the Lady is concerned. The problem lies in the potential for violent competition among the men in the story. One of Elias's major themes in the early part of *The Civilizing Process* is "the transformation of elementary urges into the many kinds of refined pleasure known to society" (1994b, 320). If knights are forced to spend much of their time not fighting and to be violent only at the command of their feudal superior, they must be provided with more peaceful diversions. Love is one of the obvious choices, as Elias points out: "encouraged above all by the presence of the lady, more peaceful forms of conduct become obligatory" (1994b, 323). He goes on to say that the change is not total and that the potential for spontaneous violence still exists. This potential violence is made more likely by the institution of the tournament, in which a knight's love for a lady and his skill as a fighter are supposed to reinforce each other: "At the tournament, each wanted to be first, to do well – if he could – to please the lady" (Marie de France 1991, lines 63–6).[7]

The four indistinguishable knights manage for some time to compete in tournaments without resorting to actual violence (as opposed to ritualized combat) and without disturbing their affairs with the Lady: "She loved and held all four until there was a tournament announced at Nantes after Easter. Men came from other countries to challenge the four lovers" (1991, lines 71–6).[8] Marie follows this passage with a list of all the areas of France and surrounding countries from which knights come to fight at the tournament. As Elias indicates, there are at this time a large number of knights who have no real wars to fight. Furthermore, these knights have only partially been brought under control: "even the *courtois* knight is first and foremost still a warrior, and his life an almost uninterrupted chain of wars, feuds and violence. The more peaceful constraints of social intertwining which tend to impose a profound transformation of drive, do not yet bear constantly and evenly on his life; they intrude only intermittently, are constantly breached by belligerence" (Elias 1994b, 468). In a tournament there is clearly always a danger that ritualized violence will turn into real violence, particularly when a knight's ability to joust is seen as connected with his status as a lover.

For some time, however, the tournament in the poem goes on without problems. The four knights cover themselves with glory as the

Lady watches: "The Lady was in a tower; she could easily distinguish her knights and their men. She saw her lovers helping each other and did not know which one to value most" (1991, lines 107–10).[9] Although the Lady can tell her lovers and their retainers from all the other combatants, she is still unable to decide which of the four should be her favourite. Throughout the lay Marie is careful to obviate any possibility that a front runner will emerge. Although the Lady could still be said to have a certain power at this point in the lay, her spatial isolation from the scene of conflict is important. The narrative situation is reminiscent of Elias's comments about the position of women in an essentially martial society: "the men of the Middle Ages, when women were generally excluded from the central sphere of male life, military action, spend most of their time among themselves ... The woman belongs in her own special room" (1994b, 326). The realities of the gender system are revealed in this tournament scene, as the mingling of the sexes typical of courtly society is replaced by the gender segregation that is necessary to the work of fighting which underwrites both courtliness and knightly identity.

As you might expect, the four knights fight brilliantly throughout the tournament. In fact, they fight *equally* brilliantly, and thus the narrative dilemma is prolonged. Like many other forms of narrative, the lay is supposed to end with a consummation. The unsuitable admirers must be dispensed with, leaving one knight who can be united with the Lady either in love or in death. In sexual terms, Elias's concept of monopoly refers to a man's undisputed possession of a woman. But rather than being the means for establishing this monopoly, the tournament has reconfirmed the impossibility of selection. It is clear that a drastic solution will have to be found: "Thus her four lovers did so well that they won the prizes; then night fell and they should have separated. They strayed too foolishly from their people, and they paid for it because three of them were killed" (1991, lines 115–21).[10] The knights suffer disaster because of their own recklessness in allowing themselves to be separated from their retinue. Furthermore, the men who struck the knights down are horrified: "They grieved greatly for them: they had not done it knowingly" (1991, lines 129–30).[11] Marie emphasizes that the situation is a tragic accident. Clearly, the potential for violence is still a real threat in courtly society. The tournament is intended to turn violence, which is the main preoccupation of the knightly class, into a ritualized activity performed in the service of romantic love.

Marie demonstrates that it is naive to think that violence can be kept under control. She illustrates how easily the pursuit of love, rather than civilizing warriors, can turn into war carried on by other means.

Furthermore, she shows that violence is in fact necessary to at least some courtly narratives. Something, after all, has to be done to reduce the number of the Lady's lovers. The disaster at the tournament would seem to be the answer to the problem, but although three knights are killed off, the wedding still cannot take place: "the fourth was badly wounded; the lance went right through his thigh and his body" (1991, lines 122–4).[12] Even if we do not take the thigh wound as a periphrasis for castration, it is clear that the surviving knight is at least temporarily impotent. His impotency and the deaths of the three other knights are the necessary conditions for the Lady's assumption of agency in the poem: "I shall bury the dead, and if the wounded one can be healed, I shall willingly do it and I shall hire good doctors for him" (1991, lines 161–4).[13] Up to this point in the poem, the Lady, although Marie has described her as an admirable and accomplished woman, has been a largely passive figure. From this point on, she assumes a certain degree of control. The action has passed from the male to the female sphere, although it is of course significant that the female sphere is the place where women attempt to compensate for the destruction caused by male violence.

The Lady buries the dead knights magnificently and hires doctors for the wounded knight, whom she attempts to comfort. She is herself uncomforted, however, and her continuing sorrow leads her to what we can see as, in context, a powerful act of self-assertion: "Because I have loved you so much, I want my sorrows to be remembered. I shall make a lay about the four of you, and I shall call it The Four Sorrows" (1991, lines 201–4).[14] Elias sees medieval lyric verse as emerging from a new and more reverent attitude towards women. In Le Chaitivel, however, the woman is the poet rather than the object of the romantic impulses recounted in the poem; indeed, she becomes a poet as a result of functioning as a love object. The Lady is not content to be fictionalized as the object of masculine emotions, and she chooses to write a poem that has her own feminine emotions as its subject. The title neatly illustrates this situation, since the four knights are to be remembered, not for themselves, but for her response to them. The Lady's position in the tower, which I earlier described as an image of feminine isolation from masculine activities, is also the vantage point of the artist who, after all, has the final say in how events are remembered.

What the Lady produces and names need not simply be considered a text or even a comment on other texts, and she need not simply be considered an artist in the traditional sense. At the beginning of Le Chaitivel, when Marie summarizes what the lay will include, she mentions "where it was born" (1991, line 5).[15] Even before we hear the lay, then, we are invited to consider it a child. By suggesting this view of the lay and then telling us that the woman in the story has four lovers, Marie is perhaps setting up a reading of the text as a search to determine paternity. At the end of *Le Chaitivel*, the Lady's role in the production of the lay seems to be a traditionally feminine one. Michelle A. Freeman says that "Marie's work (1) explains an existing artifact by means of capturing the moment of inception and (2) depicts, in a celebratory manner, the artifact's subsequent existence as a private gift ... between a man and a woman. In this sense, might not the gift represent a kind of sublimation of the child not borne by the woman for her lover?" (1984, 861). Inception, then, is a substitute for conception. The lay stands in for the child whom the knight is incapable of begetting.

Unfortunately, the wounded knight is well aware that a work's title is not simply descriptive, that it can also be taken as an instruction on how to read the text itself. By continuing the refusal to distinguish among the four knights, the Lady's title would commemorate her original independence and sexual freedom. When she tells him her plan, he quickly cries out, "Lady, make the new lay, but call it The Wretched Man" (1991, lines 207–8).[16] He tells her that the other knights' troubles are over while his continue, and he insists that the title should commemorate him: "If the lay is to be called after me, let it be called The Wretched Man. Whoever calls it The Four Sorrows will be changing its real name" (1991, lines 225–8).[17] A man's monopoly over a woman, his undisputed possession of her, extends not only to the woman herself but also to what she produces. Nevertheless, if the lay is a sort of child, then it is clear that the paternity is uncertain. In naming the lay, the knight attempts to set himself up as the father and to avoid the prospect of being declared a cuckold by the sexual pluralism evident in the lay's original title. But although he insists on naming the lay, there is no indication that he will write it or even that he will recite it. The parallels to childbirth and child-rearing could hardly be clearer. Thus the situation at the end of *Le Chaitivel* can be read as a narrative rendering of the fear that Marie expresses at the end of her fables: poems, like children, take their father's name, even though the woman has all the *labur*.

The poem does not end with the impotent knight's assumption of potency. Although the Lady gives in to him, Marie is careful to point out both at the beginning and at the end of the poem that either title is suitable. At the end she says that those who first recited the lay called it *Four Sorrows*, while *The Wretched Man* is the currently accepted title, thus giving the female title the claim of priority at least. In the very last lines of the poem, Marie draws attention to the lack of closure: "Here it ends; there is no more; I have heard no more;

I know no more; I shall tell you no more" (1991, lines 238–40).[18] These lines can be read as an acknowledgment that the poem is unfinished because the story it recounts is unfinished. The couple in *Le Chaitivel*, alone of all the couples in Marie's lays, does not achieve narrative closure, which comes from union either in marriage or in death. The knight may at first be thought to have triumphed because the title of the lay suggests that his story is the central one in the poem, but this triumph is compromised by Marie's statements that his is only a possible title and by the fact that she ends the poem by calling attention to his impotence. His insistence on his singularity actually works against him: "this 'one' … is only produced by the text on the basis of exclusion of sexuality" (Huchet 1981, 429).[19]

The poem thus ends with a narrative impasse in which, as Samuel T. Cowling points out, "the narrator's commentary upon the naming of this *lai* explicitly restores in an unresolvable equilibrium the impulses that have been operating throughout" (1974–75, 687). This ending of the poem is hardly a triumph for the Lady, but neither is it a defeat. Although the violence that Elias reminds us is always just beneath the surface of courtly life has erupted, the man has been no more exempt from it than the woman, and the lay that remains to tell the story testifies to the woman's strength and skill. Marie has shown, to return to Elias's formulation, one of the ways in which women have "special opportunities to overcome male dominance." Although men may have a monopoly on the violence that underwrites the feudal system, a women who writes can at least ensure that they do not have the monopoly on how events are perceived and remembered.

NOTES

1 Al finement de cest escrit,
   Qu'en Romanz ai treité e dit,
   me numerai pur remembrance:
   Marie ai num, si sui de France.
   Puet cel estre, que clerc plusur
   prendereient sur eus mun labur:
   ne voil que nul sur li le die.
2 Tant furent tuit de grant valur,
   Ne pot eslire le meillur.
   Ne volt les treis perdre pur l'un.
3 Ce groupe, qui porte dans son chiffre – celui des quatre saisons, des quatre vents, des quatre éléments du cosmos et du corps humain – réalise une sorte d'ensemble parfait; mais aucun de ses membres ne peut accéder à une existence distincte et individuelle.

4 En Bretaine ot quatre baruns,
  Mes jeo ne sai numer lur nuns.
5 ... mut erent de grant beauté
  E chevalier pruz e vaillant,
  Large, curteis e despendant.
6 K'i peüssent gloser la lettre
  E de lur sen le surplus mettre.
7 A l'assembler des chevaliers
  Voleit chescuns estre primiers
  De bien fere, si il peüst,
  Pur ceo qu'a la dame pleüst.
8 Tuz quatre les ama e tint,
  Tant qu'aprés une Paske vint,
  Ot un turneiement crié,
  Pur aquointier les quatre druz
  I sunt d'autre païs venuz.
9 La dame fu sur une tur,
  Bien choisi les suens e les lur;
  Ses druz i vit mut bien aidier,
  Ne seit le queil deit plus preisier.
10 Si quatre dru bien le fescient,
  Si ke de tuz le pris aveient,
  Tant ke ceo vint a l'avesprer
  Que il deveient desevrer;
  Trop folement s'abaundonerent
  Luinz de lur gent, sil comparerent,
  Kar li treis i furent ocis.
11 Mut esteient pur eus dolent:
  Nel firent pas a escïent.
12 E li quarz nafrez e malmis
  Par mi la quisse e einz el cors,
  Si que la lance parut fors.
13 Les morz ferai ensevelir,
  E si li nafrez poet garir,
  Volentiers m'en entremetrai
  E bons mires li baillerai.
14 Pur ceo que tant vus ai amez,
  Voil que mis doels seit remembrez;
  Des vus quatres ferai un lai
  E *Quatre Dols* le numerai.
15 U il fu nez.
16 Dame, fetes le lai novel,
  Si l'apelez *Le Chaitivel*.

17 Pur c'ert li lais de mei nomez:
   Le Chaitivel iert appelez.
   Ki *Quatre Dols* le numera
   Sun propre nun li changera.
18 Ici finist, nen i ad plus,
   Plus n'en oï ne plus n'en sai
   Ne plus ne vus en cunterai.
19 ce "un" ... n'est produit par l'écrit que sur fond d'exclusion de
   la sexualité.

9 Writing in the Face of Death: Norbert Elias and Autobiographies of Cancer

ULRICH C. TEUCHER

In *The Loneliness of the Dying*, Norbert Elias writes about the problems of aging in modern societies. Many of his observations also apply to those who must live with a life-threatening illness. Cancer, for example, is a serious illness that disrupts life in many ways. Not only do patients find it difficult to cope with their overwhelming emotions of fear, loss of control, and sustained uncertainty; they must also face the fears and insecurities of family, friends, and colleagues who do not know how to respond to an unexpected brush with mortality. However, cancer patients find support among each other and in support groups. In Vancouver, for instance, the British Columbia Cancer Agency facilitates such groups. Typically, they begin with people sitting in a circle. Taking turns, they tell each other, usually in few words, what is on their minds. For some, the news may be happy, while others may be facing a recurrence of their cancer. Following this exchange, people lie down on mattresses, lights are dimmed, and the group leader begins to guide the participants, with the help of imagery, into a state of relaxation. This exercise is carefully and yet spontaneously orchestrated as a number of assistants, including music and massage therapists, complement the leader's soothing suggestions from different parts of the room. Many of the images involve visions of nature or transformational journeys and suggest an abundance of space and care. These messages reassure the participants that they are not alone but part of an interdependent whole. Finally, the participants close the session with another circle by holding one another's hands.

The experience of interdependence in cancer care can counterbalance the anxieties and isolation caused by fear, loss of control, and uncertainty that invariably accompany a diagnosis of cancer and the vicissitudes of its treatment and outcome. In a support group it is possible to speak about hopes and fears, for life and death are never far apart. Many share what one member at the end of a session described as follows: "Thank God for the circle, because you know how I feel and I know how you feel."

The themes of isolation, interdependent caring, and acknowledgement of death are also on Elias's mind when he writes, at the age of eighty-five, about the problems of aging in *The Loneliness of the Dying* and a postscript, *Aging and Dying*.[1] Here he provides a socio-historical analysis of changing cultural attitudes towards death and dying, namely, the current deferral of death as an abstract and distant closure of life and the resulting isolation of the aging and dying. Changing attitudes, however, leave room for different ways of thinking about life and death. I trace these possibilities as Elias describes them in *The Loneliness of the Dying* and examine the equivalents of his ideas in English and German autobiographical accounts of persons living with cancer. These autobiographies confirm his observations that interaction with one another can make life bearable in the face of death.

NORBERT ELIAS: THE LONELINESS OF THE DYING

Elias observes, in *The Loneliness of the Dying*, that today "dying and death have been pushed further than ever out of sight of the living and behind the scenes of normal life" (1985b, 85). We cannot accept that human life is finite, and this denial of death affects our attitudes towards aging and illness. However, it is not so much death itself that instills fear in us, but the collective and individual fantasies that humans create about death and dying. Elias notes, "We cannot ignore the fact that it is not actually death itself that arouses fear and terror, but the anticipatory image of death" (1985b, 44).

The nature of these collective and individual fantasies has, however, changed over time. According to Elias, the oldest and most common form of how humans try to come to terms with the finiteness of life is by mythologizing death, by inventing an afterlife in Hades or Valhalla, in hell or paradise (1985b, 1). Until the end of the Middle Ages in Europe, humans felt that they had little control over their lives. Generally, life expectancy was short, dying was often more painful than it is now, and the fear of punishment after death had been institutionalized as an official doctrine. However, dying and death were far more public; usually, family and neighbours were involved in caring for the dying, and death was accepted as part of an individual's possibility and as part of life (1985b, 16). Since the Renaissance, however, a number of mutually influencing developments have led to some changes. These developments and changes are well known to any reader of Elias's work and here will only be listed cursorily. For one, the progress particularly in biological knowledge has led to a considerable increase in life expectancy. Therefore humans no longer see death as a metaphysical intervention but as a distant end to processes that are now believed to be "natural" and thus subject to understanding, control, and exploitation. However, a prolonged life expectancy invites a deferral of thinking about death, which in turn contributes to a poverty of language when we speak about the end of life and a lack of identification with those who are aging.

The lack of identification with the elderly and dying is also increased by what Elias calls a powerful acceleration of individualization (*Individualisierungsschub*; 1985b, 58). At the end of this process emerges the isolated subject, the *homo clausus*, whose self-image suggests independence from others, an inner world cut off from the outer world of fellow human beings. It is not surprising that this "windowless monad," isolated in life, will think of itself as isolated also in death (1985b, 60). Such beliefs would explain the community's lack of identification with the aging and dying and their tacit exclusion from the living, a fate that is, according to Elias, one of the most prominent features of industrial societies.

Having traced our ways of thinking about death and dying in the course of social development and with regard to specific groups, Elias suggests that attitudes towards death and dying are neither unalterable nor accidental and that alternatives are possible (1985b, 84). These may begin with changes at the individual level. For example, psychological work might uncover and resolve childhood guilt fantasies over wishing a parent dead. We might reconsider our preference for individual identity and instead acknowledge that our lives depend on natural resources such as light, air, and food and the fellowship of our parents, families, and peers. We might want to contemplate the approaching dissolution of our own person as we age and empathize with the physical, social, and emotional problems typical of old age or illness. We might also want to rethink our construction of nature and life as ordered natural processes that are subject to our control (1985b, 81–2), especially in the face of events as random and meaningless as cancer.

Finally, Elias points out, the high incidence of death by accident and individual or organized crime should remind us that life statistics provide no certainty about an individual's time of death (1985b, 50). Indeed, the high incidence of life-threatening illnesses surely strengthens his argument. As the sociologist notes, we tend to forget that even in advanced societies an objective danger of death is always present. How, we may ask, are we to conduct our lives, aware that death may be possible at any time? Elias suggests that life is fulfilled and meaningful if a person has been able to set goals and reach them, and it is meaningless for a person who feels that he or she has missed opportunities. Not surprisingly, given his emphasis on interdependence, Elias considers the involvement of a person with his or her fellow human beings, whether by personal conduct or work, as most important for a meaningful life and death (1985b, 62ff.). However, if death is possible at any time, it follows that goals should be set and reached, not in the far distance, but in a continuum. That is, life should be conducted in a meaningful way, according to Elias, by seeking involvement with one's fellow human beings.

Now we may understand why he insists that death is a problem of the living. The latter can chose whether they deny death and alienate themselves from the aging and dying, or acknowledge death as a constant possibility of the human condition and identify with the aging and dying. Thus the living may attain "a clearer awareness that humanity is a community of mortals" (1985b, 3). According to Elias, our task is to demystify death and give it new meaning by accepting it as an inevitable part of human existence. The company of family and friends and their emotional support can help to make the process and event of dying as simple and comfortable as possible.

While Elias is concerned with problems that are associated with aging and death, his observations may also be helpful when we consider life with a life-threatening illness. Usually, as Glenna Halvorson-Boyd points out (Halvorson-Boyd and Hunter 1995), we see the world as conveniently divided between the living and the dying, the healthy and the sick. However, in life-threatening illness the lines are blurred. Because of the sustained uncertainty of a cancer prognosis, death is no longer an absolute boundary but presents a "possibility of an infinite approximation" ("Möglichkeit der unendlichen Annäherung," Noll 1991, 178). Faced with the fragility of life, patients who live with a cancer must struggle not only with their own fear of dying but in addition with the fears of the healthy. A study of English and German autobiographies of cancer finds various narrative strategies for coping with a life-threatening illness, ranging from heroic battles for a healthy future to fragmented, open-ended narratives that, in the face of uncertainty, appreciate life and meaning in the present.

AUTOBIOGRAPHIES OF CANCER

According to the late Peter Noll, personal accounts of life with cancer have become a literary genre of their own. In their autobiographies, writers describe how they cope not only with their illness and its treatment but also with helpless and awkward reactions of family, friends, colleagues, and health professionals (Noll 1991, 194). Such reactions may, on the one hand, be explained by a lack of suitable means of communication and a lack of identification, as Elias would suggest. For example, medical staff often appear to have little interest in the patients. As Kathlyn Conway notes, "We are a job to them. If they were to make contact with us, they might know that we are frightened and would have to talk to us; they could not move us through so efficiently" (Conway 1997, 28). A number of authors note the contrast between their fears and a "relentless cheerfulness" (Korda 1996, 46) in major cancer centres – "Cancerlands" with "chirping receptionists" (Wadler 1994, 100). On the other hand, a person with a life-threatening illness confronts those who are healthy with their denial of their own mortality, an experience that may create much anxiety. Conway, who suffered three cancers within twenty years, notes that healthy people often do not know how to respond to her. Some, to quell their anxiety, simply tell her cancer stories that they have heard (1997, 3), while others reassure themselves that eating carrots and exercising will prevent them from developing cancer (1997, 57). By suggesting in subtle ways that the patient is responsible for his or her cancer, healthy people contribute to the isolation that a patient feels.

It is through sharing their experience that patients with cancer move out of their isolation and fears and interact with, and educate, their family, their friends, and the public (Tausch 1995). Narrators find that writing provides them with a "freedom to be honest in a way that [is] not always possible in conversation" (Conway 1997, 2). The majority of cancer narratives originate in the personal experience of the author.[2] Often authors enlist the help of experienced writers, who organize, shape, and even write large sections of the emerging narrative.[3] When a writer does not live to complete or publish his or her story, partners, relatives, or friends may step in to edit and bring the narrative to a closure.[4] The collaboration between author, co-writer, partner, and editor in writing the narrative may emulate the collaboration between the ill and those who care for them during recovery and recuperation. For example, Linda Pratt Mukai's narrative *Living with Dying* (Mukai and Chan 1996) acknowledges the contribution of her family and caregivers to her life with cancer by embedding their first-person narratives in her own autobiographical account. These different narratives in turn interact in a narrative constructed and edited by Mukai's co-writer, Janis Fischer Chan. A similar approach can also be observed in Rita Koerber's narrative *The Book of Rita's Living* (Koerber et al. 1990).

Those who live with cancer write about their experience and the decisions that they make (or made) so as to encourage other patients and their friends, families, and caregivers and to prepare them for what they will have to undergo (Adjei 1994, 9; Bloor 1996, 18; Mukai and Chan 1996, 2). Some authors believe that they found specific therapies, diets, exercises, or other ways of dealing with their illness which they want to share with others who are ill (Gawler 1989; Fraehm and Fraehm 1992; Mae and Loeffler 1992; Richardson 1995). Laura Evans describes her book on breast cancer and climbing mountains (both literally and figuratively) as "a manual on following *your* dreams" (1996, xii; emphasis added). Thus the form and the intended message of these autobiographies vary. Authors may convey life during and after illness in the form of a novel (Beutler 1989), diary (Adjei 1994), manifesto (Friebel 1996), parable (Zorn 1994 or Dalhoff 1991), or self-help book (Fraehm and Fraehm 1992).

Autobiographers themselves may read and refer to other writers' personal accounts. Some want to read success stories only (Dehn 1995, 47), while others wish to learn about a complete journey from life to death. For example, Christina Middlebrook, who lives with metastasized breast cancer, regards *Cancer in Two Voices*, *Grace and Grit*, and *Diary of a Zen Nun* as her "treasures"; their authors speak matter-of-factly of their approaching deaths, though not "without fear, anxiety, anger, and grief" (1996, 205–6).

Many begin to write because this activity helps them to cope better with their illness. Some discover the benefits of writing during their illness and treatment (Adjei 1994, 184; Mechtel 1993, 50, 52) and find that only after they write can they put a distance between themselves and their illness (Conway 1997, 3; Dehn 1995, 90). Kathlyn Conway appears successful in writing her way out of a depression in the aftermath of her breast cancer (1997, 2, 240). While writing, she values the act of remembering, organizing, and describing her experience, an act that "draws together all the stray parts of [her]self." Conway feels as though she is "writing to save [her] life" (1997, 240). This process can be immensely painful. Yet it appears necessary to construct a continuity of the self by writing about events that were so harrowing that there may not even be a personal memory of them (Middlebrook 1996, 57ff.). Peter Noll, who knows (at the time of writing) that he will die soon, hopes that his writing can help him and his readers to understand death and dying better, while he and they are still alive (1991, 227). Autobiographers may return to their writing as readers, for example, in order to gather courage from an earlier determination that they would have forgotten had they not written about it (Mechtel 1993, 97). Others want to learn more about difficult aspects of their self during their illness, a self that they find hard to identify with (Conway 1997, 259).

Rereading the personal past may lead to a rewriting of the past. The patient's immediate and distant life history before the diagnosis, as well as earlier suspicious signals of the body, may take on new meaning in light of the diagnosis and the patient's attempts to construct meaning. Some authors contemplate prior stressful experiences, such as work overload (Wadler 1994) or lifestyle (Bloor 1996), while Laura Evans debates whether unresolved grief over the death of family members, personal wrongdoing, or her fast-food diet may have contributed to her breast cancer. From hindsight, earlier signals of the body, previously disregarded, may be recounted as markers of the oncoming illness. Jackie Stacey notes that "these new narratives of the body rescript the story of [her] life with ruthless editorial authority. While the mind had been full of stories of life, the body had been planning another story: the threat of death" (1996, 8). Cancer patients are aware of the vagaries of their illness and its treatment and consider that their future life may be difficult to predict. At the same time, many hope that cancer presents only a temporary brush with mortality and that they can return to where they had left off in life before the illness. As Middlebrook notes, patients and the public alike prefer to think of cancer remission as cure. Such beliefs may lead to renewed denial and a hope for closure that becomes apparent as autobiographers search for fitting narrative structures. Conway writes: "During my illness I searched for narratives that would structure my experience and offer me a vision of the future in which breast cancer would end ... I studied my diagnosis and statistical survival rates to find material with which to compose a story that had a future in which I would be healthy" (1997, 158).

A narrative structure which many autobiographies of cancer adapt is that of the mystery, with its elements of innocence, first suspicion, the shock of detection of a deadly threat, historical and medical research, pursuit, and arrest. Although the suspect is often identified early on, even on the first page, the element of mystery and fear spreads because the enemy often cannot be identified easily. Moreover, the suspect turns out not to be an intruder but, rather, a member of the family, so to speak. In fact, and generally most frightening, the suspect is revealed to be a part of the assailed and may resist the attempts of the writer to separate him or herself from the threat by objectifying or externalizing it. The boundaries between self and other become blurred, and the suspect all too often resists apprehension. These conditions add to the frightening mystery of cancer stories. Not all mysteries, however, result in the identification of the suspect and closure. Some plot lines are left open-ended, a structure that seems to suit many cancer narratives well.

Usually the narrator meets the threat with a stance of defiance. Great, previously unknown resources are mustered in order to "triumph over illness" (Evans 1996, 264). Often the imagery of battle is employed to achieve "triumph." Such imagery may be helpful in fostering a sense of control of the illness during long periods of uncertainty. In a battle a defendant can fight the enemy, even if the latter is not visible, whether the enemy is externalized as an alien invader or internalized as an image of past personal failings. In both cases, the image of cancer as the "other" provides a field on which to project one's energies. Some autobiographies even announce their defiance in their titles, as evident in the following examples of German and English autobiographies: *A Time to Heal: Triumph over Cancer* (Bishop 1996); *Ich habe Krebs! Na Und?* (Friebel 1996);[5] *Krebs greift nicht das Herz an* (Lenker 1993);[6] *A Cancer Battle Plan* (Fraehm and Fraehm 1992); *Diagnose Unheilbarer Krebs: Wie ich meine Krankheit besiegte* (Adjei 1994);[7] *Surrender or Fight* (Hoek and Jongsma 1995); *Weniger als ein Jahr: Unser Kampf gegen den Krebs* (Borst 1988);[8] *Mars* (Zorn 1994); *Ich habe meinen Krebs besiegt* (Becker 1982);[9] *You Can Conquer Cancer* (Gawler 1989); *The Cancer Conqueror* (Anderson 1995); *A Warrior in the Land of Disease* (Jones 1996). These are twelve titles out of more than one hundred autobiographies currently available in English- and German-speaking countries. Although images of battle and its triumphs do not occur in all the titles, they are frequently used within the narratives. Even if some narratives use battle metaphors sparingly, they are still characterized by a stance of defiance. In the following section, I discuss some aspects of battle metaphors and narratives in English and German autobiographies.

The narrative *Autobiography of a Face*, by Lucy Grealy, deals with the problems of growing up with a Ewing sarcoma of the jaw and facial disfigurement following the surgical removal of the tumour and approximately thirty cosmetic operations from the age of nine onwards. Grealy is twenty-nine years old when she writes her autobiography, and her great hope is that there may be a moment when she looks in the mirror and discovers the image to be her own.

Throughout childhood and into early adulthood, she must endure the stares and taunts of other children, mainly boys and young males. Her mother, who grew up with the truism that there is nothing to fear but fear itself, raises her daughter to conquer her fears, and so the young girl resolves never to cry again (1994, 79). Grealy believes life to be generally cruel and sets out to defy existence by surviving it. She views her face as a battle scar and a badge of honour (1994, 187). She is horrified by the war in Cambodia. Its images let the writer, she says, bomb and starve and persecute her own suffering right out of existence (1994, 126).

The image of a battle scar or a badge of honour can be found in many cancer autobiographies, whether they are written by women or by men. Likewise, many cancer narratives historicize a person's confrontation with the illness by referring to current or past wars. While German writers refer to the Second World War, North American autobiographies allude to the Gulf War, the Vietnam War, and Second World War battles such as Iwo Jima. When Joyce Wadler writes her account of living with breast cancer and lumpectomy in *My Breast* (1994), the Gulf War is raging. Confronted with her diagnosis, she feels under attack, with Scud missiles "raining" on her head. Wadler, too, refers to the scar on her breast as a "battle scar" and a "badge of honor." Her chest tattooed for radiation and the empty cavity of the tumour marked with metal staples, she feels like "a war hero with shrapnel in her breast" who is about to be "nuked." Tattoos accompany an important childhood memory of Wadler's, namely, the concentration camp numbers on the many vacationing Jews in the resort town where she grew up. The Holocaust, as a crime against humanity, is a frequently used image in cancer narratives.

English writers comfortably use the image of a "total war" (Price 1995; Korda 1996), a phrase that is absent in German autobiographies, probably because of its unpalatable association with the Nazi concept of war. Michael Korda, who recounts his experience with prostate cancer in *Man to Man*, notes that we wage the equivalent of "total war" against cancer more than against any other disease: "It's kill-or-be-killed time, we throw in everything we've got to destroy the enemy before the enemy destroys us" (1996, 240). Similarly, Reynolds Price, who suffered from spinal cancer and writes about it in *A Whole New Life*, perceives his "skirmish" as a "total war": "The bigger assaults of fear and pain, in whatever life they crash against, are indiscriminately strong. Only one creature bears the brunt; and the brunt slams down with no regard to the quality of the roof overhead, the cooking that's served or the presence of love or solitude. All the care and cash on Earth, however welcome, are a flimsy shield when the prospect of agonized death leans in" (1995, viii).

Perhaps writers hope to draw additional strength from using battle narratives if these are historicized and visualized with reference to specific military battles. The battle narrative, however, can also double as a symbol of religious or social opposition. Writers with a strong religious leaning may view their confrontation with cancer in terms of their faith. In her book *Fight or Surrender*, Beatrice Hofman Hoek, a devout Christian, felt that she lost control of her life after cancer entered it: "The cancer seemed to take over everything" (Hoek and Jongsma 1995, 44). Inspired by Christ's battle with the enemy, and with the help of God, she decided to face her enemy head-on and to fight back: "I began to fight with every ounce of strength and courage I had." The Swiss writer Fritz Angst, on the other hand, interprets his life with lymphoma as a parable of social decay. He published his autobiography, *Mars*, under the pseudonym Fritz Zorn (1994). The writer identifies his cancer as a voice of the emotions that his bourgeois parents have taught him to repress. Initially, Zorn hopes to integrate what he believes to be a neglected part of the self. However, his cancer turns out to be incurable. Running out of time, he transforms his anger against his parents into a desperate attack on the decadence of society; hence the title evokes the Roman god of war. For a generation of German-speaking young people, *Mars* became an instant icon for the apparent lack of social conscience in their bourgeois societies.

For the American poet Audre Lorde, it is the condition of U.S. society that becomes a focal point of her confrontation with cancer. Both in *The Cancer Journals* (1980) and *A Burst of Light* (1988), she sees herself and other women with breast cancer as warriors who bare their scars in the war against a polluted environment and the silencing of women (1980, 60). Lorde saw her participation in the medical decisions about her body as a crucial strategy and responsibility for doing battle in all other areas of her life, such as fighting racism, heterosexism, and apartheid. She hoped that writing about her experience would encourage her not to give in to what she feared to be a numbing acceptance of death.

Others extend their warfare against cancer into a battle with a medical institution that they find intimidating and imprisoning. The defiance that Gisela Friebel signals in the title of her autobiography *Ich habe Krebs! Na und?* (I have cancer! So what? 1996) is directed not only against her illness but also against her physicians, whom she considers to be patronizing and merely interested in profit and filling hospital beds. For Herbert Dalhoff, in *So krank wie die Erde* (As sick as the earth; 1991), the hospital takes on Kafkaesque overtones in his description of towering facades, looming portals, and long corridors. Chapter titles such as "Die Einweisung" (The admission), "Die Untersuchung" (The examination), and "Die Unterbringung" (The accomodation) underline the depersonalizing character of the hospital and the sense of isolation that accompany Dalhoff's battle with his illness. For him, the polluted body becomes a metaphor for the pollution of the environment.

However, triumphs over cancer may also be imagined in terms of exceptional natural challenges. Some women choose, for example, mountain climbing, literally and figuratively, as a metaphor for their confrontation with cancer. When Geraldine Bloor writes "Peak Experiences" (1996), her title is meant to draw attention not only to fundamental changes in the wake of her diagnosis with cancer but also to her success in climbing Mount Killarney, at 3,000 feet the second highest peak in Ireland. Peak experiences are also at the centre of Laura Evans's autobiography *The Climb of My Life* (1996); having recovered from breast cancer and a bone-marrow transplant after high-risk chemotherapy, she organizes a successful mountain-climbing expedition of women with breast cancer to the peak of Argentina's Mount Aconcagua (22,841 feet), the highest mountain outside the Himalayas. The advertisement of a sponsor (Jansport) celebrates this "23000 foot assault on breast cancer" in a poster that seems to show Evans during a three-point climb up a vertical wall of ice. Wielding her pickaxe, she appears to chisel into the mountain a message that is foregrounded in the poster: "When diagnosed with breast cancer, women may go through many stages: Denial. Fear. Self-Pity. Or in Laura Evans' case, the insatiable urge to kick ass." As she announces in her preface, her book chronicles her journey "from the brink of death and depths of despair to the summits of some of the highest mountains on the far reaches of the planet: It is a story about the parallels between climbing and surviving crisis. It is a manual on following your dreams" (1996, xii). Evans's autobiography closes with the wish "May we triumph over illness" (1996, 264).

Because of the enormous pain, loss, and fear and the many changes to the body and the self, it is not surprising that many narratives of cancer employ metaphors of battle in order to celebrate defiance. Susan Sontag investigates such metaphors in *Illness as Metaphor*. However, the use of battle metaphors presents many problems. First of all, such analogies are divisive. War usually ends with victory for some and defeat for others. Those who survive celebrate their "triumph" over cancer, but unfortunately, there are many whose disease turns out to be incurable. The dualism of the battle narrative suggests to these patients that they have lost their struggle, that they have failed to gain control of their bodies and their disease, that they have not worked hard enough, and that they must end their life defeated.[10]

Furthermore, the concept of waging "total war" against an illness such as cancer may be a cause for even more anxiety. To be victorious in war, one cannot dwell on fear, despair, or grief. Beatrice Hofmann

Hoek, for example, finds out that the battle against cancer can be long and arduous. After nine months, she feels overcome by her anxiety and her continuous hovering on the brink of mortality. Depleted, she surrenders – she surrenders her fate to God – and recovers. Hoek notes the apparent irony: "I could only win when I stopped fighting ... the power that defeated my cancer came from God, and I was healed only when I admitted my own powerlessness" (Hoek and Jongsma 1995, 77). While her narrative is an example of the anxiety caused by a militant attitude, its solution unfortunately suggests to those who do not recover that God must have elected not to help them, perhaps because their surrender to their faith was not sincere enough.

Other authors stumble over the fact that there is an inherent problem with the image of cancer as the enemy. As Joyce Wadler lies on the radiation table, she realizes that the beam will kill the cancer cells – which are cells of her body, which are her cells. For a moment the externalization of the enemy is interrupted by a painful admission of her intimate relationship with her cancer: "All I know is somebody is going to aim a beam at my chest and kill a bunch of cells – my cells. I find myself feeling bad for them. Even if they are cancer, they are living things too" (1994, 143).

There is one further problem in the use of battle metaphors. Korda notes that prostate cancer or any other kind of cancer is a moving picture, not a still one. "The cancer grows, moves, mutates, shrinks, recurs; clinical tests can only show you what its status is today, now, not predict what it will be tomorrow, or five years from now" (1996, 80).

As Glenna Halvorson-Boyd and Lisa Hunter write in their collaborative autobiography *Dancing in Limbo*, cancer resists our modern belief that illness is caused by a known agent and can be cured; that if we follow the dictates of a healthy lifestyle, we are protected from sickness and even death; and that we can choose when and how we die (1995, 108). Thus cancer leaves us with the frightening realization that we may indeed have little control over life. To use Norbert Elias's terminology, the process of cancer, unpredictable as it is, and the process of constructing meaning in terms of expectations for the future are opposed to each other. Halvorson-Boyd and Hunter call the space created by this conflict "limbo." "After we wake up in limbo, we face the rest of our lives stripped of the protective barrier between ourselves and death. Death is real and close at hand. Although we may want to proceed as if nothing has changed, for most of us such efforts are only partially successful. We cannot escape the fact that we know how vulnerable we are and that others know the truth as well" (1995, 27). For many cancer patients and their supporters, this truth is exceedingly hard to cope with, for patients can never be certain whether, in their life with cancer, turns for the worse are merely temporary – perhaps unrelated to the illness – or signal a decline. Thus they often find themselves torn between hope and fear. The distress of having a life-threatening illness, hoping for a healthy future, and worrying about the possibility of death is narrated most movingly by Joachim Seiler, the author of *Lügenzeit* (Time of lies, 1996). The writer leaves his readers reeling from the drama of a couple who struggle to learn how to talk to each other in the face of death. On the one hand, Seiler and his wife, Edith, who suffers from cancer, are repulsed by the awkwardness of outsiders and the impersonal routine of medical professionals whose body language betrays the partial truths they dispense. On the other hand, Seiler wonders if it is possible at all to cope with the terrible truth of cancer and its treatment. He suggests that lies may preserve some remnant of dignity and love, for the progression of cancer may come quickly, overwhelming patient, partner, and reader. He portrays this acceleration as the narrative picks up speed. He races his car and his wife through the streets of Berlin, taking Edith to and from radiation treatments, picking up her medication from the drug-store, and finding that the morphine dosage continues to increase. In the ensuing chaos, neither he nor the reader is prepared for the sudden death of his wife, which leaves the narrative suspended as if in mid-air.

Not surprisingly, those who are uncertain of their survival tend to be more introspective and to reflect on life and death more extensively. However, such thinking may not make the idea of dying any easier. Peter Noll, who has rejected medical treatment for his cancer of the bladder and has a year left to live, grapples with the knowledge of death in *Diktate über Leben und Tod* (Dictations on life and death). On the one hand, he argues, everyone should be made aware that he or she could be the next one to die "because death is always around us, we should think about death while we live" (1991, 23). However, it appears that human psychology may be overwhelmed by such a task: "We must live as if we were immortal. Life will not and cannot know death" (1991, 35). Nevertheless, the author appears relieved of the pressures of long-term plans for the future and sets out to write, in the face of death, his observations about life. He comments on ordinary, as well as deeply philosophical, concerns and finds words of encouragement in his study of Montaigne, biblical sources, and the conversations with his friend, the writer Max Frisch.

When a friend spoke of an "enlightened death" to Middlebrook, she felt offended and told him that she was interested only in an "enlightened life." That, however, was before the discovery of her metastases. Now she "cannot imagine an enlightened life without including thoughts of an enlightened death" (1996, 201). When she is asked by her daughter whether she would be ready to die, Middlebrook responds: "'Ready' is an inhuman word. Let's say I am more familiar with the idea." She tells her daughter that she is going to live her life as richly as she can. Middlebrook is grateful for the support of her children, her husband, and her friends, who continue to accompany her through joy and pain.

But also to those who are more hopeful about their survival, it may seem futile to deny death and worry about an essentially unknowable future, given the fact that time is limited. According to Halvorson-Boyd and Hunter, the healthy and the ill alike should expend their energy on living each day as if it were the last (1995, 77). Joyce Wadler arrives late at such insights in *My Breast*. Her autobiography is an example of a narrative in which the author temporarily struggles with the uncertainty of her condition and hopes to return quickly to the busy routine of her previous life. In fact, Wadler's book was designed to end immediately after her final treatment (1994, 149). However, the writer has to resume the narrative when a sudden phone call from the hospital informs her, about a year later, that her cancer has been reassessed as a much more aggressive kind and that she should undergo additional chemotherapy. Only now Wadler realizes that "this whole cancer thing" is not over and that "death ... may not come when I am 85 and weary, or after I have solved all my problems or all my deadlines" (1994, 165). Thus she decides to finally leave a difficult relationship, make more time for her friends, and enjoy her life more fully.

While many patients find it difficult to share their experience of life with cancer because of the insensitivities of those who are healthy, some discover that there are people who are ready to help. Reynolds Price, who must ask for help and assistance because of a debilitating spinal cancer, has many friends on whom he can literally lean in hard times and in good. Despite all his pain, he concludes that the recent years, since the arrival of what he calls "full catastrophe," "have brought more in and sent more out then ever – more love and care, more knowledge and patience, more work in less time" (1995, 179). Price attributes this experience to no longer asking "Why me?" but asserting an open-ended "What next!" (1995, 185). He thinks of his old self as having died and his new self as "radically altered and trimmed" for a whole new journey, one over which he has little control but which he will face nevertheless (1995, 189). The theme of open-endedness is reflected in the cover of Price's autobiography: a photographic view through wide open doors into a spacious, empty, and light-filled room from which other doors lead into more rooms.

Middlebrook transforms her autobiography, *Seeing the Crab*, from a battle narrative to that of an open-ended journey. The image of a soldier introduces an extended narrative of battle, historicized with references to Vietnam and the Second World War. Her imagery of war, however, takes a Jungian turn: enemies are not to be annihilated but to be integrated; the enemies are the indeterminable forces of nature. Middlebrook imagines her soldier as a boy. In the language of Jungians, this is the contra-sexual figure, also known as the animus; he is non-heroic and anonymous, acceptant, fears death, and is inclined to sur-render. She notes: "I find great relief in surrender. Surrender means I can stop worrying and fretting and figuring out what I am supposed to do. I can forget about beating odds and just live my life. I don't need to work harder than I already have, because I have already done everything that I can and because I didn't do anything wrong in the first place" (1996, 201–2). Thus the battle narrative, itself transformed, serves as an example of Middlebrook's transformation of living with a life-threatening illness. She acknowledges that, ultimately, individual control is limited and that the forces of nature, called by Jung the psyche, are stronger. Hence the metaphor is one of the open-ended journey; thus Middlebrook chooses to leave her narrative open-ended.

Some autobiographers make both the open-endedness of their expe-riences and the continuous reassessment of their lives in the face of death central to the fragmented structure of their narratives. In *Fuss Fassen* (1989), the autobiography of the Swiss writer Maya Beutler, the occasional inclusion of official medical status reports appears to suggest a controlled, continued management of the disease. The per-sonal narrative, on the other hand, consists of a number of isolated individual episodes that have hardly any relation to one another. By subverting the continuity of the narrative and leaving it open-ended, this strategy may emphasize the disruption of life by cancer. Beutler's first chapter covers not more than half an hour of her first day back at work, but in such detail that it extends over thirty pages. As the author recreates dialogue and writes in the present tense, the action slows down and involves the reader. Beutler's attention to detail, her description of what is being said – and what is not – creates nuance, enabling us to feel her self-consciousness and awkwardness. The nar-rative becomes a metaphor of her struggle with her illness: the writer continuously dies and writes herself back into life, from discrete moment to discrete moment.

Whether autobiographers choose triumphant or open-ended narra-tives, whether they contemplate or deny the possibility of death, many come to value the importance of family, friends, and colleagues during their illness. The American poet Audre Lorde and the Vancouver writer Rosalind MacPhee both find respite from the stress of battling their illness by seeking the support and company of other women. While

the lovers of some may find it difficult to accept the changes brought
on by a life-threatening disease (Wadler 1994, Duncker 1996), others
discover the pleasures of new love during the course of their illness
(Benedict 1989, 1993; Lenker 1984, 1993). In many narratives the
support of others becomes a mutually beneficial experience and con-
firms Elias's thesis that the experience of community can make life
bearable in the face of death.

In addition, the narratives of those who (must) come to view their
life with cancer as not only a passing experience resist the tendency to
construct meaning in closure. On the contrary, meaning is contem-
plated and created continuously in the sustained involvement with
family, friends, and the public, and the translation of this involvement
into open-ended narrative. With some, it is recreated anew every
moment, in the present tense of a narrative's dialogues – not only
among the characters of the autobiography but, most importantly,
between the writer and the audience. These cancer narratives accom-
plish what Norbert Elias hopes for with regard to the problems of
aging: to remind us that we are "a community of mortals" (1985b, 3).

NOTES

1 Revised version of a lecture delivered at a medical congress at Bad
   Salzufen in October 1983.
2 One might refer to Smythe 1986; Dosdall and Broatch 1986; Mae and
   Loeffler 1992; Hoek and Jongsma 1995; and Mukai and Chan 1996.
3 Some narrators write autobiographies about their life with a partner
   who has cancer (e.g., Borst 1988; Joesten 1994; Seiler 1996).
4 Wander 1979; Koerber 1990; Wilber 1991; Butler and Rosenblum 1991;
   Thielscher-Noll and Noll 1994; Zachert and Zachert 1996.
5 I have cancer! So what?
6 Cancer does not attack the heart.
7 Diagnosis incurable cancer: How I defeated my illness.
8 Less than a year: Our fight against cancer.
9 I have defeated my cancer.
10 See also Jackie Stacey's discussion of success/failure binarie in Stacey
   1996.

10 The Changing Balance of Power between Men and Women: A Figurational Study of the Public and the Private Spheres in Western Societies

ANNETTE TREIBEL

Apart from the self-dynamics of the debate on construction and deconstruction, most representatives of today's feminist approaches endorse the following basic consensus: to be a woman or a man is always based on *social processes* and is not simply a biological fact. The perception of gender is linked to an interactive process of gender performance, on the one hand, and gender perception, on the other. Consequently, this process varies within and between different societies. One will "have" a gender only if one has it for others (Hirschauer 1993b, 34). Like many other sociologists,[1] but more insistently, Norbert Elias continuously hesitates to believe that something is simply "given" and "fixed," but always stresses the importance of process. He should therefore be an ideal author of and for gender theory. Why is it, then, that Elias has hardly ever been noticed by women and gender studies?

ELIAS'S NEGLECT BY FEMINIST THEORISTS

Until recently, feminist-oriented female sociologists neither agreed with Elias nor criticized him to any broad extent; Gabriele Klein's monograph entitled *Frauen – Körper – Tanz: Eine Zivilisationsgeschichte des Tanzes* (1992) is the most important publication referring to him. Indeed, whenever any interest was paid to his work by feminists, it was usually provoked by *methodological* questions; certainly, the demand for impartiality that characterizes the original impetus in women's studies also figures prominently in Elias's work. Gudrun-Axeli

Knapp, for example, referring directly to him, maintains that women and gender studies should not allow political perspectives or personal desires to influence their research (1988). The point is to find a reflective, (self-)critical way to deal with one's partiality.

According to Elias's way of thinking, for research purposes, women could take advantage of their gender-specific experience of being in many ways still underprivileged. However, personal affection alone is not enough. When we look at the methodological program of recent gender sociology, it is apparent that basic research instead of partiality is at issue. According to the title of a publication of the Sektion Frauenforschung (Section of Women's Studies) within the Deutsche Gesellschaft für Soziologie (German Sociological Association), experience alone is not enough anymore; what we need is *experience with method* (Diezinger et al. 1994).

I suppose that Elias's approach is too balanced, considering that it has scarcely been discussed up to the present. He is suitable neither for a so-called standpoint theory (Collins 1992) nor for a (new) method for the deconstruction of patriarchal postmodernity. I do not think it is by chance that feminist theorists prefer to work hard on so-called critical social theories, that is, on Adorno and Horkheimer (compared with the so-called Hanover approach, represented by Becker-Schmidt 1997 and Knapp 1988, 1995), on Habermas (Fraser 1989), on Freud (Irigaray 1980), on Marx (Beer 1990, 1992; Haug 1990; Heise 1993; and the so-called Bielefeld approach), on Foucault (Butler 1990; Fraser 1989), on Bourdieu (Frerichs and Steinrücke 1993), or on Beck (Beer 1992). Approaches such as those of Weber and Elias do not seem to warrant critical attention. In the case of Elias, the fact that his work is not generally known and established as a classic makes a discussion of it even more difficult.

Although it was not at the center of his considerations, the relations between men and women was of great sociological interest for Elias.[2] However, being a women or a man, as a fundamental question of identity and its construction, did not occupy him scientifically. Elias's typical reserve towards political statements and terminological-theoretical definitions (especially when he considered them static) may also be observed in his view on the relations between women and men. His "art of questioning"[3] is characterized by weighing and relativizing, rather than by arriving at definite answers. Consequently, he often runs the risk of generalizing too much and skipping over certain key differentiations. For example, he fails to distinguish between white and black women, women of different ethnic, national, and social backgrounds, and women with different professional status, categories repeatedly highlighted by women in gender studies (see Knapp 1988).

Nor does his notion of labour include extended concepts such as housework, a topic that has marked women's studies since the 1970s.[4] It is true that Elias describes the conflicts faced by modern women in his preface to *Frauen im Zwiespalt* (van Stolk and Wouters 1987), but housework as a central dimension, autonomously and historically belonging to the genesis of bourgeois society, is no subject for him. More-concrete aspects of labour and changes in the labour market specific to gender are not part of his focus either, and like the majority of his contemporaries, he tends to adopt a traditional androcentric perspective. Thus men have a professional function, or at least *do* something, whereas women *are* something. "All these interdependent functions, those of the factory director or the fitter, of a *married women without a profession* or of a friend or a father, are all functions which one person has for other people, an individual for other individuals" (1991a, 16).

In stark contrast to his other categories of research, Elias considers gender to be a static, rather than dynamic, term. For him, it is biologically unalterable and only partially variable socially. Consequently, the relatively new idea of gender as an exclusively social category[5] does not seem to be integratable into figurational sociology. I would like to reduce the problems of the linkage between figurational sociology and feminist theory, however, by recalling components of Elias's figurational sociology which have scarcely yet been referred to, but which I believe may be of great use for the field of gender studies. Certainly, his concept of power balance may be the desideratum of a gender power theory. Before I start to illustrate this concept, though, some indicators of the relations between women and men will be reviewed.

INDICATORS OF GENDER RELATIONS: EQUALIZATION ON THE SURFACE

Women are usually more visible in modern societies than in traditional ones. They may rise socially, and their acquired status may be disassociated from the ascribed status (which was a minor one up to this point because of gender affiliation). Compared to their grandmothers, women have more options today: educational degrees and drivers' licences make them more mobile. If they want to and have the necessary financial means, they can travel. Partners for life and marriages can be choosen freely – within a certain social context – and different ways of life are open to them. On closer examination, it becomes clear as well that such a development is not typical for women alone: men, too, are more free and mobile than their grandfathers. Women and men alike are less attached to the constraints of their social backgrounds and therefore are able to treat each other as equals, at least in principle. The modern relationship of the "couple" is supposed to be based on partnership, to be egalitarian, flexible, and tolerant but also responsible. Consequently, men and women do not live in clearly separated worlds anymore; their living conditions have become more alike, more equal. Equalization has taken place in tandem with individualization, and within this push for individualization women have been strongly and obviously involved. Some examples taken from German life will be listed; they include areas not necessarily noticed by the public or considered to be significant:

1 Women have become increasingly mobile: girls and women engage in male domains, such as riding motorcycles. In 1994, 200,000 motorcycles were licensed to women; ten years earlier the number was 80,000. At present, nearly every third driver's licence for a motorcycle is issued to a woman.
2 Efforts to increase female political participation are made through structural-political measures.
3 The assimilation of gender roles from the men's side is acknowledged institutionally. For example, the head of the Deutsche Hausfrauen-bund (German Housewives' Association) has decided to admit men as members: "considering the social realities, this honourable eighty-year-old organization has renamed itself Berufsverband der Haushalt-führenden [Professional Organization of Housekeepers]."[6]
4 Female ministers in federal and state parliaments not only receive traditionally female departments, such as the Ministry for the Family (see Cornelissen 1993), but also have recently been appointed to head the Ministry for Development Aid, the Ministry of Justice, and the Ministry of Defence (Hoecker 1995, 135)

These indicators at least show tendencies towards equalization. Equal rights and equality have been demanded, and traditional gender roles are being assimilated. However, equality has not been reached yet. Numerous indicators illustrate that traditional gender relations continue to persist.

TRADITIONAL ATTITUDES UNDER THE SURFACE

At the World Conference for Demography and Development in Cairo in 1995, it was repeatedly pointed out that good education for women is the key to solving the world's overpopulation and its development problems. A good education would increase the likelihood for a woman to demand her own emancipation and decide for herself how many children she would have. But as may be observed in industrial countries, that education is no guarantee of real equality. In fact, women are constantly better educated in the West, but their qualifications gradually disappear. In the case of the Federal Republic of Germany, an insignificant female minority holds leading positions in the economy, politics, and science. The changes in the private sphere are not significant either; for example:

1 Nine per cent of the 1.1 million managers in the Federal Republic are women. Of these, only 0.6 per cent are in companies with more than 5,000 employees. The contingent of female chief physicians amounts to 2 per cent.
2 The situation does not look better at universities, where recent numbers show a continuous decline. Among those with doctorates, women make up a mere 28 per cent. "There is nothing left to be said; it has been the same for years" (Limbach 1994).
3 According to a Forsa survey, men still do hardly any house or family work: "Only shopping is divided equally between men and women. But 87 per cent of women still have to do the laundry, 67 per cent the house cleaning, and 68 per cent the cooking. Men only do some repairs."[7]

Consequently, today's relations between men and women are two-faced: on the surface they seem egalitarian, but in reality, traditional precepts still condition the makeup of relations between the genders. How does the concept of the power balance offered by figurational sociology help to explain this situation?

FIGURATIONAL SOCIOLOGY: POWER BALANCES AS A COMPLEX GAME

The Concept of the Power Balance

Elias points out that any discussion about the phenomenon of power suffers from the everyday language we use. He criticizes the materializing tendency in language that opposes process and interdependency. Elias's approach to the phenomenon of power once again illustrates his reservations about questions of value:

One may say that somebody "has" power and leave it at that, although such a usage, which implies that power is a thing, leads down a blind alley. A more adequate solution to problems of power depends on power being understood unequivocally as a *structural characteristic* of a relationship, all-pervading and, as a structural characteristic, neither good nor bad. It may be both. We depend on others, others depend on us. In so far as we are more dependent on others than they are on us, more directed by others than they are by us, they have power over us, whether we have become dependent on them by their use of naked force or by our need to be loved, money, healing, status, a career, or simply for excitement. (1978c, 93; italics added)

The term "balance" suggests a relatively peaceful starting position. It only makes sense to talk about a balance of power if one side does not have or keep a preponderance of power, if no violent assaults on the weaker are possible. Strictly speaking, the term "power balance" seems to make no sense: either one side has power over the other or it does not. If it is exchangeable which group has the power, the term "power" (understood as an asymmetrical relationship between at least two actors), expressing social inequality in its pointed form, is of no use. "Balance" is reminiscent of "equality," power of "inequality."[8] Nevertheless, sociologically the term does make sense, as Elias shows.

Power balance as a figure of argumentation has been developed and illustrated by Elias throughout his work. Time and time again, he shows how, in a developed society where one group will have more means of power than another, it will use this power continuously and consistently in order to maintain the power differential in relation to the subordinate group. The more powerful group will invent a series of defence and exclusion mechanisms against the less powerful group. This is illustrated most clearly in *The Established and the Outsiders* (1965):

1 The more powerful group establishes a claim to a higher understanding of civilization and to have developed its own access to this privileged position. It thinks itself cleaner, more organized, nicer, "better." Elias calls this attitude "group charisma," a term inversely corresponding to the label of "group disgrace" given to the less powerful.
2 The best characteristics of the best and most prominent members are ascribed to the whole of the dominant group, whereas the worst and most shameful qualities of the most notorious individuals are carried over to identify all in the outsiders' group. Elias calls this mechanism a *pars pro toto – distortion*.
3 The more powerful group is characterized by a relatively strong cohesion and monopoly of its power resources. So-called praise gossip about its members and so-called blame gossip about the members of the strangers' group also strengthen the cohesion. Earlier hostilities are buried for the sake of unified behaviour against "the others."

Elias emphasizes that it is nevertheless not possible to hold onto power forever: unchallenged, no group can continuously be in power. On the one hand, the pressure exerted on individuals within the more powerful group in order to keep the ranks closed is increasingly felt to be compulsive. On the other hand, the behaviour of the less powerful changes as well: having supported the power differential for a long time (sometimes for several generations) by keeping silent and through "identification with the aggressor," the excluded will one day resist. They will not accept the label of "group disgrace" any longer; they will develop their own group solidarity and "we-feeling," created out of the denigration or derision of "the upper ones."

Game Models

A systematic, sharpened illustration of Elias's power concept in the form of a figurational analysis may be found in the third chapter of *What Is Sociology?* (1978c). There he presents various forms and evolutionary stages of the power balance as "game models." These have rarely been noticed so far. Elias uses the game models to demonstrate and at the same time abstract the concepts of "process" and "figuration." Like all sociological terms he introduces, the game concept is relational as well. Elias transfers the social analysis to another level: the members of a society become players, and just as in a football or chess game, they have to follow certain rules and have to be familiar with certain constellations in order to participate in the game. The models vary according to the number of participating persons, their game power, and the number of given levels.

The players at the lower levels gradually become stronger, the conflicts increase, and the game becomes more and more complicated. Elias emphasizes that the more complex the type of a game it becomes, the weaker will be the possibilities for the stronger players (considered as individuals) to influence the game. The profits of complexity go together with a loss of power for the individual person. Complexity demands circumspection, foresight, and the postponement of drives. It may cause frustrations, especially among those established at the upper levels. For the involved persons, the "higher order of interdependencies" is not comprehensible any longer; that is why they defend themselves against it. Comparable to the tensions of the civilizing process, every change in the balance of power is often attended by anxiety and must be seen in a detached, thoughtful way. "After a while, it becomes easier to understand that as power differentials lessen between interdependent groups, there is a diminishing possibility that any participants, whether on their own or as groups, will be able to influence the overall course of the game. But chances to control the game may increase again as people become more and more distanced from their own intertwining network and gain more insight into the structure and dynamics of the game" (Elias 1978c, 97).

Direct participation in the game minimizes the ability to perceive what is really going on; indeed, most often it is the arbitrators and spectators who have the definitive reading of what is happening. If those directly participating wanted to regain control opportunities and power resources, they would need more distance and insight. Elias illustrated this phenomenon in his earlier essay "The Fishermen in the Maelstrom" (1987b).

Summed up, then, balance of power means that within a constellation of power, superiority of the stronger group is never absolute; rather, it always stands in relation to the weaker group. The social processes that go along with such a constellation may be considered a swing of the pendulum. Once the pendulum swings in one direction, it cannot help but return in the other. In this relation of the strong and the weak, if the reciprocal dependencies are very high, the swings of the pendulum will be proportionally extreme.

Changes in the Gender Balance

Investigating gender relations in Elias's sense means comprehending them as a dynamic category. They are seen as a "figurational stream," which means that they are not static, with women always subordinated and men always in positions of dominance. Men and women are interwoven by chains of drives and affects, as well as by chains of work and property. Because of these exceptionally strong reciprocal dependencies (compared to other social constellations and interactions) gender relations will have an exceptional structure. They are, to be sure, the most unequal among all the social relations. Earlier studies, especially from the Netherlands, have illustrated this point before, and Stephen Mennell, who summarized and commented upon these studies in his introduction to Elias and figurational sociology, notes that in traditional gender relations, as in all established-outsider figurations, women worry more about men than vice versa. Consequently, it would be an indicator of a changing power balance in favour of women if men worried more about women and tried to get their understanding.

Illustrating gender relations in the following sections as a balance of power, I will direct my attention, on the one hand, to the gender relations created in the public within German politics and, on the other hand, to the privately formed relations of love, friendship, and marriage. But first, I will point out that formulations such as "women" and "men" express tendencies that do not concern every single man or woman.

THE GENDER-GAME MOVES: THE BACK-AND-FORTH OF POWER BALANCES

Quota Systems within German Political Parties

The decision of the European Court on 17 October in favour of a male candidate for an administrative job in the Bremen Department of Agriculture again attracted public attention to the issue of quota systems, a topic that at times has seemed to be overlooked in juridical, philosophical, and specialized political science circles. The fact that the male candidate was preferred over a female one, despite the court's adhering to guidelines for women's support, made the case particularly interesting. In the first version of this chapter, written several months before this decision, I held the thesis that even the Christian Democratic Union (CDU) would not close its mind to a quota system for party posts. I took this as an indicator of a changed power balance in favour of women. But at the CDU's federal party conference on 18 October 1995 (one day after the decision of the European Court) the attempts of General Secretary Hintze, president of the German parliament Süßmuth, and even then-chancellor Helmut Kohl to pass an appropriate resolution failed. Since then, it has appeared reasonable to interpret the development as an unequivocal setback and swing to the right. The long-lasting consequences of these decisions are not foreseeable yet, but it is surely helpful to look at the way in which discussion of quota systems has developed. In the following section I concentrate on this discourse within the political parties; the debate in the public service and other social fields will be largely ignored.[9]

The Greens gave the initial signal for a stronger presence of women in politics, facilitated by guidelines for posts and mandates. They passed a target regulation in 1980 and six years later introduced the quota system. In 1986, at the party convention in Hanover, the equal gendering of all committees was established. This frank, clear, and uncompromising decision (not 30 or 40 but 50 per cent) may be explained by the congruence – at least during the founding years – of the political aims of the Greens and the women's movement. But nonetheless, as Cornelissen states, "the strong individualization process, the desire for economical independency, and the increasing demands of women for professional and public participation had to be taken into account by all the other German parties" (1993, 330). Where this has not happened, such as the continual failure to produce stronger representation of women in "high politics" through self-regulation, structural and political coercion has been seen to be required through the introduction of quota systems.

Within the Social Democrats (SPD), the opinion that self-regulation was sufficient predominated for a long time. The Association of Social Democratic Women (ASF), founded in 1973, repeatedly made attempts to introduce a quota system. Nevertheless, they all failed as a result of the self-satisfied view that the SPD had no need for such regulations. In 1983 the Young Socialists (Jusos) decided in favour of a 40 per cent quota, but only at a party convention in 1988 was a quota system for the whole SPD passed: 40 per cent of all posts up to 1994 and 40 per cent of all mandates until 1999 were to be held by women. "In the year 2013 male and female comrades may draw a deep breath. At that point, the quota system will be crossed out from the statutes. The 'woman problem' of the SPD will be solved at that point" (Lang 1989, 106).

Although the Liberals (FDP) hold on to the concept of self-regulation and considers the quota system to be superfluous, consequently relying on its liberal self-image, the party passed a support plan for women in 1987. The general secretary of the CDU, Peter Hintze, in 1994 was also inclined to consider a quota system for the CDU. However, he did not have in mind the 50 per cent quota of the Greens or the 40 per cent quota of the SPD, but only a 30 per cent quota. This action was motivated by the loss of votes among young, eligible, educated women.[10] The rule of giving 30 per cent of places on the party lists and of committee positions to women was originally supposed to be in force until 1999; no quota would be introduced for direct mandates. In autumn 1994, 416 delegates voted for this approach, supported by the party leaders; 361 voted against it (Sauer 1994, 109). One year later the two-thirds majority necessary for a change in the statutes was not achieved: 496 voted for the quota, 288 against it; 501 votes would have been needed.

In summarizing the discourse on quotas up to now, we should note that the intrusion into male power allowed by the quota system was not universally supported by women's groups (Lang 1989, 72–4). As well, women's partly "deviant," unconventional concept of politics has had the consequence that they are more predisposed to work in initiatives than in political parties. This pattern strongly favoured the presence and representation of women within the Greens. As for the rest, the patriarchal mechanisms of exclusion still repeatedly apply: the representation of women in the present German parliament amounts to 57 per cent; it is 43 per cent in the Democratic Socialists (PDS),

33 per cent in the SPD, 17 per cent in the FDP, and 14 per cent in the CDU/CSU (Christian Social Union) (Hoecker 1995, 137).

Men do not act unanimously: some men's groups, especially those of the left and liberal-conservative elite, suppose that it will be favourable to give themselves an emancipatory, egalitarian image. Publicly, fewer and fewer men dare to act patriarchally. Thus the behaviour of male party members towards women's efforts for equal status within the parties may be described as follows: they are "more or less benevolent allies of the women" (Cornelissen 1993, 335). But the rejection of a simple 30 per cent quota by the CDU federal party convention may indicate a new counteraction in Germany. From an internal perspective, the introduction of a minimum quota of 30 per cent would have been advisable, considering the potential loss of female votes. But after the decision of the European Court, the proposal was left up in the air. Consequently, the discourse on quota systems itself demonstrates that it is never an institutional or organizational matter.

The attitude of women towards the quota system has undergone changes as well. In the 1980s one section of the women's movement criticized the quota and fought against it, arguing that it was too defensive – that it merely stabilized the patriarchy, supporting the career-oriented, "collaborative" women. Today's opponents believe that the quota does not help and/or that they do not personally need it. The existence of both feminist and female supporters, as well as opponents, to the quota system may be interpreted on a number of different levels. On the one hand, the differentiation of viewpoints illustrates that women may afford to have different opinions. The period of isolation, in which only one true feminist position had to be found and supported, has passed. On the other hand, the development could be regarded as a newer adaptation of women to the male society. "The decision of the European Court proves to men that patriarchal resistance is fruitful. This is horrible in times of crisis and harder still in battles of distribution ... It fits right here with the fact that more and more women distance themselves from the quota system – in the hope that they may escape the stigmatization of their sex that way. The divisions between men and women and between woman and woman in the society have just heated up" (Jansen 1995).

From my point of view, the fact that women's opinions on the quota system vary strongly and are discussed in public is an indicator of the normalization of the women's emancipation movement, rather than a rebound. Elias's model of a two-level game may be applied to the changed gender relations, within which women are less helpless and increasingly organize themselves. "Imagine a two-level model in which the strength of the lower-level players is growing slowly but steadily in relation to the strength of the upper-level players ... Usually the lower-level players exercise only latent and indirect influence, one reason for which is that they lack organization. Among the manifest signs of their latent strength are the never-ending vigilance of the upper-level players and the closely-woven net of precautions serving to keep them under control, and which is often tightened when their potential strength increases" (1978c, 89).

In the meantime, one may derive from the degree of women's organization the perception that the game has become even more complex and that one may talk not only about two levels but about a house needing an elevator in order to service all the different (especially upper) floors. The newest decisions against the quota, which were taken within the parties and at the level of industrial law, let the pendulum swing in favour of established men, as they demonstrate their desperate "last stand."

Private Gender Relations: Men and Women in Permanent Struggle?

In the preface to *Frauen im Zwiespalt* (van Stolk and Wouters 1987), Elias makes the comment that, "In this as in other cases, emancipation not only is a fight against power but also a fight within the person itself." Here he is referring to women who are trying to free themselves from the violence of their partners. One of the reasons why this liberation works only slowly, and in many cases not at all, is that the "struggle within the person" stays unconscious and may therefore not develop into an open and obvious "struggle outside the person." For Elias, the less powerful are never only victims. With the concept of "complicity" created by Christina Thürmer-Rohr, a more open power concept (one that would be supported by Elias) has been introduced into gender theory (see Thürmer-Rohr 1989). According to this concept, women contribute to the perpetuation of male dominance through inactivity, rituals of subordination, and "idolization" of heroic male acts. Although, as outlined above, women are in principle capable of caring for themselves and their social betterment, many still prefer a status derived through their partners or husbands.

In their study *Frauen im Zwiespalt* (1987), mentioned earlier, Bram van Stolk and Cas Wouters created the concept of "harmonic inequality as figurational ideal." The ideal is especially supported by women. According to a newer investigation (Meulenbelt 1994, 34), women strive, even if unconsciously, to subordinate themselves within at least one of three categories: age, professional status, or physical height. If the man is younger and less qualified than his female partner, then he must at least be taller than she is. This ideal seems to correspond to real gender figurations more than to the figurational ideal of an egalitarian partnership, as I illustrated it at the beginning in the "public face" of gender relations.

According to Cas Wouters's newer observations, the private sphere is characterized by a permanent constraint to "self-reflection and reflection of others," as a result of increasing individualization (1994a). It is definitely chic to express and show feelings or to be spontaneous, but at the same time one should not demonstrate strong superiority or inferiority. However, even if superiority is not shown, that does not mean that none is felt. Because of the lip service paid to equalization and modernity, the inward tension grows even higher. The newspapers are full of how often a trivial incident can release an explosion in many relationships. Apparently, the "long-lasting breath" that is necessary for the construction of modern, self-chosen relationships exhausts itself far too often (see Beck and Beck-Gernsheim 1994). Women's individualization process, with its private and public consequences, also increases the tensions. Better education and impulses by the women's movement did support women's tendency to move from a "we-I" balance to an "I-we" balance, a tendency that Elias observes for all modern individuals. Possibly, the reference to the women's movement may serve as a healthy corrective to many women's "I-identity."

It helps to understand that women are not "we-less egos." Consequently, they are still part of the women's collective, an anchor that has survived the socialist brotherhood of leftist, progressive males, despite all sister conflicts between difference theoreticians, "new mothers," and deconstructionists. "To the extent to which solidarity between women supports them in their posture to demand it, it also weakens marital ties, the relationships based on partnership even more than the patriarchal ones. Apparently, men do not have the potential for quick self-transformation that is often credited to them" (Hondrich and Koch-Arzberger 1992, 75). From this perspective, the claims for quota systems might be confronted with even greater skepticism. On the one hand, the subjective emotional tensions of men lead to the viewpoint that women may well help themselves and therefore do not need the support of preferential treatment. On the other hand, many women tend to cut off the process of individualization by overdoing it, by retreating, and/or by only going into competition with other women (see Geiger 1993). If they continuously remind themselves instead that they are not "we-less egos," they may hold on to the once-gained strength.

Figurations and Figurational Ideals:
Diverse Ambivalences and the Rhetoric
of the Equal-Rights Debate

Relationships that tend towards equality are by and large those most prone to conflict: nothing is self-evident; everything has to be reflected on and bargained over, the everyday as well as institutional reciprocal contacts. Women's groups, men's groups, advisers on relationships, partner therapies, houses for women, quota systems – these indicators are not the expression of a fight between the sexes, controlled with effort, but rather "normal" indicators of a power balance, within which the pendulum swings extremely strongly both ways. The concept of the struggle between the sexes is based on a dichotomous division: men, on the one side, women on the other, in an antagonistic, partially hostile constellation. The concept of the power balance makes clear that conflicts such as those between women and men have obviously to be seen as costs of modernity, and that they have to be accepted, not necessarily politically but certainly sociologically.

CONCLUSION

The figurational ideals of the genders, especially those of women, have changed, but the figurational patterns themselves have not changed very much. Partly bcause of the specific contradictoriness of their figurational ideals, women contribute to the fact that the power differential with men has not become (even) smaller. Attitudes have changed, but behaviour much less so. Jutta Limbach, for example, points out that the partners of female lawyers talk and think in extremely egalitarian fashion, but their actions do not reflect the same lofty ideals. On the institutional as well as on the private level, equality remains pure rhetoric, all the while maintaining a self-dynamic that men especially think of as real.

Considering the increased game power of women and the multipolar dependency of men (on women, on the public discourse, on institutions), I believe the concept of the power balance to be adequate for discourses of gender relations. Women are no longer without power, and considering Elias's model, they in fact never were. After the women's movement, strategies of isolation and separation, the phase of retreat, seem to have come to an end. The group charisma claimed by men to be more "civilized" and "rational" than women becomes tenuous in the face of the requirements for communication that they must confront. The mechanisms of defence and exclusion, the exclusive possession over power resources and power monopolies, can work only restrictively today. Men, traditionally the inhabitants of the upper echelons of society, have not only accepted the growing game power of women; indeed, they have fought with no holds barred.

Within Elias's argumentation, no group can be unchallengeably in power. Here the word "unchallengeably" is very important, for it begs the question of how violent and extreme the attempts of the more powerful group to maintain its dominance will be. As men and women are confronted with networks of relationships at the private and the public levels, new figurations that have obvious equalization, if not equality, as their consequence become less probable. This pattern will occur even more the less women care about stronger rules of the game that leave the field to the more power-experienced and -spoiled men. Male dominance will only end if women use their power resources and do not gamble with the cohesion already achieved by the women's movement.

NOTES

The German version of this chapter, "Geschlechterverhältnis als Machtbalance: Figurationssoziologie im Kontext von Gleichstellungspolitik und Gleichheitsforderungen," appeared in Gabriele Klein and Katharina Liebsch, eds., *Zivilisierung des weiblichen Ich* (Frankfurt am Main: Suhrkamp, 1997). Translation into English was by Friederike Kautt.

1 Here I think especially of representatives of phenomenological approaches, symbolical interactionism, and ethnomethodology.
2 The so-called Leicester Paper, a text written by Elias on the "Wandlungen des Geschlechtergleichgewichts" (the balance of power between the sexes) has not been published yet.
3 So called by Helmut Kuzmics and Ingo Mörth in their informative preface "Norbert Elias und die Kultursoziologie der Moderne" (1991, 7–31).
4 For an overview of this approach, see Treibel 1995, 67–85.
5 This concept has been developed since the middle of the 1980s by Ursula Beer and others; see Beer 1987.
6 *Die Tageszeitung*, 20–21 1995: With reference to the change in the statutes, the journal of the association states: "the name of the association was changed from Deutscher Hausfrauenbund Berufsverband der Hausfrau [German Housewives' Professional Association of the Housewife] to Deutscher Hausfrauenbund Berufsverband der Haushaltsführenden [German Housewives' Professional Association of Housekeepers]. The term *Haushaltsführende* [housekeepers] is broader than the term *Hausfrau* [housewife]. Men are not excluded verbally anymore. The generalized term also includes people who are employed outside of house. The term *Haushaltsführung* [keeping, in the sense of

management] shows what kind of work a housewife mainly has to do: the management of a small business, care for people, listing and control of the budget, storekeeping, public relations, education, health care, and the like" (*Moderne Hausfrau: Aktuelle Informationen für die Frau in Haushalt und Beruf* 7/8 [1995]:10).

7 *Westdeutsche Allgemeine Zeitung*, 3 March 1994.

8 The term "power balance" was originally developed by political scientists. It was and still is applied to a change of relations between states. Here the flexibility of the participating states and/or governments is very important. Thus a "new power balance" is noted for Europe after the Second World War. However, "because of the great disparity of power between the two superpowers and all the other nations, the latter lost that freedom of movement that previously had made for a flexible balance of power. Instead, the allies, clustered around the two superpowers, tended to transform themselves into two stable blocs, opposing each other across a rigid boundary line" (*Encyclopedia Britannica*, 2:1065). Probably, the term will be less applied after the breakdown of the Eastern bloc as a superpower.

9 With the decision of the European Court (in the committee of judges were – without a quota system – fifteen men) not all state regulations implementing support for women are automatically invalid. According to this ruling, the "absolute and compulsive" priority applied to women in their appointment and promotion, as Bremen's regulation on equal status requires (see *Westdeutsche Allgemeine Zeitung*, 18 October 1995), is inadmissable. Consequently, the introduction of an automatic, strict quota into German industrial law was rejected. The ruling from Luxembourg now goes back to the Federal Industrial Tribunal. On the discussion on quota systems outside the political parties, see Maschner 1993.

10 With 14 per cent, the proportion of women within the CDU is the smallest of all the parties in the German federal parliament, and there is only a 0–10 per cent presence of female CDU politicians at the state and municipal levels.

11 Symbol and Integration Process: Two Meanings of the Concept "Nation"

GODFRIED VAN BENTHEM
VAN DEN BERGH

This chapter deals with the long-term development of the concept and idea of "nation." I will argue that nations should no longer be seen as entities in the same way as states or communities. They are best understood as either symbols and ideal images or as integration processes. The first difficulty in thinking about nations from a process perspective is that in ordinary language "nation" has become a static, unchanging entity. As Elias would have said, "The time has come for a great spring cleaning."

HUNTING FOR MYTHS: STATES AND THE CHANGING MEANING OF "NATION"

The idea of the nation as the unit on which states should be based developed first in dynastic states in western Europe, beginning in France and England. Germany and other European states followed during Napoleon's empire. Dynastic states, like empires, had a pluriform population. Homogeneity was neither a fact nor an ideal. They did not have a standard language or culture, but their people often possessed a number of dialects with a common root, as well as distinct local or regional cultural traditions. The heterogeneity of their populations did not concern monarchs: they saw these people as their subjects, valued instrumentally for their capacity to pay taxes and produce food. The power balances in dynastic states were highly uneven. Such states were thus very different from the later nation-states that were claimed to be homogeneous in terms of language, religion, culture, or ethnicity. Ordinary people had no rights, merely obligations.

The idea of the nation and the nation-state can only be understood as an aspect of the development of states, in which the population changed from subjects into citizens and in which the properties of the ruled became more important for the character of the state than the properties of the rulers. The development of dynastic states into nation-states is closely connected to power balances within states becoming more even, a process that Elias has called "functional democratization"; this is a precondition for political democratization (1978c, 63).

Though older meanings, derived from antiquity, also played a role (Greenfeld 1992; Kohn 1961), the development of the idea of the nation has two trajectories. In the first, nation took over the meaning of "state" as a political community to which philosophers held monarchs to be responsible (Skinner 1978). When entities that we now define as states first emerged – as characterized by the twin monopolies over the means and the legitimate use of violence and taxation – the concept "state" was not yet a synonym for the dynastic realm. The latter was seen and treated as the private property of the king. Louis XIV's famous remark "The state? I am the state" was both a rejection of the meaning of "state" as a public institution and an usurpation of the concept for his claim to absolute power over his realm.

After dynastic realms had become states, "state" – as a term indicating opposition to the king's power – lost its meaning. The term "nation" took over this meaning and function. In France, for example, it began to refer to the neglect by the court of the interests of the merchant and entrepreneurial classes, on which the prosperity of the state was claimed to be resting. From the medieval meaning of groups of students from a particular region or country, *nationes*, it thus came to mean a cultural and political elite (Greenfeld 1992, 4–5) representative of the whole. That could be the aristocracy, as in Poland (the Schlachta), Hungary, or England, but also the Third Estate, which the Abbé Siéyès identified at the beginning of the revolution as the French nation. The term "nation" could also refer to representative political institutions, such as Parliament in England (Breuilly 1993, 84–93). It did not, however, become identical with the whole of a dynastic state-society before the French Revolution.

The second trajectory is connected with the competition between states. The following quote illustrates well how that meaning of "nation" has developed: "ordinary people began to recognize and emphasize the difference in dialects, customs, religion, culture among the states ... Pride in local distinctions and loyalty became more pronounced. The significance of this development was that princes could more easily organize peasant militias and armies to fight their wars for them. In turn, peasants and townsmen believed that they were fighting not just as a duty to a feudal lord but for the independence and honor of their own state" (Walker, quoted in Holsti 1992, 56). This passage does not describe a development in Europe, but the struggle of the warring states in the fifth to the third century BC in China. Should we regard such "we-feelings" and images as "popular proto-nationalism" (Hobsbawm 1990, 6–80) or as Armstrong's "nationalism before nations"? That would be anachronistic, since the idea of the "nation" did not yet exist at the time. It can be added that interstate rivalry forced princes – as soon as they had the means for it – to expand and improve the bureaucratic and transportation infrastructure of their states, thus unintentionally making traditional and localized societies into more centralized and unified ones. This change also occurred in Europe. To make competing societies more prosperous and close-knit was an imperative in elimination struggles at all levels, from dynastic territories to "balance of power" regions and the world at large.

The idea of the nation and nationalism thus had two sources: opposition to dynastic rule and competition between dynastic states. Both were connected to changes in power balances, between the rulers and the ruled as well as between social classes. The French Revolution is less of a caesura, then, than is often supposed. The idea of the nation at first developed slowly, and the concept was used less consciously and in more meanings then after nationalism had developed as a doctrine.

The idea that nations determined the legitimate boundaries of states hardly existed before the French Revolution. For Louis XIV, "France" had little meaning. One reason for the sudden popularity of the new meaning of "nation" was probably the doctrine of popular sovereignty, which replaced that of divine right. Sovereign rule required a clearly defined unit. Humanity was too large and unspecific. But why should existing states be the units within which popular sovereignty was exercised? Still, after the abolition of dynastic rule, a country such as France could be pictured as a community formed by a sovereign people, as a nation upon which the state could be based. The invention of that "we-image" made it possible for the former dynastic state to continue in a new, more legitimate form. Though the boundaries of state and nation were made to coincide, the *French state* remained "them" for most French people, and *France as a nation*, "us." Opposition and "we-feelings" were reconciled in the idea of the nation.

The new meaning of "nation," as the people as a whole, received its strongest impetus from the call to arms for the new French nation, the *levée en masse*. Surprisingly, the revolutionary irregular armies turned out to be superior to the standing armies of dynastic states. Mercenary soldiers lacked the conscripts' fervour of identification and willingness to die for their nation. The superiority of the revolutionary and Napoleonic armies resulted in a French bid for hegemony in Europe. In turn, the formation of the Napoleonic empire in Germany kindled thinking about German national unity as the means for making the country into a great power.

In Germany, elimination struggles were still going on when they had long been finished in France and England. Though many small entities still played a role, two great powers fought for control of German territory, as defined by the myth of the Holy Roman Empire – the Deutscher Nation – Prussia (the Hohenzollerns) and Austria (the Habsburgs). The two rivals were forced to become allies in order to drive Napoleon out.

At the time, the concept "nation" had two meanings in Germany: the entity that should become a great power for the aristocracy and the image to which the "we-feelings" of the German intelligentsia were attached.[1] Fichte combined the two meanings in his *Rede an die Deutsche Nation*. But for Herder "nation" was not to be linked to "state" but to "culture," in line with the self-image of the middle classes (Elias 1978a, chap. 1). His idea of the nation as being based on language and culture did prepare the way for the nationalist assumption that nations were entities in their own right with their own unique character. The next step was the idea that they had the right to their own state.

But did German nationalism lead to the unification of Germany in 1871 (van Osta 1967, 379–82; Zwaan 1996, 392–404)? Was it an example of a nation-first state, as conventional wisdom has it? Nationalism did play a role, first, in response to the humiliation of being conquered and ruled by the French and, second, as a substitute for being excluded from political power for the middle classes. The political power of these nationalist strata remained small, as the fate of the National Assembly in Frankfurt in 1848 illustrated. But the idea that a German nation existed unintentionally helped and justified the attempt of Prussia to eliminate Austria from the struggle for control over "Germany." Austria was a member of the Deutsche Bund, though not of the Customs Union (Zollverein). Bismarck used conflict about reform of the Bund to force war on Austria. Prussia was militarily so clearly superior that it achieved hegemony in the German territory. The victory over France in 1871, the annexation of Elsass-Lotharingen (Alsace-Lorraine), and the creation of the German empire ruled by the Hohenzollerns was the final step in the elimination of Austria by Prussia. But the middle-class elites, as the carriers of German nationalism, remained excluded from political and military power as before.

In both Germany and Italy, unification was therefore primarily state formation that came about through the same elimination struggles as had occurred earlier in other territories in Europe. The devastation of the Thirty Years War, the resulting weakness of German states until the rise of Prussia, and the domestic problems of the Habsburg empire kept the German territory divided. Coming relatively late, the formation of the German Reich (more a dynastic state than an empire) received more support among the population – thanks also to the three victorious wars that produced it – than would have been the case before the rise of nationalism.

German unification was therefore not the natural consequence of the existence of the German nation, which had already come about long before the German state. It was to some extent influenced by German nationalism, but in this way indirectly and unintentionally. German unity was more the result of the dynamics of dynastic state formation than of the German nation acquiring its own state. For true German nationalists, not only should Austria belong to that nation, a relationship that Hitler later concretized, but also the German part of Switzerland: a claim seldom mentioned in connection with the German nation.

The modern meaning of "nation" developed in Europe as part of the process of the transformation of dynastic states into nation-states. The identification of states with nations did not result just from the influence of nationalists, but also because that "ideal-image" legitimated the continuation of states after dynastic rule was overthrown and popular sovereignty had replaced the divine right of kings. The reification of nations – and their personification in international relations – is due to their becoming seen as identical with states. But nationalist ideology also implied that nations were entities prior to states. The ideas of popular sovereignty and self-determination made this doctrinal extension politically feasible. In this way the "ideal-image" of "nation" could not only justify exclusion and even persecution of outsider groups but also became the main justification for independence and emancipation movements, especially in classical and colonial empires, but also in conflicts started by outsider groups against established nation-states. The experience of oppression and discrimination is what these movements share. The idea of the nation was most effective to mobilize people, especially against foreign rule and against enemies, real and imagined. That is why nationalism spread over the world as a whole.

One can now distinguish between different kinds of nationalism that emerged since the beginning of the nineteenth century:

1 Nationalism as part of the transition from dynastic into nation-states in western Europe, in the form both of official and opposition party ideologies and of popular "we-feelings."

2 Nationalism as unification movements in the territories that became Germany and Italy. Similar pan-national or greater-national movements followed, but lacked the same conditions for success.

3 Nationalism as emancipation and independence movements of those population groups treated as second-class citizens in dynastic empires (Habsburg and Ottoman) in central Europe and the Balkans. Here these nations came into being mostly through international politics.

4 Nationalism as part of the attempt of the independent states of Japan and Thailand to reform in order to resist the power and expansion of the West. Similar motives were important in China.

5 Nationalism as ideology and political movement in colonial territories to justify and mobilize people for independence struggles. These ideologies and movements were historically far from uniform, depending both on the nature of pre-colonial polities and on the structure of colonial rule. In some cases, pre-colonial polities already were dynastic states, such as Vietnam or Burma, or civilizations and state systems or empires, such as India and China. In other cases, colonies were no longer populated by indigenous peoples but by the descendants of slaves and indentured labourers, as in the Caribbean and Surinam. Post-colonial states are either successors to a colony as a whole, as in Indonesia or Nigeria, or to administrative units of colonies, as in the French African states or the three parts of French Indochina.

6 The nationalism of secession movements either in established states, for historic reasons and because of political frustration, or in post-colonial states, as the result of being blocked in obtaining a share in political power at the central level.

7 The nationalism of "nationalities" in the Soviet Union, not necessarily coinciding only with the Soviet republics that became independent states in 1991 (Motyl 1992). That nationalism was the result of the privileged position of Russia in the czarist and later Soviet empire; in that sense it was perhaps quite similar to the nationalism directed against the control of the Habsburg empire by German speakers.

8 The "successor" nationalism following the disintegration of the federation of Yugoslavia. A hegemonic war between Serbia and Croatia followed, partly directly and partly indirectly, for the control of Bosnia and Herzegovina. Nationalist propaganda was used to justify the practice of removing and killing people in order to control their territory. Though this was called "ethnic cleansing," its purpose was unlike the goal of "purification" that led to the Holocaust. It served the age-old war aim of conquering and controlling territory, including besieging cities.

Nationalisms learned from each other and took over each others' arguments and myths. But the problem is that, while one can say with reasonable certainty that "this is a state" and "that is not a state," one cannot do so with the "nation." If nations cannot be identified on the basis of generally agreed upon criteria, however, such arbitrariness supported by power could and can lead to bloody conflicts (Ignatieff 1994).

THE HIDDEN WEAKNESS OF NATIONALISM

The different strands in the development of the meaning attributed to "nation" came together in what became its standard meaning in nationalist ideology. As Kedourie succinctly formulated it, "Nationalism is a doctrine invented in Europe at the beginning of the nineteenth century. It pretends to supply a criterion for the determination of the unit of population proper to enjoy a government exclusively its own, for the legitimate exercise of power in the state, and for the right organization of a society of states. Briefly, the doctrine holds that humanity is naturally divided into nations, that nations are known by certain characteristics that can be ascertained, and that the only legitimate type of government is national self-government" (1961, 1). Nationalism was "invented" and "it pretends"; though the doctrine could serve different political purposes, it was not self-evident. France could be seen as a "natural" unit because of its long and continuous dynastic history. Later claims to nationhood had to be projected back into history.

This doctrine, though, hides a crucial weakness. A necessary condition for its validity is "that nations are known by certain characteristics that can be ascertained." If nations could be known in this way, consensus could be achieved as to whether "this is a nation and that is not a nation." Then humanity could indeed be divided into nations as "naturally" legitimate bases of states. But as nations can not be known by a set of given characteristics, many, if not most of them, can be contested – as to their boundaries if not their very existence. Claims abound for autonomy or secession of nations from established states, which themselves claim to coincide with nations. Such claims cannot be reconciled by defining the "nation."

This flaw seriously weakens the doctrine of nationalism. It should provide a general legitimation for the claims of specific nations, but if nations cannot be known by specific properties that can be objectively ascertained, the doctrine crumbles. Whether nations are real because people perceive them as real (the "Thomas theorem") does not help. That may be so, but it does not make any difference for the conflicting claims and problems of legitimation which the idea of the nation raises.

If the characteristics of the "nation" cannot be objectively ascertained so that consensus can be achieved, can the doctrine of nationalism be saved? In 1882 the French philosopher Ernest Renan presented at the Sorbonne his famous speech "What Is a Nation?" which had precisely that aim. He wanted to demonstrate that France was a nation deserving support and loyalty; he realized, however, that this claim was not self-evident in terms of nationalist doctrine. In 1871 France had lost Alsace-Lorraine to Germany, territories considered so incontestably French that they justified a *revanche*. But the inhabitants of those parts of France spoke German. So as a nation, France did not fulfill the most important criterion for being a nation. Renan had to look elsewhere. What did make France into a nation? He completely rejected the assumption that objective characteristics could define nations. Not language or ethnographical character (which for Renan implied descent as well as culture), religion, economic interests, or geography would do as a basis for a general definition of nations. Most contemporary students of nations and nationalism agree. How then to distinguish nations from non-nations?

Renan's solution was later called the "subjective" definition of nations. Its criterion is whether the people making up a nation see it as and want it to be a nation. His description of nations as a "daily plebiscite" has remained rightly famous, but it does not go beyond the Thomas theorem. It is a tautology: a nation is formed by the people who want to form that nation. But Renan did try to give it a more objective basis. He saw "history" as having moulded the special character of particular nations. When the postulated nation coincides with an established state such as France, its history turned into myth can be made plausible. As we have seen, "we-feelings" towards competing and warring states developed before the idea of the nation. Renan argued that nations are formed by shared memories, which impel people to want to keep on living together. Glory and suffering – recorded or symbolized in hero-worship, monuments, flag and anthem, ceremonies and history writing – then become the most important ingredients in claiming a nation. Renan added, "shared suffering unites more intensely than joy." And "as to national memories, mourning is worth more than triumph, it implies obligations and demands, and joint efforts." One hears the song of *revanche*.

Renan believed that identifying with a nation can motivate people to a common purpose. The national vocation can make individuals sacrifice themselves for the survival of the whole. The idea of the nation strengthens the state in its relations with other states and gives its people a feeling of solidarity and of being united, a shared "we-feeling."

The rhetorical force of Renan's definition in English comes through in the following passage:

A nation is a soul, a spiritual principle. Two things, which in truth are but one, constitute this soul or spiritual principle. One lies in the past, one in the present. One is the possession in common of a rich legacy of memories; the other is present-day consent, the desire to live together, the will to perpetuate the value of the heritage that one has received in an undivided form ... The nation, like the individual, is the culmination of a long past of endeavours, sacrifice and devotion. Of all cults, that of the ancestors is the most legitimate, for the ancestors have made us what we are. A heroic past, great men, glory (by which I understand genuine glory), this is the social capital upon which one bases a national idea. To have common glories in the past and to have a common will in the present; to have performed great deeds together, to wish to perform still more – these are the essential conditions for being a people. (1990, 19)

But Renan's objectified subjective definition of the nation, as based on shared memories and expectations, can apply only to state-societies with a long and continuous dynastic history (such as France). It is much more difficult for new states that have developed from units of (classical or colonial) imperial rule. If these can refer to older units (to dynastic states such as Thailand or Vietnam or civilizations such as India or Greece) as their precursors, they can more easily use history in the way that Renan has used it. As we have seen, "we-feelings" before nationalism attached themselves primarily to survival units. Stories of war and resistance with heroes and villains can be used to develop national images, supported by artistic or literary achievements. If all these are not available, it is more difficult to successfully imagine a "nation." Belarus is a good example of this problem. Nations as images cannot do without myths that make them unique. Renan's definition clarifies why states as successful "nations" possess a virtual repertory of myths and stories; that characteristic applies also to nations which have been independent survival units in the past, such as Tibet or the Baltic states.

One could rephrase Renan's perspective as follows: a nation is a state with which its people (citizens) fully identify and are prepared to work and make sacrifices for to ensure its survival or its greatness. Renan's definition is state-centred. In his time the rulers of great powers came to depend more on the "we-feelings" and loyalty of the ruled than ever before. His perspective on the nation is instrumental: nationalism provides social cohesion and compensates for class differences. That populist trait of nationalism makes it highly useful for autocratic regimes too.

At the time when Renan gave his lecture at the Sorbonne, a large number of the inhabitants of France would not have understood his question. Their horizon and "we-feelings" were confined to their own village and, at most, region. Most of them did not yet see themselves as French. "We-feelings" towards the French nation-state only developed under the impact of an extended railway network, obligatory primary education, and conscription (Weber 1976).

GIVEN OR INVENTED?

Renan's definition can only have value if a nation coincides with a historically continuous state. What does that mean for the claims of "new" nationalist movements or for states that have recently come into being following the collapse of an empire? How does one separate the chaff from the wheat? Renan is right that objective characteristics do not work. The criteria most often used, such as language, culture, or religion, are neither necessary nor sufficient. A common "national" (in fact, state) language is the product of government policies, not a primordial characteristic of a nation. But even if such criteria would work, there are many nations with the same language or with more than one language. The argument also applies to culture: national cultures (and characters) become specific the longer and more continuous the history of the state. Still, even to claim a national character for cultural achievements is anachronistic. The content of a specific "national" culture is not easily separated from those of wider or narrower cultural areas or regions. Cultural boundaries are much more diffuse than the boundaries of nation-states. European culture is a good example.

State bonds or specific historical trajectories, especially if they include foreign rule and discrimination, are therefore more important for the success of a nationalist movement in claiming the existence of a nation than given characteristics. Language and culture, of course, can be very important criteria to justify nationalist movements, but so too is religion. The claim of Pakistan to constitute a nation is based on its Islamic identity. But then what of the national claim of Bangladesh? If there can be many nations based on the same religion, how can religion be a criterion for demarcating specific nations?

In recent years ethnicity has again become fashionable as an objective criterion for nationhood, serving also as an explanation for the origin of intrastate wars, such as those in the former Yugoslavia. Ethnic nationalism and conflict are often asserted to be the primary cause of these wars, as of those in other parts of the world. Gagnon (1994–95), however, has demonstrated that the thesis of "ancient ethnic hatreds" having produced the wars and "ethnic cleansing" in the Balkans is wrong. It is curious that before "ethnic" became popular to explain integration conflicts within states, nationalities were seen as the groups that might acquire their own states. Ethnicities or ethnic groups, on the contrary, were seen as minorities that were either too weak and small or too dispersed to qualify for more than cultural autonomy and special protection from government. Examples are Indian tribes in the Americas, Aboriginals in Australia, and Gypsies in Europe. But late-coming immigrants in the United States, such as the Italians, Poles, or Irish, were also called ethnic groups, set against those of British origin, while the black descendants of slaves were seen as a "race" (Moynihan 1993). As in the original meaning of nation, "ethnic" and a fortiori "race" are used to designate groups of foreigners, usually stereotyped. Migrants in contemporary Europe are thus also labelled "ethnic." In Africa "ethnicity" has been substituted for "tribe," as a less pejorative and more objective term, but not necessarily as a more accurate one, given mass migrations, colonial creation of "tribes," and political manipulation of conflicts (Ranger 1983).

The very different groupings all designated as "ethnic" only share the characteristic that they are supposed to be objectively different from other groups. This difference does not have to be a common descent, though that is often the implied or hidden meaning. Such a supposition seems self-evident when "ethnic" groups possess recognizable physiological characteristics, especially skin colour. But physiological characteristics in fact are just that, nothing more. They do not mean that people have the same culture or language or that they come from the same state. To speak of "ethnicity" in such cases can lump people together who have little or nothing in common. If "ethnic" is understood as common origin or descent, it must imply genetically determined characteristics, and it becomes a euphemism for "race." A counter-argument often made is that "ethnic" does not have to refer to common descent at all. It simply refers, it is said, to a common culture. But as we have seen, that view does not solve the problem of definition.

As an objective criterion for demarcating nations, ethnicity could therefore only work if it were possible to identify genetically specific, homogeneous groups. But mass migration, conquest, crossover marriage patterns, warfare, and slavery have shaped human societies much more than living in isolation; Iceland may be an exception. Humanity is, in any case, one in the sense that it has a single genetic potential that makes physiological differences irrelevant. That is clearly demonstrated in the capacity to learn; that physiology nevertheless matters so much is the consequence of stigmatization of outsider and minority groups by established groups, in order to maintain their power and privilege. It is what explains the recurrent search for objective criteria (such as postulating genetic differences in IQs) to demarcate human groups from each other.[2] In that respect, the idea of "nation" can serve a similar ideological purpose as the idea of "ethnicity": to defend the privileges of the powerful as justified by their special character. But nation and ethnicity have the same weakness: confusion about what they in fact refer to.

A prominent researcher of the relationship between states and nations, Hugh Seton-Watson, had to come to the conclusion that "nations" (and by implication, "ethnicities") cannot be defined on the basis of scientific – that is, objective – criteria (1977, 5). Since he saw nations as objectively existing entities, this problem baffled him: "Thus I am driven to the conclusion that no scientific definition of a nation can be devised, yet the phenomenon has existed and exists." If neither the subjective nor the objective ("scientific") ways to define nations have succeeded, what does it mean to say, "yet [the nation] has existed and exists"? What is it that exists? Are we back where we started?

In the recent literature on nations and nationalism, most authors adopt the subjective perspective, though not Renan's hortatory approach. Nations, they say, are invented or constructed by actual rulers or the leaders of nationalist movements as potential rulers. In that vein, Ernest Gellner writes, "Nationalism is not the awakening of nations to self-consciousness: it invents nations where they do not exist" (1983, 48). Once invented, though, nations become real entities (though they coincide with states) since they are not invented at will but because they fulfill necessary functions – mobilization, legitimation, cohesion – for modernizing societies.

The historian E.J. Hobsbawm agrees: "With Gellner I would stress the element of artifact, invention and social engineering which enters in the making of nations." He adds, though, that forgetting – of horrors committed in the past – is just as necessary as invention. Renan knew this already: "Forgetting, I would even go so far as to say historical error, is a crucial factor in the creation of a nation" (1990, 11).

This perspective on the forming of nations has been elaborated further by Benedict Anderson. Nations, he argues, are too large and too populous to form traditional "face-to-face" communities (1991, 6–7). Their members cannot all know each other. To feel as a "we," they will have to identify with anonymous societies and imagine these to be communities. What Anderson does not mention is that communities have to be homogeneous, contrary to the pluriform dynastic states. Homogeneity is the most important implication of the idea of nations. What Anderson says is that people will be more prepared to identify with, and make sacrifices for, a homogeneous community than an anonymous entity. So, one can conclude, dynastic rulers had to present their states as nations in order to stay in power. Independence movements also derive their legitimacy from claiming a nation for what at the time is often no more than a unit of imperial or colonial administration with a pluriform population.[3]

This emphasis on invention, creation, and imagining quite obviously refutes the idea that nations are God-given or natural entities. But the modernized subjective approach is not quite satisfactory either. Why were precisely these nations invented and not others? Why do some attempts at invention succeed and others not? In theory, there is no limit to the number of potential nations to be invented. Why could France become a nation, but the Habsburg empire could not? Why did a Soviet nation fail to develop, while the American nation did? And what are the characteristics of nations once they have been invented or imagined?

These questions bring us back to the objective approach. Should there not have been prior identification with an already existing entity for people to identify with a newly created nation? If so, do nations not then develop out of an already existing ethnic "we-identity"? If they cannot be invented at will, must they have an ethnic origin, an objective base, as Smith and Armstrong argue? Smith sees what he calls "ethnies" as the entities preceding all nations. He does recognize that these have come about, not by genetically specific descent, but by the development of cultural boundaries. But that argument brings us again to the weakness discussed earlier. As an entity, "ethnie" faces exactly the same problem of ascertaining its characteristics as "nation." Smith assumes the existence of preceding entities instead of prior "we-feelings" directed to dynastic states and myths about battles and heroes (for example, Jeanne d'Arc) that help in the transformation of dynastic into nation-states.

ENTITIES OR SYMBOLS?

There is thus still no satisfactory answer to the question "What is a nation?" The political impact of nationalist doctrine has contributed to the confusion. The global spread of nationalism has made it appear increasingly self-evident to treat nations as particular kinds of entities demarcated from each other. That view implies that (national) minorities are equally entities which are separable from the real or proper nation, a concept that, in turn, can easily make them into outsiders, people of lesser value, who can be treated as second-class citizens – or worse. National minorities, "ethnic" groups, or indigenous peoples can become separate and distinct entities only because the idea of the nation as a homogeneous entity that claims the state justifies it and makes it self-evident. In dynastic states, especially in cities, population groups with different origins and characteristics could, as is self-evident, live together in reasonable harmony.

Curiously enough, the authors who stress that nations have to be invented or constructed see them after the moment of creation as really existing entities clearly demarcated from each other. In Anderson's perspective, that view is quite clear: when imagination has done its work, actual nations have been formed. But what ascertainable characteristics do these then have? By what kind of criteria are they demarcated from each other? And why does imagining work for a majority and not for minorities? All that remains in the dark.

It is therefore necessary to re-examine the assumption that nations are a kind of observable entity. If it is impossible to ascertain their characteristics in such a way that they can be demarcated from each other without anyone being able to contest the outcome, can the self-evident treatment of nations as entities be maintained? Once we stop seeing them as given or invented entities, it becomes clear why Seton-Watson had to resort to his paradoxical statement giving a ghost-like existence to nations.

Nations are not entities with concrete boundaries. They are best understood as being a special kind of symbol and ideal-image, the content of which is filled and sustained by myths. The doctrine of nationalism is a myth that all nationalists share. But as symbol and ideal-image, each nation needs its own myths and stories to be unique. "Nation" is a more normative, hortatory concept than a descriptive one. States are entities; nations are integrative symbols. States are politically organized on the basis of at least two central monopolies, the reach of which determines the boundaries of their control and demarcates both territories and peoples. Nations appear to be entities because they coincide with states and can conceptually substitute for them, as in United *Nations* or in *nation*-state. Political leaders, for symbolic reasons, often prefer to speak of their goals for the nation than for the state.

My proposed shift in perspective goes against the established ways of thinking about nations. Nationalism, as an ideology, needs to see them as entities with specific characteristics. As a symbol, "nation" can refer as well to the image of a Third Reich, purified and powerful, as to the cohesion and solidarity of democratic states such as Norway or the Netherlands or to a new state that has emerged from a former empire. In themselves, the symbol and ideal-image are neither good nor bad. It all depends on what goals the symbol is used for. It can be used for different purposes and in different ways. Nations are not "imagined communities"; they symbolize existing or desired state-societies as communities that should be homogeneous, solitary, and free from foreign rule. The concept "nation" can also symbolize the need for sacrifice and the need to prepare for war against rivals or foreign oppressors.

TWO MEANINGS OF "NATION"

In ordinary language, "nation" is used as part of both "nationalism" and "nation-state." That fact points already to the term's having two meanings. It can refer to a quality possessed by a state; nation-states are indeed different from dynastic, colonial, or imperial states. As "nation" in nationalism, the word can refer to "we-feelings" (patriotism), as well as to the political movements and ideologies, based on the general doctrine described by Kedourie, and to the specific myths that any "nation" as symbolized entity needs. The two meanings in ordinary language have in common that "nation" refers to a homogeneous entity. This definition implies that groups which do not belong to the proper nation are seen as objectively being "national minorities" that do not have equal rights as citizens. If the object of nationalism is defined by reference to language, religion, culture, or descent, people who do not fit those criteria will ipso facto be outsiders, if not subhumans who may be eliminated. As nationalist ideology has determined the meaning of "nation" in ordinary language, it has been successful.

All nationalisms, in fact, have to develop myths to claim their nation as unique. Such myths draw the profile of the nation in question with the help of selective assertions about history and culture, and they include language, religion, or other identity-establishing characteristics. Their most persuasive components are often "we-they" images, based on the "best-worst" stigmatization mechanism discovered by Elias and Scotson in established-outsider relationships between neighbourhoods of a small English town (1995, xix–lii). They also contain stories about fateful historical events, about "our" heroism and "their" atrocities. Nationalist movements of outsider groups need boundary criteria to demarcate their nation's territory both from the state they are part of and from its neighbours. They have to show their nation as being united and demonstrating solidarity and as providing a better future for its members. The nation as symbol is further expressed by a national flag and anthem, by monuments and museums, and by commemorative celebrations, parades, and festivities.

This meaning of "nation" is ideological and political. The other meaning, as referring to integration processes of states or to the phase in state formation that follows dynastic or imperial states, is not tied to a specific ideology. It does not postulate specific characteristics that include and exclude. It derives its meaning from an existing state, old or new. For nationalist ideology, it can be "arbitrary" (the meaning is not based on a specific named people). The problem is that the boundaries of all dynastic, imperial, or colonial states are "arbitrary" in that sense, since they do not result from "natural" entities, but from war, conquest, or sale. Their level of integration derives at first from the infrastructure (transport, security, education, economics, administration) developed by prior rulers.

"Nation" in this sense is the symbol for a process in a particular direction best described as integration. For former dynastic states, the beginning of this process can be indicated in the way that Elias observes in his 1970 paper "Processes of State Formation and Nation Building": "We can begin to speak of a nation if the functional interdependencies between its regions and its social strata as well as its hierarchical levels of authority become sufficiently great and sufficiently reciprocal for none of them to be able to disregard completely what the others think, feel or wish" (1970a, 274). "Nation" here refers to existing states that begin to develop in a particular direction: "we can begin." Any beginning implies a direction – becoming more highly integrated – and an end. The ideal-image of a nation, as can be found in the writings of nationalist intellectuals, is a unified, egalitarian, harmonious, and democratic society. Elias has given the concept of "nation" the combined meaning of "phase" in the state-formation process and "ideal-image" – the symbol of the end result of that process. In that way, "nation" becomes a process concept.

From this perspective, other categories than the supposed characteristics of "nations" become crucial. Integration implies denser interdependencies, more even power balances, and more encompassing patterns of identification in the relations between rulers and ruled, between social classes, and between the regions of a state. The development in the direction of the ideal-image of the nation can then be seen as an aspect of a more general transformation of society, for which industrialization and democratization (modernization for Gellner) are shorthand formulas.

The integration perspective can be elaborated further. Interdependencies have two aspects: territorial and functional. The first refers to the development of what is often called a "national" economy, a network of interdependencies that become more coterminous with the state territory as a whole than with local or regional markets. Such a statewide network of interdependencies could only develop after a prince had pacified his realm, making it safe for trade and transport. The second aspect is the increasing differentiation of social, bureaucratic, and economic-financial functions that makes the interdependencies and the power balances between rulers and ruled and between social classes less uneven than before. Industrialization helped this process along. During the nineteenth century it was furthered by conscious government policies, pushed by the military and economic rivalry between states. Under their aegis, statewide infrastructure and communications networks, in material terms (roads, railways, canals, harbours) and in human terms (especially compulsory primary education but also conscription and, later, social-insurance arrangements), were created. Governments thus engaged in what one can call "nation building" or development. That included the centralization of rule and the use of the nation as a symbol justifying this activity, which Anderson has called "official nationalism." Regions became more integrated into the state, both socially and economically. In terms of changes in "we-feelings," this mutation occurred slowly. Weber has shown that for France, considered the most highly integrated nation-state in Europe, only after 1871 did peasants begin to see themselves as Frenchmen instead of identifying with their village or region.

Widening patterns of identification are an integral aspect of the development of nation-states. Its popular, democratic associations made the nation a better symbol of the crystallization of "we-feelings" than the state. Before the French Revolution, neither the aristocracy nor the central rulers identified with the common people. They did not even see them as human beings. Aristocrats did not identify with the state but with the person of the monarch they served, with their own families, and in a wider sense, with aristocratic society at home and abroad. They came to identify with the state in which they lived not much before the end of the eighteenth century, probably in England first because the English monarchy was too weak to assume "absolute" power (Greenfeld 1992, chap. 1). In contemporary nation-states it has become unthinkable that ambassadors or high civil servants could move in their functions from one state to another. But in dynastic states, monarchs regularly employed foreigners in the highest positions precisely because their loyalty and dependence was to the rulers only. In the nineteenth century the czar offered Bismarck, then leaving St Petersburg as the ambassador of Prussia, an appointment as ambassador of Russia.

For the aristocracy, class identification for a long time remained more important than nation or country. For the Third Estate or bourgeoisie, the situation was different. As we have seen, in France "nation" was already in the eighteenth century a term of opposition, implying a demand for reform of state policies to take more account of the interests of the bourgeoisie, claimed to coincide with those of France in its competition with England. That view led the Abbé Siéyès to state that the Third Estate was the "nation." For the German bourgeoisie, identification with Germany as a nation – with its language and culture – was a way for the bourgeoisie to distinguish itself from the aristocracy.

The development of "we-feelings" follows changes in power balances. In the relation between rulers and ruled that pattern is quite clear. Until the Industrial Revolution, the power balances between rulers and ruled changed very slowly; then a working class with latent power resources began to form. The socialist intellectuals claiming to be its representatives at first saw the working class as an international class, as was the aristocracy before. In their Communist Manifesto Marx and Engels wrote: "workers have no fatherland; one cannot take away from them what they do not have."

That they speak of "fatherland" instead of "nation" may indicate that "nation" had not yet become as self-evident as today. But they were right: workers were not yet represented at all in politics. For them, the state was primarily the police. Marx and Engels's theory even caused the International to believe that working-class solidarity would prevent war in Europe. In 1914 that expectation came to naught. The national "we-feeling" of social-democratic parties, represented in parliaments, proved too strong.

Why did the internationalism of the working class slowly but surely disappear? The main reason was that to obtain political influence, it had to organize itself within the political framework of its own state. In response to the fear of its growing power, governments, with Bismarck leading the way, initiated social-insurance legislation. It was meant to weaken the social-democratic movement, but it unintentionally strengthened it, because trade unionists managed to staff the administrative institutions needed to implement the new legislation (de Swaan 1988, 192–7). In that way, workers gradually obtained a "fatherland" and acquired a stake in politics and the state, so that they could then feel part of the nation too. During the First World War, socialists for the first time joined coalition governments. After 1945 the development of the welfare or service state was a further stage in the process of nation formation, although it is unclear whether such high levels of national integration will be maintained. But it may be concluded that nation formation or national integration of states is not an either-or question. It refers to a complex and gradual process in which all the aspects of Elias's definition have to be examined. The degree of density of interdependencies and of asymmetry of power balances between rulers and ruled, between social classes, and between regions, including the degree of reciprocal "taking account" in the political system, can be used as an indicator to assess the level of national integration – or the chance of disintegration.

The differences between the degree or level of national integration processes in different parts of the world are great. What I have described above is no more than an orienting model based primarily on western Europe, where the transformation of dynastic to nation-states first began. A more comprehensive theoretical perspective must, for example, take account of the consequences of the Meiji revolution in Japan, of the reforms of the Thai dynastic state, and also of post-imperial and post-colonial states.

In the present world of states, "nation" is still a powerful symbol. All states are supposed to be nation-states, even though their levels of integration are very different. That nations are symbols rather than entities can make nationalist rhetoric very strident and uncompromising. Nationalist movements and parties fear losing legitimacy and popular support, and therefore stick to their guns. The image of a nation can appear to have coercive force: "To what end, and in whose name, I ask myself, this senseless nationalist imperative, which enforces membership of a nation to which you are driven and in which you are instructed ... Don't count on me; I won't go along with you. You won't teach me to hate anyone. And to tell you the truth, the more you call on me and remind me of my nationality, the less I feel I belong to it. The more you appeal to my patriotism, the less patriotic I feel" (Glenny 1992, ix–x).

Nations as symbols are not self-evident. Boro Todorovic, speaking in 1991 on YUTEL independent television in Belgrade, showed that not all designated members of a "nation claimed" think and feel alike. To see "nation" as a symbol implies that more attention has to be given to its political uses. If rulers talk about the nation, they are likely to want something from the ruled.

SIMILARITIES AND DIFFERENCES

The general doctrine of nationalism has been very successful. With few exceptions, the world is now fully covered by states claiming to be based on nations. Few states do not claim that they are so based. To prevent the rise of centrifugal forces, Indian leaders at first did not want to see India as a nation. Its cohesion came from its being an age-old civilization. But then a common culture is supposed to be a distinguishing characteristic of a nation. Where culture was seen to includes religion, it created problems for India and led to its partition even before independence (Devji 1996).

Homogeneity, as a supposed property of nations, is usually more myth and ideal-image than reality. If it becomes a political goal to be enforced, it can lead from discrimination of minorities to "ethnic cleansing." Homogeneity is a result of long-term integration processes that make minorities disappear. The Scandinavian countries, the Netherlands, and France are examples of such highly integrated state-societies, though long-distance migration now disturbs the self-evident character of their "we-feelings." The United States has always combined a high level of national integration with a recognition in politics of different "we-groups" named according to their country of origin – the "ethnic vote." Members of the black minority, however, were for a long time treated as second-class citizens. And the more recent Asian and Latin American immigrants were, if at all, very slowly admitted to mainstream American society; still, compared with the former Soviet Union or Yugoslavia, the United States's nationalism has been successful. Though all nations as symbols and images have to be invented, not all attempts to do so have succeeded. Why has the number of nation-states remained limited? It is not so difficult to develop the mythology to justify the historical and present existence of a nation. In 1500, western Europe still had about five hundred separate independent political entities, of which twenty remained in 1900 (Tilly 1961, 24).

Relatively few of these have now become a justification for centrifugal movements. These need a specific developmental explanation, such as Hechter's "internal colonialism" (1975). They are not signs of a general revival of nationalism. Neither is the breakup of the Soviet Union, since its successors were Soviet republics that did not necessarily coincide with entities claimed as nations. What, then, are the conditions making for a high level of national integration in established states or in "nations" aspiring to become states? There are few comparative studies of national integration processes available, so I can only make some general remarks.

As to established states, an important condition is "age" and "continuity." The more durable the "we-feelings" towards a national image are, the more self-evident and reified they become. The newer the states are, the more likely it is that their level of national integration is low. If they have waged a war of liberation, they may remain highly integrated for some time afterwards, until centrifugal forces – regional, class-oriented, or in the form of warlords – become stronger, while fighting for control over the central state monopolies.

As to new entities claimed as "nations," they will be the more cohesive, the more their populations are discriminated against and treated as second-class citizens. It helps if they can invoke a prior state, whether a nation or a dynastic state. They mostly do not satisfy the last condition. Colonial empires and colonial states or administrative units are designated for pragmatic reasons as "nations" by national liberation or independence movements.

Classical empires, such as the Habsburg, Ottoman, or czarist-Soviet empires, by definition could not develop into more highly integrated nation-states. They might not have disintegrated if they had been regarded by the general population as nations in the sense of objects of "we-feelings." Instead, in all three cases, "we-they" images developed towards the core groups ("nations") of their pluriform populations, whether Austrian, Turkish, or Russian. However, the population of many now-established nation-states was as pluriform when they were still dynastic states. But these states did develop into relatively highly integrated nation-states.

Will "nation" and nationalism remain as influential as they were? In a time when many interdependencies, especially economic, financial, and technological ones, are becoming increasingly global, when massive long-distance migration especially makes established nation-states more pluriform again, "nation" is no longer an attractive symbol and image. Many established nation-states are forced to return to the pluriform and cosmopolitan composition of dynastic states. Homogeneity has always been more of an ideal than a reality. But as an ideal it may become counterproductive when it decreases, rather than strengthens, the integration of states as a necessary condition for providing all citizens with decent living conditions.

NOTES

1 That is the beginning of German nationalism, the development of which has been described and explained by Elias (1996a, 134–71) as a change from an orientation of the middle classes to humanity and the moral problems that it raises towards national culture and the morality of power politics.

2 For another argument that this search is bound to fail, see Hobsbawm 1990, chap. 2. In a line of reasoning similar to Renan's, he sees as the only way in which nations can have a partly objective or historical basis "the consciousness of belonging or having belonged to a lasting political entity." The contrary view is still defended by Smith (1986), who is convinced that all nations are successors to an "ethnie" (his term).

3 McNeill (1986) argues that political or survival units in the past have always been polyethnic. The idea of homogenous nations could only arise in western Europe because states in fact were more ethnically homogenous there than in other civilizations. Migration, however, now begins to make the ideal of homogeneity and the idea of nations obsolete. One may argue, however, that the populations of dynastic states were not so much homogeneous as melting pots which had become integrated to such an extent that their differences were no longer important.

12 The Second Pillar of State Power: Figurational Explorations of the State and Money

REINHARD BLOMERT

In *The Civilizing Process*, Norbert Elias compares the French court with a stock exchange, in which "people ... exert pressure and force on each other in a wide variety of different ways" (1994b, 475). By this, he means that people's physical behaviour is being shaped without the threat of physical force. He describes the way of life at court in the following manner:

Every individual belongs to a "clique," a social circle which supports him when necessary; but the groupings change. He enters alliances, if possible with people ranking high at court. But rank at court can change very quickly; he has rivals; he has open and concealed enemies. And the tactics of his struggles, as of his alliances, demand careful consideration. The degree of aloofness or familiarity with everyone must be carefully measured; each greeting, each conversation has a significance over and above what is actually said or done. They indicate the standing of a person; and they contribute to the formation of court opinion on his standing ... The court is a kind of stock exchange; as in every "good society," an estimate of the "value" of each individual is continuously being formed. But here his value has its real foundation not in the wealth or even the achievements or ability of the individual, but in the favour he enjoys with the king, the influence he has with other mighty ones, his importance in the play of courtly cliques. (1994b, 476)

In the first week of December 1996, the New York Stock Exchange was troubled by the so-called Greenspan shock, which affected the financial market deeply. Alan Greenspan, the chairman of the U.S.

Federal Reserve Board, had talked about the "irrational exuberance" of the asset values in stock markets. On 5 December he had put forth the question, "How do we know when irrational exuberance has unduly escaped asset values, which then become subject to unexpected and prolonged contractions?" The British *Financial Times* wrote: "Few people in the world choose their words as carefully as central bankers. Every phrase and nuance of everything they say is scrutinized by financial markets. Billions of dollars can be knocked off the value of assets by a single stray adjective" (1996, xii). The stock exchange is famous for the quickness with which its shares can change their values: they go up one day and down the next. It looks like the game at the French court that Elias describes, where the opinions about persons or circles would change from day to day, from minute to minute. In the days and weeks following Greenspan's remarks, stock brokers sold stocks, and the expanding supply led to falling prices. In Tokyo, stocks went down by as much as 3 per cent, and Wall Street was down by 2.5 per cent. Greenspan is not a king, and the stock exchange is not a court. Nonetheless, his words carry weight the world over on stock markets, like the words of a king at Versailles. In this context, however, he did not question the ranking of some of his courtiers but, rather, the value of shares. The *Financial Times* commented further: "Mr. Greenspan was, on the face of it, simply restating orthodox central bank policy that due weight should be given to the movement of asset prices when forming monetary policy judgements. But it was the timing of the remarks that made them so critical" (1996, xii). Greenspan's words had been understood as a warning of a possible bubble effect. Such an effect had pulled down Japanese stock values since the late 1980s into the worst recession since the Second World War.

What differs and what is similar between the court and the stock exchange? Brokers do not have to look for the personal grace of Alan Greenspan. They listen to his words because his comments can mean thousands of dollars of gain or loss when "he" decides to raise or lower interest rates. And losses and gains mean ruin or new investment opportunities for companies and their workers. The rumours at the stock market resemble the rumours at court, with one specific difference: the stock exchange motions are not directed at individuals and their well-being, but at the expectation of future market prospects. Not the value of a courtier but that of the shares of a company is subject to the opinions which float around stock markets.

Elias grew up in the first part of the twentieth century, one of the most climactic half-centuries the world has ever seen – fifty years that brought about the complete changeover to a secular orientation in western Europe. When the First World War came to an end, the European order had lost the most important of its monarchies. The state of the post-aristocratic epoch was now oriented to economic performance and its two pillars, production and finance. The European states of the nineteenth century in general were governed by a coalition of two classes, aristocrats and the middle class. These ruling classes tried to maintain production by keeping the working class down. Workers had not yet reached the status of equality with aristocrats or members of the bourgeoisie. They had limited rights with regards to voting, and for many it seemed that Marx was right: the state was merely a tool of the ruling classes. Production was organized in a military-style order. For some time the Social Democrats, the worker's party in Germany, were even proscribed by Bismarck. Strikes and demonstrations were not allowed, and the state intervened with its police force whenever this rule was broken. In Germany this was the heroic phase of the workers' emancipation movement, which led to the legalization of their party. The end of the Kaiserreich brought about an important change in rulership: the parties of the two "outsider" groups – the Catholic party and the Social Democrats – came to power in combination with a small group from the liberal middle class (the so-called Weimar Coalition). The aristocrats and also to a great extent the middle class did not accept the emancipation brought about by the workers' party. The Weimar Coalition instituted the legalization of strikes, demonstrations, and collective bargaining and introduced labour laws, labour courts, and unemployment insurance. Thus it improved basic working conditions and stabilized the results of workers' emancipation through laws; indeed, many of these gains are the mainstays of labour codes in Germany today.

The defeat of Germany in the First World War had been sealed with a treaty that forbade the country to maintain armed forces of more than 100,000 soldiers. After hyperinflation, Weimar Germany recovered with the help of American capital and was stabilized economically by the mid-1920s. Yet the finance and currency situation in the industrialized world was weak. Throughout the First World War and the 1920s and 1930s the currencies of the industrial countries moved to and fro, now abandoning, now maintaining the gold standard. This fluctuation brought about serious trouble for the financial markets, which before the Great War had been as global as they are today. Trade and monetary exchange had been at a high level; mutual acceptance of currencies on the basis of the gold standard gave basic security. When the gold standard was given up, the mutual acceptance of currencies and international trade became much more unsteady. Animosities, reparation claims, and fears poisoned the atmosphere: "With the erosion of credibility, international cooperation became even more important than before the war. Yet the requisite level of cooperation was not forthcoming. Three obstacles blocked the way: domestic political constraints, international political disputes, and incompatible conceptual frameworks" (Eichengreen 1995, 10).

There were other obstacles that impeded the functioning of cooperation: the newly established Federal Reserve Bank of the United States "disrupted the clubby atmosphere with which the European central bankers had managed the pre-war system" (Eichengreen 1995, 11). The power of Social Democratic politicians at the same time politicized the decisions of the central bankers further in an unknown manner.[1]

A series of international conferences on war debts, currency standards, and reparation questions held at this time should have led to the recovery of credibility and currency security for international trade and commerce. The political atmosphere, however, was so embittered that such difficulties had no chance of being overcome. All such commissions and conferences in the end led to only a single institutional currency agreement, the Bank for International Settlements (BIS), formed in Basel in 1930. In October of 1929 the international monetary order began to break down, and when, in 1931, American capital was simultaneously drawn out of Germany, it signaled a strong setback for the legitimacy of the Weimar Republic.[2] The republican order, which had been built upon economic potential, seemed defeated. Immediately after this development, the military option was resumed again by the German government, ultimately leading to the Second World War.

Peace after the war brought about the division of the world into two parts under the respective leaderships of the United States and the Soviet Union. For West Germany as well as Japan, this outcome meant the end of military autonomy and sovereignty. The newly established West German army in 1956 was put under American authority. Its priority was to shoulder part of the military and financial burden of the Cold War. The West German army never got access to atomic weapons and therefore always remained a minor partner in the NATO alliance. On the economic side, there were two main commercial alliances within these two camps – Comecon and the OECD.

I will focus here on the dimensions of the relationship between state and currency that resulted in some characteristic changes after the catastrophic breakdown at the end of the 1920s. The most important step was the Bretton Woods agreement of 1944. It led to a financial order with fixed exchange values and capital controls for the nations involved. At this point, "Global foreign exchange trading ... was negligible in the late 1950s" (Helleiner 1994, 1), and the capital transfers were small. There was no pressure from interest groups to leave the system of fixed exchange rates. At the end of the 1960s the international finance markets evolved and reached by "the early 1990s a daily value of roughly $1 trillion" (Helleiner 1994, 1). Deregulation had opened the borders, and capital controls were successively abandoned. Beginning with Britain, which "abolished its forty-year-old system of capital controls in 1979" (Helleiner 1994, 146), a dynamic competition in liberalization took off which further eroded capital controls. The financial markets had won a degree of freedom "unparalleled since the 1920s" (Helleiner 1994, 146). Countries that would not give up these controls lost confidence, and their currencies sank in value.

The security of production and of currency systems must be the primary economic task of states. Keeping production going is, of course, no problem for old industrial states with elaborated industrial relations,[3] but as capital is mobile and able to cross borders, the state becomes involved in competition with other states within the world market. The conditions for capital investments are evaluated by the different states in terms of their tax system, the quality of their human capital, including the bargaining processes that influence the inflation rate,[4] and their social and ecological requirements for production.

In a lucid speech, Wolfgang Streeck (1997) has pointed to the civilizing effects that the threat of capital evasion now has on state action. To react to the threat of disinvestment, which would endanger production and currency and ultimately the credibility of any ruling party, the state has two options: to arrange international standards for the condition of investments, such as capital taxes or social standards for companies; and to make the first move in a process of liberalization.

The first option is reached only by international agreements, and the result of such negotiations will depend on the balance of power between industrial countries. So most states attempt the easier path and choose the second option. Such deregulation leads to a competition of liberalization between the big industrial states. The disadvantage of this option is that it might result in domestic problems of lower social standards (which seem to "rise to the bottom") and possibly raise taxes for their fixed factors of production. On the other hand, the competition between states may also result in unintended benefits for consumers: for example, the raising of ecological standards[5] or of health standards.[6]

If states do not want to lose the capital of stockholders, they have to keep their currency convertible and hold domestic prices and exchange relations stable. On 3 September 1996 the New York Times commented, "Inflation has at last been tamed, if not mastered." At a meeting of central bankers and economists from different countries, the chairman of the Federal Reserve Board said that this was "a testament to the effectiveness of the conduct of monetary policy around the world in bringing inflation to heel over the past 15 years or so." And he seemed to celebrate a victory over a long-hated enemy: "And now for the first time in at least a generation the goal of price stability is within the reach of all major industrial countries as well as a substantial number of others." There is no doubt that central bankers have lived up to the challenges of the markets since the breakdown of the Bretton Woods system. What are the means available to the central banks? The value of the currency does not rest on the stores of gold bullion at Fort Knox; rather, central banks keep deposits of foreign exchange and safety values of all kinds and try to maintain the currency at a balanced level using a vast assortment of instruments. The set of tools that central bankers use to maintain the international status of their domestic currency has evolved and been refined during several of these crises, dating back to the one that caused the collapse of the Bretton Woods system in 1971.

I will give examples of the two sorts of reactions to the challenges faced by national and international monetary systems. They demonstrate the two options for national economic policy described above. Each of these reactions followed a crisis that troubled the financial markets, and each showed how the system of balances between the economic powers works. In most Western countries the state has control over domestic banks, because these institutions are the promulgators of the national currency. The controlling institutions are the central banks. When a bank fails, a part of the circulating money is destroyed, and in major bankruptcies, confidence in the national currency is jeopardized. The possible consequences of masses of people plundering their accounts would bring the money circulation into deep crisis.

HOW TO TAME BIG MONEY

"In the late afternoon of June 26, 1974, Bankhaus I.D. Herstatt of Cologne [one of the oldest private banks in Germany] was closed by German authorities." What had happened? "The bank had suffered huge losses in its foreign exchange department, which it had covered up with fraudulent bookkeeping. In particular, the bank had speculated wildly in currency markets, borrowing in different currencies from banks around the world, and it had lost the gamble" (Kapstein 1996, 39). Some other institutions, such as the Franklin National Bank, the twentieth largest bank in the United States, and six years later the Banco Ambrosiano at the Vatican,[7] were also involved in this gamble. It brought about a new situation for the central banks: they had to actively stem the speculatory pressures on their currency. How could the state and its national currency be protected against the pitfalls of free-moving capital? How could fraudulent speculators be kept in check?

The Herstatt failure left thousands of customers of small foreign banks unpaid. Because the German authorities handled the case as a domestic bankruptcy, they were bluntly criticized by foreign institutions: "outstanding issues between the German authorities and Herstatt's creditor banks were dealt with bilaterally, either at the official level (that is, between the central bankers of Germany and other countries) or at transnational levels (that is, between the banks and authorities directly)" (Kapstein 1996, 40). Bankers asked the Deutsche Bundesbank (the German federal reserve) to honour Herstatt's debts and intervene in the foreign-exchange markets in order to support the smaller banks, which had suffered from the failure or were even about to go bankrupt. But the German central bank's mandate did not extend this far, and so it refused to act as lender of last resort.[8] Rather, the German response to the bankruptcy was to establish a private bank fund which would provide private insurance for German banks in the case of future failures. "Nonetheless, the Herstatt crisis did force banking supervisors in different countries to begin speaking with one another on a regular basis and sharing information, and soon that process would become formalized by the Group of Ten central bank governors" (Kapstein 1996, 41). Thus the Herstatt scandal was, first, the result of the collapse of the Bretton Woods system, which was built on fixed exchange rates. After the end of the fixed price system of currencies, a floating of exchange rates began, which became a field of commercial action as well as allowing access to some criminal bankers. Secondly, it was the starting point of regular consultations by central bankers, later formalized in the supervisors' group of the G-10.

The state had delegated a part of its sovereignty. Its power to set its own standards of action in a particular field had become useless, since this area had grown beyond the borders of the state's realm of influence. As long as banks worked primarily on a national level, exchange rates mattered only for trading and transnational purposes. When they expand into foreign countries and the interdependencies between foreign and domestic banking become more and more intertwined, national currency autonomy is eventually "up for grabs." So to what extent should a commercial foreign bank be allowed to act like a domestic bank? How can this branch of a foreign bank be controlled? Who is responsible for any loss that it might incur?

The series of scandals from Herstatt, Franklin National, and Ambrosiano to the Bank of Credit and Commerce International scandal and the Baring's collapse has improved the rules for cooperation among the G-10 central bank governors. The solution to the question of who controls the foreign branches of banks came to be "international cooperation based on home country control" (Kapstein 1996, 2). So how could good money be sheltered against speculation? How could the state tame the pressures of financial markets? There was no other means than the control of banks, the supervision of the balance of their engagements in different fields of commerce. And it is clear that this supervision had to refer to information from abroad, when the borders for capital were opened in the early 1980s. The Basel accord of 1988 shows that international cooperation is a solution for a problem that brought high risks for all highly developed industrial countries and was not limited to a national level. The interdependence of markets and money circulation is growing fast, but the state has not yet lost its control over multinational companies and the international flow of money. Instead, it has strengthened supervision, but its independence to act unilaterally, which it used to have in the 1920s, has been lost; the autonomy of national decision-making has been eroded through multinational commissions and accords such as the Basel accord. These international rules involve quality standards of banking, such as minimum capital adequacy: "risk weighted standards" of deposited assets,[9] which allow one to estimate the security of a bank. These standards make banking business more open to evaluation. Private rating agencies have also established more precise standards of confidence for bank companies, ranging, for example, from category AAA to category CCC, the latter being the worst situation, where investor confidence hovers near zero.

In the aftermath of the Basel accord and the Iraqi invasion of Kuwait, several Japanese banks got into trouble and went bankrupt because the minimum capital adequacy standard had not been reached. As Japanese banks used to fall easily within the ranking of the top twenty banks in the world, the value of the yen went down only a few points, but the great "bubble" has not yet been forgotten in the Japanese economy.

HOW TO TAME AN ECONOMIC OUTSIDER'S POLICY

The main sort of solution at hand tends to strengthen state control over the actions of private banks, while at the same time weakening its autonomy through the implementation of international standards of supervision. The limits of action for private banks are not really defined, but the crossing of limits that are set by the new standards are calling into question the credibility of those banks which fail to maintain these standards. It is a type of civilizing process for behaviour that banks are having to undergo. There is another sort of restraint, which does not concern private subjects of economy but, rather, state action. The case of the British economy in the 1970s shows the high degree of interdependency between the states of the free-market monetary system and at the same time the new limits of national solutions for domestic economic policy. "Britain had borrowed extensively in international financial markets in 1974–76, but in 1976 British authorities suddenly found that operators in those markets, particularly those in London, began speculating heavily against the pound (even though Britain's current account situation was improving and inflation was decreasing)" (Helleiner 1994, 124–5).

Does it matter whether this was only a logical reaction of financial markets or a reaction of financial markets in alliance with monetarist theoreticians?[10] The effect was that "the pound's depreciating value reinforced domestic inflationary pressures, which only further undermined confidence in the pound" (Helleiner 1994, 125). "Faced with this growing currency crisis, the Labour government initially sought offsetting financing from the IMF and foreign central bankers. Because the pound was subject to what IMF Managing Director Witteveen called 'unreasonable exaggeration,' a $5.3 billion credit was extended in June by the BIC, Switzerland, and most of the G-10 countries" (Helleiner 1994, 125). This was the first step. Colleagues of the central banks of other nations helped by lending money to support the endangered British currency. In this phase there was no attempt to interfere with British domestic affairs. But as the crisis continued, and "it became apparent, that more money would be required," the central bankers changed their attitude. "In response to Prime Minister James Callaghan's further requests for financing, the United States and West Germany stated that they should extend more money only if Britain agreed to an IMF stabilization package that included strict monetary targets and spending cuts" (Helleiner 1994, 125).

Did British policy-makers lose authority in favour of the speculators? U.S. economist James Tobin "proposed a cooperative intitiative in which all states would impose a transaction tax on spot foreign exchange transactions in order to 'throw some sand in the wheels of our excessively efficient international money markets'" (Helleiner 1994, 126). His recommendation, to support the idea of state autonomy against market forces, "fell like a stone in a deep well" (Helleiner 1994, 126). The British government had only two choices: to accept the IMF program or to insulate "the domestic economy from external financial pressures by imposing ... comprehensive exchange controls

... [which] would be extremely costly and would effectively shut down London as an international financial center" (Helleiner 1994, 127).

After intense sessions of the Labour cabinet, in the end the IMF package was given the support of the British government. This, as Helleiner puts it, was a turning point in relations between the industrial countries: the balance of power in deciding economic policies had significantly shifted to those decisions make by supranational commissions of experts. The cost of having insulated British capital controls would have exceeded that of maintaining the nation's policy autonomy.

The British case was not unique. When the American administration called for co-operative support from West Germany and Japan for its weak dollar in 1978–79, it won assistance at first because "a dollar depreciation would be harmful to [Japanese and German] domestic exporters, for whom the United States was still the most important foreign market. The OPEC countries were also major defenders of the dollar in this period because both the revenue from oil exports and a large proportion of their assets were denominated in dollars" (Helleiner 1994, 131). But when the U.S. administration seemed to make no effort to reduce the federal deficit and curb inflation, confidence in the dollar began to sink again. This downturn had dramatic consequences: "Saudi Arabia began to sell its dollar reserves and warned of an oil price increase ... West European governments signaled their dissatisfaction with US unilateralism by beginning negotiations that led to the creation of the European Monetary System (EMS) in March 1979, resulting in the establishment of relatively stable European exchange rates and a new currency, the ECU" (Helleiner 1994, 131).

In the U.S. Treasury Department some consideration was given to ending the role of the dollar as the world's key currency. But at the last minute the idea was abandoned for the same reasons as the British administration had earlier realized – abandoning a role in the world monetary system turned out to be more costly than simply accepting a certain amount of discipline imposed on the state by private investors and other national governments. And so we see that the globalization of financial markets compels the governments of the industrial countries to submit their domestic budgets to supranational standards. The world's financial markets, once deregulated by liberal politicians, have led to the establishment of relatively strong economic constraints which clash with domestic autonomy. The European efforts to construct a fixed system of currency exchange value relations[11] is to be seen as a consequence of the U.S. financial policy at the end of the 1970s. As a smaller regional version of the Bretton Woods system, it has some protective capability for the European market to stave off the volatile U.S. dollar. But it is certainly not a shelter for the autonomous policies of European states. Kapstein writes here: "For nation-states, financial globalization has complicated the formulation of both economic and foreign policy; indeed, it has largely eradicated the distinction between the two. First, on the economic side, public officials have discovered that it has become increasingly costly to defend economic policies against market pressures, given the unimpeded flow of international financial transactions. Such policies are immediately translated by foreign exchange traders into currency valuations, and consequently result in a money flight into or out of the country. Several European states – notably Great Britain – were reminded of this lesson during the summer and autumn of 1992, when the pound sterling was battered by currency markets and ultimately forced to leave the European Community's Exchange Rate Mechanism (ERM). These developments, in turn, created severe tensions within the community, especially between Germany and Britain" (1996, 6). Thus foreign relations are to an increasing degree subject to economic constraints.

There are two points still left open on the agenda of the G-10. How can they control the dirty money that covers the world with nearly $500 billion a year and endangers economic policies? How does one deal with states that are not party to their settlements? How to deal with tax havens? These problems, as far as they are economic ones, are interwoven with the general problem of the degree of internationalization present in co-operation. Tax paradises are sometimes territories of minor sovereigns, princes, or dukes from the extinct Holy Roman Empire, long-forgotten private fiefdoms of the British crown such as the Channel Islands and governed by the British Parliament or the Vatican, which has special autonomy (and its own coins) but no borders with the Italian state – in short, places where "state" applies in a sense that Elias never intended, and where the *ancien régime* can survive by using the niches these territories possess between the state powers. Every scandal that comes out of these areas simply strengthens the pressure of the European Union, as well as of the G-10 nations, to compel these "states" to enter into the international settlements.

The pillars of state sovereignty have changed: decisions under national policies have to be attuned to the rules of international commissions; national rules are subject to standardization, which is the result of compromises between independent states. These states have some basic political elements in common – democratic rules, relatively free markets, convertible currencies, relatively open borders to trade and commerce – and they have the same interest in mitigating chain reactions, such as the one that went from New York to Europe in October 1929, when the money system was so deeply shaken. The politics of war, games of national isolation, and state regulation went on for nearly two generations after that crash. States are now beginning to furnish new nets that will set highly "civilized" standards of behaviour in the financial markets. The question still arises, however, whether and how states will manage the increasing domestic competition concerning the distribution of taxes and the social burden that will ensue as a result of these new regulations.[12]

NOTES

1 We read in Eichengreen, "The monetary authorities were attacked from the left for upholding outdated monetary doctrines and from the right for pandering to the demands of the masses. They consequently lost much of the insulation they once enjoyed" (1995, 9).

2 "Although international markets flourished in the late nineteenth and early twentieth centuries, they were almost completely absent from the international economy during the three decades that followed the financial crisis of 1931" (Helleiner 1994, 1).

3 It seems to be a problem in Asia, with its young industry, as the recent strikes in South Korea might suggest.

4 See, for example, Hall and Franzese 1996.

5 Streeck has pointed to the so-called California effect, which occurred as California set higher environmental standards for automobile equipment. The costs for car manufacturers to furnish this equipment simply for the Californian market would have outweighed the cost of providing all cars in the U.S. market with such upgrades.

6 The BSE scandal that troubled the farmers of the European Union will in the end raise the health standards and controls for beef.

7 Its chairman, Roberto Calvi also chairman of the Franklin National Bank. His well-publicized death – he was found hanging by his neck from Blackfriars Bridge in London on 18 June 1982 – led to the revelation of the strange connections between the Vatican and the Italian-American Mafia. Aside from alleged crime-organization connections, though, these cases remind us of the recent Baring's Bank scandal; the failure of this bank showed the problems with the low level of bank regulation in Britain.

8 There are some distinct differences in the legal construction of central banks that concern not only this "lender of last resort" function.

9 The overall risk is differentiated between the risks of the two so-called tiers: common stocks and securities.

10 "an interplay between the views of these [monetarist] commentators and the financial markets, which seemed to reinforce each other" (William Keegan and Rupert Pennant-Rea, quoted in Helleiner 1994, 125).

11 The European Union's Exchange Rate Mechanism, or ERM.

12 As a postscript, we should note that Asian banks did not satisfy the requirements of the Basel accord; it is linked to systems with balances of power and democratic control, thus to systems that include people with long-term interests. Fuelled by trends and expectations of hyperprofits, risk capital of different origins accumulated in Asia. The Asian crisis followed, and not only did it destroy capital, but the impaired financial system also shattered some political systems and their superficial democracies. Bankers, economists, and politicians have now turned their attention to new foreign-exchange controls in an effort to correct the exuberances of deregulation.

13 The American Civilizing Process

STEPHEN MENNELL

Sombart once famously asked, "Warum gibt es in den Vereinigten Staaten keinen Sozialismus?" The question which prompted this paper is an adaptation of that one: "Warum gibt es in den Vereinigten Staaten keinen *Eliasismus*?"

I have long been puzzled by the failure of Norbert Elias's work to make much significant impact among sociologists in the United States – still the world's largest, best organized, and perhaps most influential bloc of sociologists. In Europe, Elias is at present less used and cited than Habermas, Foucault, or Bourdieu, but there is a significant minority of social scientists and historians actively employing his ideas. In the United States, however, one can list on the fingers of one hand sociologists who have shown an active interest in him. Such attention as he has received has been overwhelmingly focused on the first volume of his first book, *The Civilizing Process*. This focus is also evident in the recent work of the American historian Peter Stearns, *American Cool*, which, while actively engaging with Elias and Cas Wouters in studying the construction of a "twentieth century emotional style," makes little or no systematic attempt to relate the formation of habitus to long-term state-formation processes, power struggles, established-outsider relations, involvement and detachment, and the rest of the concerns that underlie Elias's theory of civilizing processes. In short, no one in the United States seems as yet to have been inspired by his achievement in "bridging the macro/micro gap" in a way that is at once theoretical and empirical, not merely conceptual. This American neglect can no doubt in part be explained at the level of the sociology of contemporary sociology. But that would be a rather tedious and pointless exercise. Indeed, I am more interested in reasons rooted in American *society* rather than in American *sociology*.

Elias's appeal is, I think, diminished by an abiding sense of American exceptionalism (Lipset 1996). Superficially at least, most of his writings seem to be concerned specifically with Europe. He writes about state formation, once again a hot topic among comparative-historical sociologists after decades of neglect, but he focuses in most detail on state-formation processes in medieval and early modern Europe.[1] He writes about aristocratic courts and the habitus of courtiers in *ancien régime* Europe, something to which, at least superficially, there was never any counterpart in the United States. Indeed, he seems to write about just those aspects of European cultural heritage which the Founding Fathers were consciously rejecting and escaping.

Nevertheless, I have a feeling that a serious attempt to apply and develop the theory of civilizing and decivilizing processes in relation to the United States may eventually prove revealing. This chapter presents only a few preliminary thoughts which are intended to grow into a book. What I propose to do is to take the four main sections of *The Civilizing Process* and connect their concerns to American history. The four sections were, to recall them, "on the Sociogenesis of the Concepts 'Civilization' and 'Culture'"; "Civilization as a Specific Transformation of Human Behavior"; "Feudalization and State Formation"; and "Synopsis." I shall take each in turn.

CIVILIZATION AND CULTURE IN AMERICAN SOCIETY

Elias was writing in the 1930s against the background of a century and a half of intellectual debates centring on the notions of "civilization" and "culture," culminating in the then-recent essays of Thomas Mann, Oswald Spengler, Alfred Weber, Sigmund Freud, Marcel Mauss, and Lucien Febvre (Rundell and Mennell 1998). So the first section of *The Civilizing Process* deals with the accretion of diverse and powerful evaluative connotations around the word "civilization." This concept, he writes, "expresses the self-consciousness of the West ... It sums up everything in which Western society of the last two or three centuries believes itself superior to earlier societies or 'more primitive' contemporary ones. By this term, Western society seeks to describe what constitutes its special character and what it is proud of: the level of *its* technology, the nature of *its* manners, the development of *its* scientific knowledge or view of the world, and much more" (1994b, 3). By the nineteenth century, the ways in which people in the West used the word "civilization" showed that they had already largely forgotten the historical and social *process* of civilization: for them it was largely a completed and taken-for-granted accomplishment that carried with it a great sense of pride and superiority.

The great American historians Charles and Mary Beard, in their 1942 book *The American Spirit*, showed that – whatever else of their European heritage they were casting off – the Founding Fathers certainly did not abandon a preoccupation with problems of "civilization." From Thomas Jefferson in the early republic to Robert MacIver in twentieth-century American sociology, American intellectuals followed European discussions of civilization and culture, contributed to them, and considered how the issues related to the United States. From quite an early date, a conception of "American civilization" became bound up with a sense of American superiority, especially over Europe (as well as over Native Americans and Blacks), just as in Europe, "civilization" had become a badge of superiority over the natives of the lands subjected to European colonialism and over the lower classes of European societies themselves. Moreover, in America there was always a strong sense of human progress, which was combined with at least as strong a sense that the virtues of civilization were, if not innate in every individual American, then at least inherent in the founding conditions of American society. In other words, Americans too came to forget the *process* of civilization through which they had arrived where they were, and now took the *state* of civilization as something very much for granted.

Thomas Jefferson is a pivotal figure, both in his intellectual dominance of the early republic and in the lasting influence that his patterns of thought have had in the United States. Contrasting the ways of *ancien régime* Europe with those of the nascent republic, he wrote in a letter to William Johnson dated 12 June 1823:

The doctrines of Europe were that men in numerous associations cannot be restrained within the limits of order and justice, but by forces physical and moral, wielded over them by authorities independent of their will. Hence their organization of kings, hereditary nobles, and priests. Still further to constrain the brute force of the people, they deem it necessary to keep them down by hard labor, poverty and ignorance, and to take from them as from bees, so much of their earnings, as that unremitting labor shall be necessary to obtain a sufficient surplus barely to sustain a scanty and miserable life. And these earnings they apply to maintain their privileged orders in splendor and idleness, to fascinate the people, and excite in them an humble adoration and submission, as to an order of superior beings. (Jefferson 1907, 15: 440)

This passage contains several anticipations of Elias's concerns a century and half later. Let us, for the moment, set aside Jefferson's comments on what Elias was to call the "court society," which Jefferson had seen at first hand at Versailles on the eve of the French Revolution; social display and conspicuous consumption were to become a characteristic of American elites only long after his day, in the Gilded Age so mordantly analyzed by Thorstein Veblen. The passage just quoted also contains an obvious anticipation of the distinction between what Elias was to call *Fremdzwang* (constraint by other people – "forces ... wielded ... by authorities independent of their will," in Jefferson's phrase) and *Selbstzwang* (self-constraint). Jefferson, however, like most earlier writers, treats the two forms of constraint as a static dichotomy rather than as a continuum, a tension balance, and the outcome of developmental processes. This difference is especially clear in a passage further on in the same letter in which he states his belief and that of his political allies

that man was a *rational* animal endowed by nature with rights, and with an *innate* sense of justice; and that he could be restrained from wrong and protected in right, *by moderate powers* confided to persons of his own choice and held to their duties by dependence on his own will. We believed that the complicated organization of kings, nobles and priests was not the wisest or the best to effect the happiness of associated man ... We believed that men, enjoying in ease and security the full fruits of their own industry, enlisted by all their interests on the side of law and order, habituated to think for themselves, and to follow reason as their guide, would be more easily and safely governed, than minds nourished in error, and vitiated and debased, as in Europe, by ignorance, indigence, and oppression." (Jefferson 1907, 15: 441; italics added)

Jefferson rightly speaks of habituation. Yet the overall impression given by his writings is that a peaceful, civilized society is more the outcome of consciously enlightened political institutions than of a long-term, unintended, and blind process of development. He appears to take for granted an American habitus in which *Selbstzwang* is relatively strong and stable, rather than in constant interdependence and tension with the forces of *Fremdzwang*. Notably, he assumes that all human beings can be governed and can govern themselves by reason, rather than seeing that as an outcome of a process of rationalization – which, as Elias emphasized, is a process of *emotional* change (more exactly, a change in prevailing standards of emotion management) or change in habitus (1983, 92). The immediate consequence of this belief seems to be that from the start, internal pacification was taken too much for granted – at least by Jefferson and his faction – and seen too much as a one-sided product of Americans' peaceful and reasonable habitus, rather than as the outcome of a two-way process over time. They thus seem to have underestimated the continuing need for an effective state monopolization of the means of violence, possibly with long-term consequences. In a similar way, Jefferson's idealism (in both senses) leads him to see the dominance of kings, nobles, and clergy in *ancien régime* Europe as something to be condemned as unenlightened, rather than to ask why agrarian societies have everywhere been dominated by priests and warriors, or to perceive the taming of warriors as a necessary element in any process of state formation.

Of course, it would be absurd to criticize a thinker of two hundred years ago for not having anticipated all the insights of modern sociology, psychology, and political science. Nevertheless, Jefferson is important as the most eloquent initiator of a tradition of social thought and social criticism which has endured to this day and which, while closely shadowing European debates about "civilization" and "culture," has stressed certain unique – or at least, exceptional – characteristics of "American civilization." The Beards identify some of the main propositions underlying notions of civilization in the early United States. They include a belief in human progress, with the United States providing special scope for it; the belief that America, though an offshoot of Europe, has never been a mere duplication of it in ideas, institutions, or practices; and a kind of multi-linear conception of social development rooted in the idea that American civilization, being fundamentally different from Europe, "must continue to differ, for history is irreversible" (Beard and Beard 1942, 162–4). In particular, from the beginning, Americans have held to a form of what, since Louis Hartz's book *The Founding of New Societies*, has been known as the "Hartz thesis." That is to say, American civilization was different because

1 American society had been founded late, in the full light of the modern age, already in the late Renaissance and the Enlightenment.
2 Its population was made up of immigrants of many different European nationalities, but mainly from the middle and working classes, not from princes, nobles, and ecclesiastics.
3 Despite poverty and slavery (widely deplored long before the conflict that led to its abolition), there was relatively great equality of social conditions.
4 Its rich endowment of natural and agricultural resources, in a vast area of land, provided abundant opportunities.

The dominant theme in discussions of "American civilization" from the earliest stages was an optimism and activism towards collective social life and the general good – an "ethical will to overcome suffering and other evils and make the good or the better prevail in individual behavior and social arrangements" (Beard and Beard 1942, 3). But from the mid-nineteenth century onwards, especially after the Civil War, a more pessimistic counterpoint becomes more assertive. One can speculate about the reasons for this change: the mood of defeat in the South; the closing of the frontier in the 1880s, with its implications for diminished opportunities; the more conspicuous social inequalities in the northern cities during the post-bellum Gilded Age. Intellectually it was linked to the rise of social Darwinism, one of whose greatest exponents, the Yale sociologist W.G. Sumner, saw civilization as artifice, disciplinary and constraining in character. He wrote that "civilization has cost mankind many inconveniences and it has, in many respects, involved experiences that we do not like. It has subjected us to drill and discipline; the civilized man is disciplined in his feelings, modes of action, the use of his time, his personal relations, and in all his rights and duties ... [C]ivilized man, instead of living instinctively, as his ancestors did only a few centuries ago, has become a *rationalizing* animal" (quoted in Beard and Beard 1942, 339). Sumner may have been influenced by the German proponents of *Kultur* in opposition to "artificial" and francophile *Zivilisation*. He more certainly anticipates the pessimism of Freud in *Civilization and Its Discontents*, as well as some of the concerns that Elias was to take up in a more detailed and sociological manner in his work.

To sum up, then, the sociogenesis of the concept of civilization in America shows strong links with, and resemblances to, the parallel process in Europe. Not surprisingly, however, the concept took on different nuances in the United States – nuances of American exceptionalism – just as Elias demonstrated the development of different emphases in France and Germany.

THE HISTORY OF AMERICAN MANNERS

Having studied the sociogenesis of the concept of civilization in France and Germany, Elias turned to the specific changes in behaviour in connection with which it had arisen. For, as he remarked, the value judgments associated with the concept were familiar, but "the facts to which they related" were much less so. What are the facts about changing manners in America? Fortunately, there are already several good studies of the history of American manners, notably the works of Arthur M. Schlesinger Sr and Peter Stearns (1994; Stearns and Stearns 1986) and the continuing researches of Cas Wouters.

American exceptionalism was again the first note struck by Schlesinger in his short but elegant study of American etiquette books,

Learning How to Behave, although the final impression he leaves with the reader is of the broad similarity to Europe. He begins by listing five conditions that flavoured the American behavioural canon from the outset (1947, viii–ix):

1 The colonies were settled for the most part by people who would not have been familiar with the etiquette of good society in the Old World.
2 There was never any native hereditary aristocracy of the kind that in Europe set standards of taste and behaviour (although Schlesinger and other American writers tend to be a little too literalistic or legalistic in making this point; after all, approximate functional equivalents did emerge in particular regions and periods).
3 There was the "necessity of taming a wilderness before cultivating the graces of living," a necessity constantly renewed as the frontier was pushed westward.
4 There was a constant influx of immigrants, "who faced all the difficulties of the native-born as well as the additional one of having to master the unfamiliar customs of their English-speaking neighbors."
5 Finally, as in many other new countries (such as Australia), for a very long time, men outnumbered women; women's role as a source of civilizing pressures on men has been recognized by sociologists since at least Sombart's 1913 essay *Luxury and Capitalism*.

Nevertheless, the main phases of development appear in much the same sequential order as in Europe. In early colonial America there were even sumptuary laws, enacting dress codes for each stratum of society, as in Europe. Civility and decorum were enforced on the poor by the law, with ducking stools, stocks, and fines for flirting. These draconian penalties were being relaxed in America, as in Europe, by the late eighteenth century (Schlesinger 1946, 13).[2] English and occasionally French and Italian manners books, and the American adaptations thereof, enjoyed considerable circulation in the colonies. Among the Founding Fathers, both George Washington, in his youthful compilation from French and English sources, and Benjamin Franklin, in *Poor Richard's Almanack*, contributed to the genre of advice and injunctions on behaviour.

Discussion of American behavioural codes is complicated by differences between the historic "sections" of the United States. The South was for long an exception to American exceptionalism. As Schlesinger wrote, "it was in the South, notably in Virginia, that conduct books had the most eager readers, for after the first toilsome years of breaking the wilderness the successful planter, dwelling on his broad acres amidst many black vassals, proceeded deliberately to model his life on that of the English landed gentry" (1946, 6).

From the early nineteenth century, however, etiquette books in America began to undergo a process of "naturalization." Between the War of 1812 and the Civil War, as Schlesinger comments, "the steady rise of countless humble folk to higher living standards, and the admission of all white men to the ballot and the right to hold office ... could not fail to leave their mark on social usages, particularly in the North" (1946, 15–16). Some American etiquette books continued to appeal to English or French usages for authority, but the majority scorned the stiffness redolent of royal courts and advocated instead a "truly American and republican school of politeness," in which all superfluous ritual would be abandoned (Schlesinger 1946, 21). Tocqueville, visiting America in the age of Andrew Jackson, remarked on the relative ease of polite social intercourse there.

This relative ease can be interpreted from within Elias's theory as a typical symptom of relatively equal balances of power between social strata (and between the sexes) compared with Europe. Of course, things were changing in Europe too at this time. Schlesinger observes that nearly all the etiquette books, whether native or foreign, in the generation before the Civil War carefully avoided references to the etiquette of inferior towards superiors (1947, 21). Elias observed the same tendency in the European books, and it is highly significant. Rather than for reasons of hygiene or other "rational" arguments, it had been for "reasons of respect," as I have noted elsewhere, that these new standards of behaviour were justified in the closing decades of the *ancien régime* (1989, 47). That was when "pressure from below" upon the stratum of courtiers was at its greatest, and when the dialectical mechanism of "colonization" and "repulsion" was operating most intensely (Elias 1994b, 507). During the early nineteenth century, reflecting a more even power ratio between the nobility and the middle classes, the canons were increasingly enunciated as applying uniformly to behaviour of all ranks of respectable society. So the trend observed in America is not unique, although there it probably progressed further and faster than in Europe. In the eastern cities there was an unprecedented demand in the immediate post–Civil War period for books on decorum, as one would expect in a period of increased social mobility, though it is doubtful how far they penetrated the rural areas and the West.

There may be some slight problem of comparability between the European and American manners books of this period. It is possible that American ones were directed on average to a slightly lower modal stratum of readers than were the European ones; literacy, for one thing, was higher in the United States than in most European countries. At any rate, in such matters as table manners the American books appear somewhat more basic than their European equivalents of the same date: some of the advice they give on behaviour at the table or spitting seems almost more reminiscent of the famous medieval examples quoted by Elias. On the other hand, in other respects the American books appear to be ahead of their European contemporaries. For instance, they strongly frown upon the tendency of the nouveaux riches to be inconsiderate to servants. And notably, the American books always stressed norms against what Wouters calls "self-aggrandizement," or, more prosaically, showing-off and boasting.

The period between the end of the Civil War and the outbreak of the First World War seems, with benefit of hindsight, to be an aberration in the history of American manners, at odds with trends dominant before and after. This was the so-called Gilded Age, the age of the "Robber Barons" – Rockefeller, Vanderbilt, Carnegie, Huntington, and others – men who made vast profits in the war and then in manufacturing, mining, railroads, and banking, as industrialization took off. This was the age in which many of Henry James's and Edith Wharton's novels are set, an age when parvenus managed to crash the "aristocratic" circles of the cities of the eastern seaboard, which had hitherto comprised old families tracing their origins to colonial times or to the very early days of the republic. In this period there was a cascade of new etiquette books, which, unlike their antebellum precursors, sought to instill a more aristocratic style of behaviour. "For the most part," Schlesinger comments, "these manners were borrowed consciously, if sometimes to bizarre effect, from Europe, where an hereditary leisure class held the position which America's newly rich anguished to attain in their own country" (1947, 29).

If this period seems aberrant in American history, in comparative perspective it fits perfectly into a common pattern of periods when the pressure from below upon established elites is at its greatest, and when rising bourgeois groups are forcing open the gates of exclusive society circles in the face of strong resistance. It is then that we can expect the strongest reaction of repulsion on the part of established groups, leading to rapid innovation in standards of behaviour, which become ever more demanding of emotion management and self-constraint; indeed, they even becoming ritualized as a means of demarcating members of established groups from outsiders. At the same time, the outsiders are "colonized," pushed both by the attempted exclusion of them and by their own "anticipatory socialization" into adopting the new standards. This pattern was true of the last century of the *ancien régime* studied by Elias in *The Court Society*. It was also true of London society between the end of the Napoleonic Wars and the

1890s, when, as Leonore Davidoff notes in her study *The Best Circles* (1973), the number of participating families more than quadrupled. And for similar reasons, it was true of late-nineteenth-century America. For example, the elaborate ritual of calling cards, a micrometer of social inclusion and exclusion, was at its height in both London and the cities of the American east coast in the latter half of the nineteenth century. It was already in decline in America, however, by the 1890s.

Attempts were even made in this period to introduce the custom of chaperoning young women. This was definitely a counter-trend. From the earliest days, European visitors to the United States had commented on the much greater freedom allowed young American women, the relative safety in which they could go about the cities, the *relative* equality of the sexes in normal social contact, and the reliance placed upon young women's self-control and propriety. Chaperoning was only ever adopted as something of a European affectation in very small circles of the very rich, was endured only from the early teenage years to the early mid-twenties, and soon died out. This is the period of relative emancipation to which Abram de Swaan has also traced the rise of agoraphobia in women; it would be interesting – if data exist – to compare the incidence of that affliction in America and Europe.

All commentators are agreed that in the twentieth century American manners have become (even?) more relaxed and that there has emerged the emotional habitus which Stearns calls "American cool."[3] Many writers have suggested causes contributing to this development. They include, in no particular order, the exodus to the suburbs, breaking up city elites as bastions of ceremonious intercourse; the popular antagonism to great fortunes and conspicuous consumption (reflecting, again, underlying changes towards somewhat more even power ratios between social classes); the greater economic and social independence of women, hitherto the main custodians of the codes of good behaviour (van Stolk and Wouters 1984); and the effect of films, radio, and television and car ownership (Bailey 1988). Schlesinger quotes one observer as early as the interwar period who made the perceptive comment that the greater "liberty of behavior" required "more real breeding" than ever; people had to have "an innate sense of the fitness of things, and sure feeling for the correct time and place" (1947, 58). "Innate" is not strictly the right word, but otherwise this remark anticipates the main thrust of Wouters's interpretation of informalization processes.

Stearns's *American Cool* (1994) is to some extent a prolonged debate with Elias, and more especially with Wouters. Stearns, I think, wastes a good deal of effort in debating when exactly the process of relaxation or, in Wouters's terms, "informalization" began. He misinterprets

Wouters as dating informalization from the 1960s, and seeks to show that it dates from much earlier in the century. In fact, Wouters would no doubt agree, since he paints a picture of waves of normalization, informalization, and reformalization. In any case, as Elias remarks, "nothing is more fruitless, when dealing with long-term social processes, than to attempt to locate an absolute beginning" (1983, 232).

More seriously, Stearns seems to have a rather crude understanding of Elias's theory. He repeatedly argues that Victorian Americans were not simply "more restrained" but that they were in certain ways also *less* restrained than their successors – for example, in the expression of anger. But that is precisely Elias's point. Although it may be possible to find incautious formulations in Elias's work where he refers simply to the *growth* of self-constraint, a careful reading makes it perfectly clear that he associates the course of civilizing processes with several much more subtle changes in habitus. He argues in particular that people's patterns of emotional control become "more even," "more automatic," and "more all-round." By "more even" and "more automatic" self-constraints, Elias means psychological changes: individuals' oscillations of mood become less extreme, and the controls over emotional expression become more reliable or calculable. "More all-round" ("more all-embracing" would be a better translation) refers to a decline in the differences between various "spheres" of life, such as contrasts between what is allowed in public and in private, between conduct in relation to one category of people as against another, or between "normal" behaviour and that permissible on special occasions such as carnivals or other events which serve as exceptions to the rules. The upshot seems to be that Stearns is doing battle with a straw man.

The most serious deficiency of most writings on American habitus, however, is their failure, except in an unsystematic way, to follow Elias in relating changes in habitus to broader processes at work in the macroscopic structure of society. In the next section, I shall tentatively make a few points which suggest how that task might proceed.

AMERICAN STATE FORMATION AND ITS BEARING ON HABITUS

There is an enormous literature on American political development, but most of it is slanted rather towards nation building than state formation, towards the construction of a sense of shared national identity rather than internal pacification and the forging of an effective monopolization of the means of violence (see, for example, Lipset 1963 and Greenfeld 1992, 397–484). Of course, the two cannot be entirely separated.

In colonial times and in the early republic, for most people their "we-image" as Bostonians or Virginians may have remained stronger than their "we-image" as "Americans." Indeed, as it is pointed out, until not long before independence, most seem to have felt themselves to be British, with a regional loyalty akin to that found in British counties (Greenfeld 1992, 407). Nevertheless, the "we-image" as Americans, or as British-in-America, was from the beginning strong enough to demarcate Americans of European stock from Native Americans. Only a little later, it demarcated them from the African slaves they imported, and it also demarcated them, a little less definitely, from French traders and settlers.

From as early as 1740 a common citizenship of the colonies was recognized, and this was codified in the 1802 Naturalization Act. The issue between the Jeffersonian Republicans, leaning towards the preservation of states' rights, and the Federalists (Washington, Hamilton, Jay, and initially Madison) was not settled until the Civil War. But many forces were at work promoting a long-term strengthening of an American national "we-image." The immigrants who arrived from Europe in their millions throughout the nineteenth century came with an already preformed image of "America," rather than of the specific colony or state to which earlier settlers had felt allegiance. Above all, the West – the rapid advance of the frontier across the Alleghenies, the Mississippi, and finally the Rockies – played an outstanding part as a unifying force. It fostered a general American loyalty, partly because the local patriotism found in the earlier states required time to develop (Greenfeld 1992, 433).

But the role of the West in American state formation was vastly important and complex, and it has been academically controversial ever since Frederick Jackson Turner published his celebrated paper "The Significance of the Frontier in American History" in 1893. The Turner thesis brings us back from nation building towards the basics of state formation, in the realities of internal pacification of territory and the emergence of a stable monopoly of the means of violence.

In Turner's view, the development of the states of the eastern seaboard was in many respects not dissimilar to what could be seen in Europe, notably "the evolution of institutions in a limited area": this included the rise of representative government, the development of more complex organs of government, and the rapid division of labour in the rise of manufacturing industry. Into this familiar picture, however, the existence and expansion of the frontier, from the earliest settlements to the 1880s, had introduced a decisively different "evolutionary" influence. The kernel of Turner's argument runs thus: "we have ... a recurrence of the process of evolution in each western area reached in the process of expansion. Thus American development has exhibited not merely advance along a single line, but a return to primitive conditions on a continually advancing frontier line, and a new development for that area. American social development has been continually beginning again on the frontier. This perennial rebirth, this fluidity of American life, this expansion westwards with its new opportunities, its continuous touch with the simplicity of primitive society, furnish forces dominating American character" (1962, 2–3).

In some respects, this passage is badly formulated: it exaggerates the tabula rasa quality of each new area. Settlers moving to the western frontier took with them a vast inheritance of knowledge, beliefs, and feelings into which they had been socialized and encultured in the settled East (Turner 1962, 22).[4] Yet Turner's statement does contain essential insights into the formation of habitus. As he observed, "the wilderness masters the colonist" (1962, 3). Recast into the terms of process sociology, his remarks indicate roughly that elements of the American population were constantly returning to conditions of greater autarky, to much higher levels of danger in everyday life, and thus to a continuous source of decivilizing pressures. For, as Elias observed, "The armor of civilized conduct would crumble very rapidly if, through a change in society, the degree of insecurity which existed earlier were to break in upon us again, and if danger became as incalculable as once it was. Corresponding fears would burst the limits set to them today" (1994b, 253n). We must, however, always bear strongly in mind that decivilizing pressures were always in tension with quite strong civilizing pressures. One reason, as I have already remarked, is that settlers on the frontier were not tabulae rasae and had by and large been raised in more settled and (in Elias's technical sense) more "civilized" circumstances. A second reason is that, although the first generation of their offspring might indeed be raised amidst a relatively high and incalculable level of danger, internal pacification of territory by the forces of the state, as well as economic development of many sorts, was rarely more than a generation behind the settlers moving west.

With that powerful qualification, it is still interesting to see certain parallels between the western frontier and the conditions of the earlier stages of state formation in Europe. Indeed, Elias was conscious of the parallel, for in discussing the "elimination contest" for territory among regional magnates in Europe, he illustrated the principle involved by referring to a settler on the western frontier of whom it was said, "He didn't want all the land; he just wanted the land next to his" (1994b, 389). The most significant thing about the western frontier in Turner's view was that it lay "at the hither edge of free land" (1962, 3). Turner began his essay by pointing out that between the 1880 and 1890 censuses the frontier and the supply of free land had disappeared for the first time since the beginning of European settlement. He anticipated profound consequences for American society. It should be possible, using Elias's work as a model, to discern consequences both in the American state and in habitus – we have perhaps already glimpsed some in the changes in American manners from the late nineteenth century. Again, there is an interesting parallel with Elias's discussion of the consequences of the scarcity of land in Europe around the eleventh century, including the intensification of social competition and the sociogenesis of the crusades (1994b, 286ff.).

Turner listed a number of ways in which the experience of the frontier fed back into American society in the more settled East (1962, 22). First, the frontier had "promoted the formation of a composite nationality for the American people." Second, the advance of the frontier had decreased America's dependence on England for supplies: as distances westward increased, it became impractical to rely on transatlantic shipments, and eastern cities began to compete with each other to supply the needs of the frontier lands. Third, more especially after independence, it was legislation to meet the necessities of the westward-moving frontier that did most to develop the powers of the central government. Apart from the great issue of slavery, legislation was enacted for railways and many other forms of internal improvements and above all for the sale and disposal of public lands. The very fact that the unsettled lands had been vested in the federal government proved crucial in the development of the power ratio between the states and Washington. Turner quotes the observation that in "1789 the States were the creators of the Federal Government; in 1861 the federal government was the creator of a large majority of the States" (1962, 24). Fourth, however, it also proved significant that federal attempts to make the public lands a source of revenue and to lease them gradually in parcels (in order to create a more compact pattern of settlement) consistently failed. The hunger of the frontiersmen for land was too intense. John Quincy Adams admitted defeat: "a system of administration was not what the West demanded; it wanted land."

This observation brings us to the fifth and perhaps most famous of Turner's consequences of the frontier for American society – its promotion of "rugged individualism." The "frontier is productive of individualism. Complex society is precipitated by the wilderness into a kind of primitive organization based on the family. The tendency is anti-social. It produces antipathy to control. The tax-gatherer is viewed as a representative of oppression" (Turner 1962, 30). Although Turner believed that frontier individualism had from the beginning promoted democracy – the first generation of frontier states after independence all had wide suffrages and forced the eastern states to follow suit – he also entered a note of warning: "So long as free land exists, the opportunity for a competency exists, and economic power secures political power. But the democracy born of free land, strong in selfishness and individualism, intolerant of administrative experience and education, and pressing individual liberty beyond its proper bounds, has its dangers as well as its benefits. Individualism in America has allowed a laxity in regard to government affairs which has rendered possible the spoils system and all the manifest evils that follow from the back of a highly civic spirit" (1962, 32).

The Turner thesis has undergone vicissitudes in the century since Turner published his first essay.[5] For some decades it was the dominant interpretation among historians of American social development, and although Turner himself was no monocausalist, many of his followers were. Charles Beard objected that many other processes need be given due weight: the rise of capitalism, class conflicts, slavery, and a whole series of other power struggles between established and outsider groups. In passing, it is also worth noting that one central established-outsider relationship, that between men and women, has been widely discussed by commentators on American society from an early stage, most of them remarking on the relatively more even power ratio between the sexes in America than in Europe. Even more central in American history have been the initially very unequal power ratios between ethnic groups, including the struggles over slavery and the genocide of Native Americans.

For a time, through its overemphasis of the frontier factor, the Turner school was eclipsed. It has, however, been revived in an undogmatic way in detailed research since the 1960s, and that literature holds distinct promise for the linking of the "macro" and "micro" in studying the "American civilizing process" (Lipset and Hofstadter 1968).

CONCLUSION

It is too early in my research to offer anything like the ambitious "Synopsis" that Elias undertook in the final part of *The Civilizing Process*. When I come to write such a synopsis, however, I shall be looking for evidence specifically of American twists to the processes that he describes there.

One process central to Elias's thesis is the advance (and possibly retreat) of thresholds of shame and embarrassment. Again, there is an extensive and relevant literature on American "social character," stemming from the culture and personality school in anthropology, though it is marred by too static and dichotomous a conception of a shame-guilt polarity. This literature is intimately linked to the issue of individualism both as a social ideology and as a mode of self-experience.

Individualism is popularly seen as the dominant trait in American culture – and indeed, of the habitus typical of American people. Although as a political philosophy, the ancestry of individualism as an idea can be traced back in British philosophy through Adam Smith and John Locke to Thomas Hobbes, and although in nineteenth-century America its transformation from political philosophy to social outlook can be seen notably in the writings of Ralph Waldo Emerson, the word as such entered the English language only in the 1830s. At that time it was Tocqueville who saw the rise of individualism as one of the prime dangers to the continuing health of democratic society in the United States. He was almost certainly the first person to use the word to denote an aspect of the habitus of ordinary people in their everyday lives, in a sense close to what Elias and later Bourdieu meant by habitus.

Yet even if the word had not been used in this sense, as *a mode of self-experience*, individualism was strongly established in America even before independence. One need only think of the writings of Benjamin Franklin, used by Max Weber to exemplify the spirit of capitalism. Elias argued that what Weber had discovered was, at best, one facet of a more general change in the Western mode of self-experience from the Renaissance onwards. This shift in the mode of experience was intellectually reflected in, but not caused by, the epistemological pre-occupation of Western philosophers from Descartes onwards with how knowledge is possible for the single, adult individual in isolation. It is highly significant that Alexis de Tocqueville, with his usual perspicacity, pointed out that Americans were implicitly Cartesians and Kantians in their outlook. American writers in the late twentieth century, however, have tended to see the dominance of individualism as a trait of the habitus of Americans at large, as a characteristic of our own times. James Collier, in his notable book *The Rise of Selfishness in America* (1991), places its rise in the twentieth century. The ideological conflict between individualism or selfishness and the more communitarian outlook in twentieth-century America is also central to the work of Christopher Lasch. Elias's warning that "nothing is more fruitless ... than to attempt to locate an absolute beginning" (1983, 232) is again highly relevant.

The overall model that Elias presents in his great "Synopsis" can perhaps help to disentangle, not so much when and whether, but how and why individualism became a dominant trait of American habitus. Central to his theory is the long-term increase in the social constraint towards self-constraint and pressure towards increasing foresight arising from people's enmeshment in longer chains of interdependence. Bound up with that change, according to Elias, are processes of psychologization and (*ceteris paribus*) increasing mutual identification, and of rationalization as a transition in *emotional* makeup and capacities.[6] Later he encapsulated many of these ideas in his discussion of "changes in the We-I balance" (1991a, 153–237). What features of the social and political development of the United States cast light on how such processes unfolded in that country and worked to give a distinctive flavour to American habitus?

First, it is clear that, until the rapid growth of the major cities with mass immigration in the mid-nineteenth century, the United States was a predominantly rural country. Even well behind the westward-moving frontier, the pattern of settlement was highly dispersed, with the majority of farmsteads isolated from each other, their owners leading a relatively self-sufficient existence (Larkin 1991; Collier 1991). Until later still – indeed, until relatively recently – small towns were the focus of life for most Americans (Smith 1966). This relative autarky, and the relatively short and dispersed web of interdependencies it involved, would *ceteris paribus* have tended to instill a strong sense of self-reliance, as Turner argued in relation to the frontier proper. But self-reliance is not at all the same thing as self-constraint. Elias's hypothesis is that it is the *steady* pressure exerted by long chains of interdependence, as well as the intersection of the web of interdependencies *within* each person, that increases the "social constraint towards self-constraint." These pressures would therefore be greater within the cities than in the remote rural areas; nonetheless, the cultural legacy of the frontier and the farm remains very strong.

I also think there are elements in Elias's arguments which may suggest that the intensity of civilizing pressures is related, not (or *not only*) to the *extent* of webs of social interdependence, but to the *rate of change* and increase of social interdependence. If that proves on further investigation to be the case, it raises the interesting possibility that if the chains cease to lengthen and the web ceases to spread, the pressures towards self-constraint may actually begin to diminish and decivilizing pressures become more dominant. This suggestion is highly speculative, but it fits in with much recent concern about the consequences of the real or perceived rise in the level of danger within American cities. For instance, Christopher Lasch in *The Minimal Self* (1994) connects the extent of mutual identification (and its narrowness, including *temporal* narrowness) with the size of what Elias liked to call the "survival unit"; he sees mutual identification as diminishing with the rising insecurity of everyday life in the cities.

Secondly, the American case may raise again the vexed question of the place of religion in the theory of civilizing processes – or rather, its absence (Goudsblom 1995). Digby Baltzell, in his comparative study of Quakerism in Philadelphia and Puritanism in Boston (1979), emphasizes how the Quaker doctrine of the Inner Light was associated with a much weaker habitual foresight than was the Calvinist doctrine of predestination.[7] One might wish to attempt to relate the doctrines and their differing degree of habitual foresight with the social strata in which they each took root in seventeenth-century England, but for present purposes it is enough to note in passing that Baltzell sees the Quaker outlook as more strongly influencing the habitus of modern America than Puritanism.

In his "Synopsis" Elias also pointed to the cultural trend towards "diminishing contrasts and increasing varieties." This observation, like his 1935 essay on kitsch, in many ways anticipates aspects of recent debates on modernism and postmodernism (Woodiwiss 1993). America in many ways led the world in such trends, even in the last century. As Elias, perhaps following Tocqueville, pointed out in conversation, the relative weakness of central institutions, including the historic lack of either a royal court or any single central "good society," shows itself in such cultural matters as relatively weak standardization of linguistic and stylistic usages.[8]

Most impressively of all, in his "Synopsis" Elias relates the processes he has been describing to the great trends of international balances of power, war, and peace. At this stage I can only signal my intent to attempt to relate the American civilizing process to the rise of the United States to world dominance and the beginnings of its decline. My model there will be especially Elias's *The Germans*, in which he writes about power struggles and the development of habitus, and extends the three-way comparison of the development of Germany, France, and Britain which he began in *The Civilizing Process*. As well, *The Germans* contains constant reminders that we should not focus only on *civilizing* processes, but remember that there are also structured decivilizing processes almost always present as counterpoints, sometimes becoming dominant forces.

Finally, to return to my initial question – why is there no "Eliasism" in the United States? The answer is probably because all the relevant questions have been debated in American intellectual circles over a very long period. But perhaps they have not been connected with each other in the way that Elias would have sought. "No-one else," I commented in concluding my *Norbert Elias: An Introduction*, "has so coherently drawn the connection between manners and morals, power and violence, states, war and peace through human history" (1992b, 269). Fitting America into the picture is surely long overdue.

NOTES

1 It is still extraordinary that Charles Tilly, Anthony Giddens, and Michael Mann can all write books about state formation without even citing the second volume of *The Civilizing Process*.

2 Among present-day social scientists, this transition may recall Foucault's *Discipline and Punish*, though in fact Pieter Spierenburg's *The Spectacle of Suffering* (1984) provides a more adequate explanation of why it came about, an explanation that draws on Elias's theory of state formation.

3 Schlesinger goes on to comment, "Oddly enough, the result was to flavor urban sophistication with a naturalness that smacked of bucolic folkways" (1947, 58).

4 The same issue arises in Elias's essay "Drake en Doughty" (1977a).

5 For a good discussion of this topic, one can refer to Cronon et al. 1992; Taylor 1956; and Wrobel 1993.

6 Many studies of the rise of science and the large-scale organization in America are relevant here.

7 Quakerism, he shows, was also connected with a strong sense of what Elias called *homo clausus* and with a marked anti-intellectualism.

8 H.L. Mencken, in his scholarly proclamation of the superiority of American over British English (1923), argued that the vitality of the latter had been sapped by the "policing" of the language by elites in the seventeenth and eighteenth centuries, although that had happened to a markedly less extent than in French. Compare Elias's "Excursus on the Modeling of Speech at Court" (1994b, 88–93).

Bibliography

Abrams, Philip. 1982. *Historical Sociology*. Shepton Mallet: Open Books.

Adjei, Karin. 1994. *Diagnose Unheilbarer Krebs: Wie ich meine Krankheit besiegte*. München: Knaur Verlag.

Anderson, Benedict. 1991. *Imagined Communities: Reflections on the Origin and Spread of Nationalism*. New York: Verso.

Anderson, Greg. 1995. *The Cancer Conqueror: An Incredible Journey to Wellness*. Kansas City: Andrews and McMeel.

Arditi, Jorge. 1994. "Hegemony and Etiquette: An Exploration on the Transformation of Practice and Power in Eighteenth Century England." *British Journal of Sociology* 45.2 (June):177–93.

– 1996. "Simmel's Theory of Alienation and the Decline of the Nonrational." *Sociological Theory* 14.2 (July):93–108.

Aresty, Esther B. 1970. *The Best Behavior: The Course of Good Manners – from Antiquity to the Present – as Seen through Courtesy and Etiquette Books*. New York: Simon and Schuster.

Armstrong, John A. 1982. *Nations before Nationalism*. Chapel Hill: University of North Carolina Press.

Arnason, Johann. 1987. "Figurational Sociology as a Counter-Paradigm." *Theory Culture and Society* 4.2–3 (June):429–56.

Bailey, Beth L. 1988. *From Front Porch to Back Seat: Courtship in Twentieth Century America*. Baltimore: Johns Hopkins University Press.

Baltzell, E. Digby. 1979. *Puritan Boston and Quaker Philadelphia*. Boston: Beacon Press.

Barlösius, Eva, Elçin Kürsat-Ahlers, and Hans-Peter Waldhoff, eds. 1997. *Distanzierte Verstrickungen: Die ambivalente Bindung soziologisch Forschender an ihren Gegenstand: Festschrift für Peter Gleichmann zum 65.* Geburtstag, Berlin: Sigma.

Bauman, Zygmunt. 1989. *Modernity and the Holocaust.* Oxford: Polity.

Baumgart, Ralf, and Volker Eichener. 1991. *Norbert Elias zur Einführung.* Hamburg: Junius.

Beard, Charles A., and Mary R. Beard. 1942. *The American Spirit.* Vol. 4 of *The Rise of American Civilization.* London: Jonathan Cape.

Beck, Ulrich, and Elisabeth Beck-Gernsheim, eds. 1994. *Riskante Freiheiten: Individualisierung in modernen Gesellschaften.* Frankfurt am Main: Suhrkamp.

Becker, Klaus Peter. 1982. *Ich habe meinen Krebs besiegt.* Unterhaching: Luitpold Lang Verlag.

Becker-Schmidt, Regina. 1987. "Die doppelte Vergesellschaftung – die doppelte Unterdrückung: Besonderheiten der Frauenforschung in den Sozialwissenschaften." In *Die andere Hälfte der Gesellschaft,* ed. Lilo Unterkirchner and Ina Wagner, 10–25. Wien: Österreichischer Gewerkschaftsbund.

Beer, Ursula, ed. 1987. *Klasse Geschlecht: Feministische Gesellschaftsanalyse und Wissenschaftskritik.* Bielefeld: AJZ Verlag.

– 1990. *Geschlecht, Struktur, Geschichte – Soziale Konstituierung des Geschlechterverhältnisses.* Frankfurt am Main: Campus.

– 1992. "Das Geschlechterverhältnis in der Risikogesellschaft: Überlegungen zu den Thesen von Ulrich Beck." *Feministische Studien* 10.1:99–112.

Benedict, Ingrid. 1989. *Laßt mir meine bunten Farben.* Bergisch Gladbach: Lübbe Verlag.

– 1993. *Ich habe keine Angst um mich.* Bergisch Gladbach: Lübbe Verlag.

Benedict, Ruth. 1946. *The Chrysanthemum and the Sword.* New York: Houghton-Mifflin.

Bernstein, Richard J. 1979. *Restrukturierung der Gesellschaftstheorie.* Frankfurt/Main: Suhrkamp.

Beutler, Maja. 1989. *Fuss Fassen.* Bern: Zytglogge.

Beyfus, Drusilla. 1992. *Modern Manners: The Essential Guide to Living in the '90s.* London: Hamlyn.

Biester, Elke, et al., eds. 1994. *Gleichstellungspolitik – Totem und Tabus: Eine feministische Revision.* Frankfurt am Main: Campus.

Binswanger, Hans Christoph. 1994. *Money and Magic: A Critique of the Modern Economy in the Light of Goethe's Faust.* Trans. J.E. Harrison. Chicago: University of Chicago Press.

Bishop, Beata. 1996. *A Time to Heal: Triumph over Cancer.* London: Arkana Penguin.

Blomert, Reinhard. 1991. *Psyche und Zivilisation: Zur theoretischen Konstruktion bei Norbert Elias.* Hamburg: Lit Verlag.

– Helmut Kuzmics, and Annette Treibel, eds. 1993. *Transformationen des Wir-Gefühls: Studien zum nationalen Habitus.* Frankfurt: Suhrkamp.

Bloor, Geraldine. 1996. "Peak Experiences." In *Fighting Spirit: The Stories of Women in the Bristol Breast Cancer Survey*, ed. Heather Goodare London: Scarlet Press.

Bogner, Artur. 1989. *Zivilisation und Rationalisierung: Die Zivilisationstheorien M. Webers, N. Elias' und der Frankfurter Schule*. Opladen: Westdeutscher Verlag.

Bolton, Mary. 1961. *The New Etiquette Book*. London: Foulsham.

Borst, Sigrid. 1988. *Weniger als ein Jahr: Unser Kampf gegen den Krebs*. Frankfurt/Main: Fischer Taschenbuch Verlag.

Brenner, Y.S., H. Kaelble, and M. Thomas, eds. 1991. *Income Distribution in Historical Perspective*. Cambridge: Cambridge University Press.

Breuilly, John. 1993. *Nationalism and the State*. Manchester: Manchester University Press.

Brinkgreve, Christien, and M. Korzec. 1982. "On Modern Relationships: The Commandments of the New Freedom." *Netherlands Journal of Sociology* 18.1:47–56.

– 1976. "Kan het civlisatieproces van richting veranderen? [Can the civilizing process change direction?]." *Amsterdams Sociologisch Tijdschrift* 3.3:361–4.

– 1979. "Feelings, Behavior, Morals in the Netherlands, 1938–78: Analysis and Interpretation of an Advice Column." *Netherlands Journal of Sociology* 15.2:123–40.

– 1984. "Verhaltensmuster in der niederländischen Gesellschaft (1938–1977): Analyse und Interpretation der Ratgeber-Rubrik einer Illustrierten." In Gleichmann et al. 1984, 299–310.

Bruck-Auffenberg, Natalie. 1897. *De vrouw "comme il faut."* Trans. Marie de Bock-Hardenberg. Leiden: Brill.

Burnett, Ron. 1996. "A Torn Page, Ghosts on the Computer Screen, Words, Labyrinths: Exploring the Frontiers of Cyberspace." In Marcus 1996, 67–98.

Butler, Judith P. 1990. *Gender Trouble: Feminism and the Subversion of Identity*. New York: Routledge.

– and Barbara Rosenblum. 1991. *Cancer in Two Voices*. Duluth: Spinsters Ink.

Cairns, E., and R. Wilson. 1985. "Psychiatric Aspects of Violence in Northern Ireland." *Stress Medicine* 1:193–201.

Carson, Gerald. 1966. *The Polite Americans: A Wide-Angle View of Our More or Less Good Manners over 300 Years*. New York: William Morrow.

Castells, Manuel. 1996. *The Rise of the Network Society: The Information Age*. Vol. 1. New York: Basil Blackwell.

Castiglione, Baldesar. 1959. *The Book of the Courtier*. Trans. Charles S. Singleton. Garden City, NY: Anchor Books.

Cavan, Sherri. 1970. "The Etiquette of Youth." In *Social Psychology through Symbolic Interaction*, ed. G.P. Stone and H.A. Farberman, 554–65. New York: Wiley.

Churchill, Winston S. 1930. *My Early Life*. London: Thornton Butterworth.

Collier, James Lincoln. 1991. *The Rise of Selfishness in America*. New York: Oxford University Press.

Collins, Patricia H. Black. 1992. *Feminist Thought: Knowledge, Consciousness, and the Politics of Empowerment*. Boston: Unwin and Hyman.

Conway, Kathlyn. 1997. *Ordinary Life: A Memoir of Illness*. New York: W.H. Freeman.

Cooley, Charles H. 1964. *Human Nature and the Social Order*. New York: Schocken.

Cornelissen, Waltraud. 1993. "Politische Partizipation von Frauen in der alten Bundesrepublik und im vereinten Deutschland." In Helwig and Nickel 1993, 321–49.

Courey, Anne de. 1985. *A Guide to Modern Manners*. London: Thames and Hudson.

Cowling, Samuel T. 1974–75. "The Image of the Tournament in Marie de France's Le Chaitivel." *Romance Notes* 16:686–91.

Cronon, William, G. Miles, and J. Gitlin. 1992. *Under an Open Sky: Rethinking America's Western Past*. New York: W.W. Norton.

Curtin, Michael. 1987. *Propriety and Position: A Study of Victorian Manners*. New York: Garland.

Dalhoff, Herbert. 1991. *So krank wie die Erde: Krebsleiden und Naturerfahrung*. Frankfurt/Main: Fischer Taschenbuch Verlag.

Davidoff, Leonore. 1973. *The Best Circles: Society, Etiquette and the Season*. London: Croom Helm.

Debrett's Etiquette and Modern Manners. 1982 [1981] Ed. Elsie Burch Donald. 2d ed. London: Pan Books.

Dehn, Mechthild. 1995. *Leben, Krebs: Entscheidung, Anruf, Suche*. Stuttgart: Radius Verlag.

de Swaan, Abram. 1981a. "Vom Befehlsprinzip zum Verhandlungsprinzip. Über neuere Verschiebungen im Gefühlshaushalt der Menschen." In Kuzmics and Mörth 1991, 173–98.

– 1981b."The Politics of Agoraphobia." *Theory and Society* 10.3:359–85.

– 1988. *In Care of the State: Health Care, Education and Welfare in Europe and the USA in the Modern Era*. Oxford: Polity Press.

Devereux, G.R.M. 1927. *Etiquette for Men: A Handbook of Modern Manners and Customs*. New ed., entirely rewritten and brought up to date. London: Pearson.

Devji, Faisal Fatehali. 1996. "Hindu, Muslim, Indian." In *Nationalism: Seminar 422*. New Delhi, June.

Dietrich, Heinz. 1934. *Menschen miteinander*. Berlin und Darmstadt: Deutsche Buch-Gemeinschaft.

Diezinger, Angelika, et al., eds. 1994. *Erfahrung mit Methode: Wege sozialwissenschaftlicher Frauenforschung*. Freiburg: Kore.

Dosdall, Claude, and Joanne Broatch. 1986. *My God I Thought You'd Died: One Man's Personal Triumph over Cancer.* Toronto: Seal-McClelland and Stewart–Bantam.

Duerr, Hans Peter. 1988. *Nacktheit und Scham: Der Mythos vom Zivilisationsprozeß.* Frankfurt am Main: Suhrkamp.

Duncker, Patricia. 1996. "The Blue Book." In *Cancer: Through the Eyes of Ten Women,* ed. Patricia Duncker and Vicky Wilson. London: Harper-Collins.

Dunning, E.G., et al. 1987. "Violent Disorders in Twentieth Century Britain." In *The Crowd in Contemporary Britain,* ed. George Gaskell and Robert Benewick, 19–75. London: Sage.

– P. Murphy, and J. Williams. 1988. *The Roots of Football Hooliganism.* London: Routledge.

Durkheim, Émile. 1965. *The Elementary Forms of the Religious Life.* New York: Free Press.

Eagleton, Terry. 1983. *Literary Theory: An Introduction.* Oxford: Basil Blackwell.

Edwards, Anne, and Drusilla Beyfus. 1956. *Lady Behave: A Guide to Modern Manners.* Rev. version 1969. London: Boswell & Co.

Eichengreen, Barry. 1995. *Golden Fetters: The Gold Standard and the Great Depression, 1919–1939.* New York: University Press.

Eichler, Lilian. 1921. *The Book of Etiquette.* 2 vols. Repr. 1923. Garden City, NY: Doubleday.

– 1924. *The Book of Etiquette.* Repr. 1934, 1948. New York: Triangle Books.

Elias, Norbert. 1921. "Vom Sehen in der Natur." *Blau-Weiss-Blätter.* 2.8–10 (Breslauer Hefte):133–44.

– 1929. "Die Bedeutung der Konkurrenz im Gebiete des Geistigen" (The significance of intellectual competition). In *Verhandlungen des 6: Deutschen Soziologentages vom 17. – 19.9.1928 in Zürich.* Tübingen: J.C.B. Mohr (P. Siebeck).

– 1935. "Die Verteibung der Hugenotten aus Frankreich." *Der Ausweg* 1.2:369–76.

– 1970a. "Processes of State Formation and Nation Building." In *Transactions of the 7th World Congress of Sociology Varna 1970,* vol. 3. Sofia: International Sociological Association.

– 1970b. *Was ist Soziologie?* München: Juventa.

– 1977. "Drake en Doughty: De ontwikkeling van een conflict. [Drake and Doughty: The development of a conflict]." *De Gids* 140.5/6:223–37.

– 1978a. *The History of Manners.* New York: Panthenon.

– 1978b. *The Civilizing Process.* Vol. 1, *The History of Manners.* Oxford: Basil Blackwell.

– 1978c. *What Is Sociology?* Trans. Stephen Mennell and Grace Morrissey. London: Hutchinson.

– 1982. *The Civilizing Process: State Formation and Civilization.* New York: Basil Blackwell.
– 1983. *The Court Society.* Trans. Edmund Jephcott. Oxford: Blackwell.
– 1984. *Über die Zeit.* Frankfurt: Suhrkamp.
– 1985a. *Humana Conditio: Betrachtungen zur Entwicklung der Menschheit am 40. Jahrestages eines Kriegsendes (8. Mai 1985).* Frankfurt am Main: Suhrkamp.
– 1985b. [1992]. *The Loneliness of the Dying.* Oxford: Basil Blackwell.
– 1987a. "The Changing Balance of Power between the Sexes in the History of Civilization." *Theory, Culture and Society* 4.2–3:287–316.
– 1987b. *Involvement and Detachment.* Oxford: Blackwell.
– 1987c. "Vorwort." In van Stolk and Wouters 1987, 9–16.
– 1987d. *Los der Menschen: Gedichte, Nachdichtungen.* Frankfurt: Suhrkamp.
– 1989. *Über die Deutschen.* Frankfurt: Suhrkamp.
– 1990. *Über sich selbst.* Frankfurt/Main: Suhrkamp.
– 1991a. *The Society of Individuals.* Oxford: Blackwell.
– 1991b. *The Symbol Theory.* London: Sage.
– 1992. *Time: An Essay.* Oxford: Blackwell.
– 1993. *Mozart: Portrait of a Genius.* Oxford: Polity; Berkeley: University of California Press.
– 1994a. *Reflections on a Life.* Trans. Edmund Jephcott. Cambridge: Polity.
– 1994b. *The Civilizing Process.* Trans. Edmund Jephcott. Oxford: Blackwell.
– 1995. *Menschen in Figurationen: Ein Lesebuch zur Einführung in die Prozess- und Figurationssoziologie von Norbert Elias.* Ed. Hans-Peter Bartels. Leske and Budrich: Opladen.
– 1996a. *The Germans: Power Struggles and the Development of Habitus in the Nineteenth and Twentieth Centuries.* Cambridge: Polity.
– 1996b. *Die Ballade vom Armen Jakob.* Frankfurt: Insel.
– 1997. "Kitsch Style and the Age of Kitsch." In *The Norbert Elias Reader: Selections from a Lifetime,* ed. Johan Goudsblom and Stephen Mennell Oxford: Blackwell.
– 1998a. *The Norbert Elias Reader: A Biographical Selection.* Ed. J. Goudsblom and Stephen Mennell. Oxford: Blackwell.
– 1998b. *Norbert Elias: On Civilization, Power, and Knowledge: Selected Writings.* Ed. Johan Goudsblom and Stephen Mennell. Chicago and London: University of Chicago Press.
– 1998c. *Watteaus Pilgerfahrt zur Insel der Liebe.* München: Edition München.
– 2000. *The Civilizing Process: Sociogenetic and Psychogenetic Investigations.* Trans. Edmund Jephcott. Ed. Eric Dunning, Johan Goudsblom, and Stephen Mennell. Oxford; Malden, Mass.: Blackwell Publishers.
– and Dunning, Eric. 1986. *Quest for Excitement: Sport and Leisure in the Civilizing Process.* Oxford: Blackwell.

– and W. Lepenies. 1977. *Zwei Reden anlässlich der Verleihung des Theodor W. Adorno Preises 1977.* Frankfurt am Main: Suhrkamp.

– and J.L. Scotson. 1965. *The Established and the Outsiders.* London: Frank Cass.

– 1990. *Etablierte und Außenseiter.* Frankfurt: Suhrkamp.

– 1993. *Etablierte und Außenseiter.* Trans. Michael Schröter. Frankfurt: Suhrkamp.

– 1995. *The Established and the Outsiders.* London: Sage.

Encyclopedia Britannica. 1963. Vol. 2. London: William Benton.

Etiquette for Everyone: Good Behaviour in Everyday Life. 1956. London: Foulsham.

Etiquette for Gentlemen: A Guide to the Observances of Good Society. 1923 [1950]. London: Ward, Lock.

Etiquette for Ladies: A Guide to the Observances of Good Society. 1923 [1950]. London: Ward, Lock.

Etiquette for Women: A Book of Modern Modes and Manners. 1902. London: Pearson.

Etiquette Up to Date. 1925. [By Burleigh]. New York: Howard Watt.

Evans, Laura. 1996. *The Climb of My Life: A Miraculous Journey from the Edge of Death to the Victory of a Lifetime.* New York: Harper Collins.

Faust, Diana M. 1988. "Women Narrators in the Lais of Marie de France." In *Women in French Literature: A Collection of Essays,* ed. Michel Guggenheim, 17–27. Saratoga, Calif.: Anna Libri.

Financial Times. 1996. 7/8 December (weekend edition).

Finkelstein, Joanne. 1989. *Dining Out: A Sociology of Modern Manners.* New York: New York University Press.

– 1991. *The Fashioned Self.* Cambridge: Polity Press.

Fletcher, Jonathan. 1997. *Violence and Civilization.* Cambridge: Polity.

Foucault, Michel. 1970. *The Order of Things: An Archaeology of the Human Sciences.* New York: Vintage.

Fraehm, Anne E., with David J. Fraehm. 1992. *A Cancer Battle Plan: Six Strategies For Beating Cancer, from a Recovered "Hopeless Case."* Colorado Springs: Pinon Press.

Franken, Konstanze von. 1951 [1957]. *Der Gute Ton: Ein Brevier für Takt und Benehmen in allen Lebenslagen.* Berlin: Hesse.

Fraser, Nancy. 1989. *Unruly Practices: Power, Discourse and Gender in Contemporary Social Theory.* Cambridge: Polity Press.

Freeman, Michelle A. 1984. "Marie de France's Poetics of Silence: The Implications for a Feminine Translation." *PMLA* 99:860–3.

Frerichs, Petra, and Margarete Steinrücke, eds. 1993. *Soziale Ungleichheit und Geschlechterverhältnisse.* Opladen: Leske & Budrich.

Friebel, Gisela. 1996. *Ich habe Krebs! Na und?* Königstein: Ariane Verlag.

Gagnon, V.P. 1994–95. "Ethnic Nationalism and International Conflict: The Case of Serbia." *International Security.*

Garfinkel, Harold. 1967. *Studies in Ethnomethodology.* Englewood Cliffs, NJ: Prentice Hall.

Garrigou, Alain, and Bernard Lacroix, eds. 1997. *Norbert Elias: La politique et l'histoire.* Paris: Éditions La Découverte.

Gawler, Ian. 1989. *You Can Conquer Cancer.* 1984. Melbourne: Hill of Content Publishing.

Geiger, Gabriele. 1993. "Postmoderner Feminismus: Über die blinden Flecken in der Theoriebildung und Alltagshandeln." *Zeitschrift für Frauenforschung* 11.1/2:133–60.

Gellner, Ernest. 1983. *Nations and Nationalism.* Oxford: Basil Blackwell.

Gerhard, Ute. 1995. "Sozialwissenschafltiche Frauenforschung: Perspektivenwechsel und theoretische Diskurse." In *Soziologie in Deutschland: Entwicklung, Institutionalisierung und Berufsfelder, Theoretische Kontroversen,* ed. B. Schäfers, 199–212. Opladen: Leske and Budrich.

Gibson, William. 1984. *Neuromancer.* New York: Ace Books.

Giddens, Anthony. 1993. *The Transformation of Intimacy: Sexuality, Love and Eroticism in Modern Societies.* Cambridge: Polity Press.

Gilgallon, Barbara, and Sue Seddon. 1988. *Modern Etiquette.* London: Ward Lock.

Gleichmann, Peter, Johan Goudsblom, and Hermann Korte, eds. 1979. *Materialien zu Norbert Elias' Zivilisationstheorie.* Frankfurt am Main: Suhrkamp.

– 1984. *Macht und Zivilisation: Materialien zu Norbert Elias' Zivilisationstheorie 2.* Frankfurt: Suhrkamp.

Glenny, Misha. 1992. *The Fall of Yugoslavia: The Third Balkan War.* London: Penguin.

Goethe, Johann Wolfgang von. 1967. *Faust: A Tragedy.* Trans. Bayard Taylor. New York: Modern Library.

– 1986. *Faust: Der Tragödie zweiter Teil.* Stuttgart: Reclam.

Goffman, Erving. 1958. *Presentation of Self in Everyday Life.* Garden City: Doubleday.

– 1963. *Behavior in Public Places: Notes on the Social Organization of Gatherings.* New York: The Free Press.

– 1967. *Interaction Ritual.* New York: Anchor.

Goldhagen, Daniel. 1996. *Hitler's Willing Executioners.* New York: Knopf.

Gottschalk, L., and Gleser, G. 1969. *Gottschalk-Gleser Content Analysis Scales.* Berkeley: University of California Press.

Goudsblom, Johan. 1977. *Sociology in the Balance: A Critical Essay.* Oxford: Blackwell.

– 1984. "Die Erforschung von Zivilisationsprozessen." In Gleichmann et al. 1984, 129–47.

– 1989. "Stijlen en beschavingen." *De Gids* 152.2:720–2.

– 1994. "The Theory of Civilizing Processes and Its Discontents." Paper presented at the Thirteenth World Congress of Sociology, Bielefeld, July.

– 1995. "Beschaving en godsdienst: Over de plaats van de religie in Norbert Elias' civilisatie theorie." *Amsterdams Sociologisch Tijdschrift* 21.4:90–101.

– 1996. "The Formation of Military-Agrarian Regimes." In *The Course of Human History: Economic Growth, Social Process, and Civilization*, ed. Johan Goudsblom, Eric Jones, and Stephen Mennell, 49–62. Armonk, NY: M.E. Sharpe.

Graham, Laurie. 1989. *Getting It Right: A Survival Guide to Modern Manners*. London: Chatto & Windus.

Graves, Robert, and Alan Hodge. 1941. *The Long Week-End: A Social History of Great Britain, 1918–1939*. London: Readers Union.

Grealy, Lucy. 1994. *Autobiography of a Face*. New York: HarperCollins.

Greenfeld, Liah. 1992. *Nationalism: Five Roads to Modernity*. Cambridge: Harvard University Press.

Groskamp-ten Have, Amy. 1939. *Hoe hoort het eigenlijk?* Amsterdam: Becht.

Gurr, Ted Robert. 1981. "Historical Trends in Violent Crime: A Critical Review of the Evidence." *Crime and Justice: An Annual Review of Research* 3:295–353.

Habermas, Jürgen. 1970. *Toward a Rational Society*. Trans. Jeremy Shapiro. Boston: Beacon Press.

Habits of Good Society: A Handbook of Etiquette. 1859 [1890]. London: James Hogg & Sons.

Hackeschmidt, Jörg. 1997. *Von Kurt Blumenfeld zu Norbert Elias: Die Erfindung einer jüdischen Nation*. Hamburg: Europäische Verlagsanstalt.

Haferkamp, Hans. 1987. "From the Intra-State to the Inter-State Civilizing Process?" *Theory, Culture and Society* 4.2/3:546–7.

Hall, Peter A., and J. Robert Franzese Jr. 1996. "Mixed Signals: Central Bank Independence: Coordinated Wage-Bargaining and European Monetary Union." Unpublished paper, Berlin, 15 July.

Halvorson-Boyd, Glenna, and Lisa K. Hunter. 1995. *Dancing in Limbo: Making Sense of Life after Cancer*. San Francisco: Jossey-Bass Publishers.

Hamlin, Cyrus. 1976. "Interpretive Notes." In *Faust* by Johann Wolfgang von Goethe, trans. Walter Arndt. New York: W.W. Norton.

Hanson, John Wesley, Jr. 1896. *Etiquette of To-Day: The Customs and Usages Required by Polite Society*. Chicago.

Harland, Marion, and Virginia van de Water. 1905 [1907]. *Everyday Etiquette: A Practical Manual of Social Usages*. Indianapolis: Bobbs-Merrill.

Hartz, Louis. 1964. *The Founding of New Societies*. New York: Harcourt Brace & World.

Haug, Frigga. 1990. "Tagträume eines sozialistischen Feminismus." In *Differenz und Gleichheit: Menschenrechte haben (k)ein Geschlecht*, ed. Ute Gerhard et al., 82–94. Frankfurt: Helmer.

Hearst, Marti A. 1997. "Interfaces for Searching the Web." *Scientific American*, May. Available at http://www.sciam.com.

Hechter, Michael. 1975. *Internal Colonialism: The Celtic Fringe in British National Development*. Berkeley and Los Angeles: University of California Press.

Heise, Hildegard. 1993. *Überlebensprinzip Spannungsaufnahme: Modernes Handlungssubjekt und Geschlechterverhältnis*. Frankfurt am Main: Campus.

Helleiner, Eric. 1994. *States and the Reemergence of Global Finance: From Bretton Woods to the 1990s*. Ithaca: Cornell University Press.

Helwig, Gisela, and Hildegard M. Nickel. 1993. *Frauen in Deutschland, 1945–1992*. Berlin: Akademie.

Hirschauer, Stefan. 1993a. "Dekonstruktion und Rekonstruktion: Plädoyer für die Erforschung des Bekannten." *Feministische Studien* 11.2:55–67.

– 1993b. *Die soziale Konstruktion der Transsexualität: Über die Medizin und den Geschlechtswechsel*. Frankfurt am Main: Suhrkamp.

Hobsbawm, E.J. 1990. *Nations and Nationalism since 1780: Program, Myth, Reality*. Cambridge: Cambridge University Press.

Hochschild, Arlie Russel. 1983. *The Managed Heart: Commercialization of Human Feeling*. Berkeley: University of California Press.

– with Anne Machung. 1989. *The Second Shift: Working Parents and the Revolution*. New York: Viking Press.

Hodge, Robert. 1990. *Literature as Discourse: Textual Strategies in English and History*. Cambridge, Oxford: Polity Press.

Hodges, Deborah Robertson. 1989. *Etiquette: An Annotated Bibliography of Literature Published in English in the United States, 1900 through 1987*. Jefferson: McFarland.

Hoecker, Beate. 1995. *Politische Partizipation von Frauen: Ein einführendes Studienbuch*. Opladen: Leske & Budrich.

Hoek, Beatrice Hofman, and Melanie Jongsma. 1995. *Surrender or Fight: One Woman's Victory over Cancer*. Grand Rapids: Baker Books.

Höflinger, Christoph. 1885. *Anstandsregeln. Regensburg: Pustet*.

Holsti, K.J. 1992. *International Politics: A Framework for Analysis*. Englewood Cliffs: Prentice Hall.

Hondrich, Karl Otto, and Claudia Koch-Arzberger. 1992. *Solidarität in der modernen Gesellschaft*. Frankfurt am Main: Fischer.

Hoole, Gavin. 1996. "Cyberlove: A Perspective." Available at http://www.aztec.cp.za/users/gshoole.

Hosin, A.A. 1987. "The Impact of International Conflict on Children's and Adolescents' National Perceptions." PhD thesis, University of Ulster.

Huchet, Jean-Charles. 1981. "Nom de femme et écriture féminine au Moyen Age: Les Lais de Marie de France." *Poétique* 48:407–30.

Humphrey, Mrs C.E. 1902. *Etiquette for Every Day*. London: Richards.

Ignatieff, Michael. 1994. *Blood and Belonging: Journeys into the New Nationalism*. London: Vintage.

Irigaray, Luce. 1980. *Speculum: Spiegel des anderen Geschlechts*. Frankfurt/M: Suhrkamp.

Jansen, Mechthild. 1995. "Bevorzugung der Bevorzugten." *Die Tageszeitung*, 18 October.

Jefferson, Thomas. 1907. *The Writings of Thomas Jefferson*. Edited by Albert Ellery Bergh. 19 vols. Washington, DC: Thomas Jefferson Memorial Association.

Joesten, Renate. 1994. *Stark wie der Tod ist die Liebe: Bericht von einem Abschied*. Bergisch-Gladbach: Lübbe Verlag.

Jones, David. 1996. *A Warrior in the Land of Disease*. West Vancouver, BC: Peace Projections.

Kahle, Brewster. 1997. "Preserving the Internet." *Scientific American*, May. Available at http://www.sciam.com.

Kapstein, Ethan B. 1996. *Governing the Global Economy: International Finance and the State*. Cambridge: Harvard University Press.

Kapteyn, Paul. 1980. *Taboe, Macht en Moraal in Nederland*. Amsterdam: De Arbeiderspers.

– 1985. "Even a Good Education Gives Rise to Problems: The Changes in Authority Between Parents and Children." *Concilium* 5:19–33.

Kasson, John F. 1990. *Rudeness and Civility: Manners in Nineteenth Century Urban America*. New York: Hill and Wang.

Kedourie, Elie. 1961. *Nationalism*. New York: Praeger.

Kemple, Thomas M. 1995. *Reading Marx Writing: Melodrama, the Market, and the "Grundrisse."* Stanford: Stanford University Press.

Killen, Mary. 1990. *Best Behaviour: The Tatler Book of Alternative Etiquette*. London: Century.

Kilminster, Richard. 1998. *The Sociological Revolution: From the Enlightenment to the Global Age*. London: Routledge.

Kim, Eun-Young. 1995. *Norbert Elias im Diskurs von Moderne und Postmoderne: Ein Rekonstruktionsversuch der Eliasschen Theorie im Licht der Diskussion von Foucault und Habermas*. Marburg: Tectum.

Kinoshita, Sharon. 1993–94. "Cherchez la femme: Feminist Criticism and Marie de France's Lai de Lanval." *Romance Notes* 34:263–73.

Klein, Gabriele. 1992. *Frauen – Körper – Tanz: Zivilisationsgeschichte des Tanzes*. Weinheim/Berlin: Quadriga.

– 1994. *Frauen – Körper – Tanz: Eine Zivilisationsgeschichte des Tanzes*. München: Heyne.

– and Katharina Liebsch, eds. 1997. *Zivilisierung des weiblichen Ich*. Frankfurt: Suhrkamp.

– and Annette Treibel, eds. 1993. *Begehren und Entbehren: Bochumer Beiträge zur Geschlechterforschung*. Pfaffenweiler: Centaurus.

Knapp, Gudrun-Axeli. 1988. "Die vergessene Differenz." *Feministische Studien* 6.1:12–31.

– 1995. "Macht und Geschlecht: Neuere Entwicklungen in der feministischen Macht- und Herrschaftsdiskussion." In *Traditionen, Brüche: Entwicklungen feministischer Theorie,* ed. Gudrun-Axeli Knapp and Angelika Wetterer, 87–325. Freiburg (Breisgau): Kore.

Knigge, Adolph Freiherr von. 1788 [1977]. *Über den Umgang mit Menschen: Herausgegeben von Gert Ueding.* Frankfurt/Main: Insel Verlag.

Koerber, Rita, Barry K. Morris, Vicki Obedkoff, and Karl Koerber. 1990. *The Book of Rita's Living.* Ed. Edith Templeton. Robson, BC: Bear Grass Press.

Kohn, Hans. 1961. *The Idea of Nationalism.* New York: Macmillan.

König, Oliver. 1990. *Nacktheit: Soziale Normierung und Moral.* Opladen: Westdeutscher Verlag.

Korda, Michael. 1996. *Man to Man: Surviving Prostate Cancer.* New York: Random House.

Korte, Hermann, ed. 1988. *Über Norbert Elias: Das Werden eines Menschenwissenschaftlers.* Frankfurt: Suhrkamp.

– 1990. *Gesellschaftliche Prozesse und individuelle Praxis: Bochumer Vorlesungen zu Norbert Elias' Zivilisationstheorie.* Frankfurt: Suhrkamp.

– 1993. *Blicke auf ein langes Leben – Norbert Elias und die Zivilisationstheorie.* Wien: Picus.

– 1997. *Über Norbert Elias: Das Werden eines Menschenwissenschaftlers.* Opladen: Leske und Budrich.

Krieken, Robert van. 1990. "The Organization of the Soul: Elias and Foucault on Discipline and the Self." *Archives europérnnes de sociologie* 31:353–71.

– 1998. *Norbert Elias.* London, Routledge.

Krumrey, Horst-Volker. 1984. *Entwicklungsstrukturen von Verhaltensstandarden: Eine soziologische Prozeßanalyse auf der Grundlage deutscher Anstands – und Manierenbücher von 1870 bis 1970.* Frankfurt am Main: Suhrkamp.

Krumrey, Volker. 1977. "Strukturwandlungen und Funktionen von Verhaltensstandards – analysiert mit Hilfe eines Interdependenzmodells zentraler sozialer Beziehungen." In Gleichmann et al., 1979, 194–214.

Kuhn, Thomas. 1970. *The Structure of Scientific Revolutions.* Chicago: University of Chicago Press.

Kuzmics, Helmut. 1989. *Der Preis der Zivilisation: Die Zwänge der Moderne im theoretischen Vergleich.* Frankfurt and New York: Campus.

– and Ingo Mörth, eds. 1991. *Der unendliche Prozeß der Zivilisation: Zur Kultursoziologie der Moderne nach Norbert Elias.* Frankfurt am Main: Campus.

Lang, Regina. 1989. *Frauenquoten: Der einen Freud, des anderen Leid.* Bonn: J.H.W. Dietz, Nachf.

Lansbury, Angela. 1985. *Etiquette for Every Occasion: A Guide to Good Manners.* London: Batsford.

Larkin, Jack. 1991. *The Reshaping of Everyday Life, 1790–1840.* New York: Harper Collins.

Lasch, Christopher. 1979. *The Culture of Narcissism.* New York: W.W. Norton.

– 1984. *The Minimal Self: Psychic Survival in Troubled Times.* New York: W.W. Norton.

Laslett, Peter. 1976. "The Wrong Way through the Telescope: A Note on Literary Evidence in Sociology and in Historical Sociology." *British Journal of Sociology* 27.3:319–42.

Leach, Sir Edmund. 1986. "Violence." *London Review of Books*, 23 October.

Lenker, Christiane. 1984. *Krebs kann auch eine Chance sein: Zwischenbilanz oder Antwort an Fritz Zorn*. Frankfurt/Main: Fischer Verlag.

– 1993. *Krebs greift das Herz nicht an: Mein zweites Leben*. Frankfurt/Main: Fischer Taschenbuch Verlag.

Lenz, Ilse. 1996. "Geschlecht, Herrschaft und internationale Ungleichheit." In *Das Geschlechterverhältnis als Gegenstand der Sozialwissenschaften*, ed. Regina Becker-Schmidt and Gudrun-Axeli Knapp, 19–46. Frankfurt: Campus.

Lepenies, Wolf. 1988. *Die drei Kulturen: Soziologie zwischen Literatur und Wissenschaft*. Reinbek: Rowohlt.

Lesk, Michael. 1997. "Going Digital." *Scientific American*, May. Available at http://www.sciam.com.

Leupin, Alexandre. 1991. "The Impossible Task of Manifesting 'literature': On Marie de France's Obscurity." Trans. Judith P. Shoaf. *Exemplaria* 3:221–42.

Levine, Donald N., ed. 1971. *Georg Simmel: On Individuality and Social Forms*. Chicago: University of Chicago Press.

Lewis, Helen B. 1971. *Shame and Guilt in Neurosis*. New York: International University Press.

Limbach, Jutta. 1994. "'Die zurückgebliebenste aller Provinzen ist die Universität': Der unaufhaltsame Aufstieg der Frauen in die Wissenschaft und die weibliche Dürre bei den Professoren." *Frankfurter Rundschau*, 8 November, 11.

Lipset, Seymour Martin. 1963. *The First New Nation*. London: Heinemann.

– 1996. *American Exceptionalism: A Double-Edged Sword*. New York: W.W. Norton.

– and Richard Hofstadter, eds. 1968. *Turner and the Sociology of the Frontier*. New York: Basic Books.

Loon, H.F. van. 1983. *Goede Manieren: Hoe Hoort Het Nu*. Amsterdam: Teleboek.

Lorde, Audre. 1980. *The Cancer Journals*. San Francisco: Aunt Lute Books.

– 1988. "A Burst of Light: Living with Cancer." In *A Burst of Light*. Toronto: Women's Press.

Lynch, Clifford. 1997 "Searching the Internet." *Scientific American*, May. Available at http://www.sciam.com.

Lynd, Helen. 1958. *On Shame and the Search for Identity*. New York: Harcourt.

MacDonald, Michael D. 1983. "Children of Wrath: Political Violence in Northern Ireland." PhD thesis, University of California, Berkeley.

McManus, George. 1975. *Bringing Up Father*. Amsterdam: Real Free Press International.

McNeill, William H. 1986. *Polyethnicity and National Unity*. Toronto: University of Toronto Press.

MacPhee, Rosalind. 1994. *Picasso's Woman: A Breast Cancer Story*. Vancouver: Douglas & McIntyre.

Mae, Eydie, with Chris Loeffler. 1992. *How I Conquered Cancer Naturally: A True Story of Courage and Triumph*. New York: Avery Publishing.

Mann, Thomas. 1980. *Tagebücher, 1937–1939*. Ed. Peter de Mendelssohn. Frankfurt am Main: Fischer.

Mannheim, Karl. 1952. "The Problem of Generations." In *Essays in the Sociology of Knowledge*. London: Routledge and Kegan Paul.

Marcus, George E., ed. 1996. *Connected: Engagements with Media*. Chicago: University of Chicago Press.

Marcus, H., and S. Kitiyama. 1991. "Culture and the Self." *Psychological Review* 98:24–53.

Marie de France. 1983. *Les Lais de Marie de France*. Ed. Jean Rychner. Paris: Honoré Champion.

– 1991. *Les Fables*. Ed. Charles Brucker. Louvain: Peeters.

Martin, Judith. [1979] 1983. *Miss Manners' Guide to Excruciatingly Correct Behavior*. New York: Warner Books/Atheneum Publishers.

– 1985. *Common Courtesy: In Which Miss Manners Solves the Problem That Baffles Mr. Jefferson*. New York: Atheneum.

– [1983] 1990. *Miss Manners' Guide for the Turn-of-the-Millenium*. New York: Pharos Books/Fireside.

Marx, Karl, and Friedrich Engels. 1948. *The Communist Manifesto*. New York: International Publishers.

Maschner, Heike. 1993. "Ohne Quote bewegt sich nichts: Bestandsaufnahme zur gesetzlichen Frauenförderung." In Klein and Treibel 1993, 125–39.

Mechtel, Angelika. 1993. *Jeden Tag will ich leben: Ein Krebstagebuch*. Frankfurt/Main: Fischer Taschenbuch Verlag.

Meissner, Hans-Otto, and Isabella Burkhard. 1962. *Gute Manieren stets gefragt: Takt, Benehmen, Etiquette*. München.

Mencken, H.L. 1923. *The American Language: An Inquiry into the Development of English in the United States*. New York: Knopf.

Mennell, Stephen. 1987. "Comment on Haferkamp." *Theory, Culture and Society* 4.2/3:559–60.

– 1989. *Norbert Elias: Civilization and the Human Self-Image*. Oxford: Blackwell.

– 1992a. "Momentum and History." In *Culture in History*, ed. J.L. Melling and J. Barry, 28–46. Exeter: University of Exeter Press.

– 1992b. *Norbert Elias: An Introduction*. Oxford: Blackwell.

– 1996. "The Formation of We-Images: A Process Theory." In *Social Theory and the Politics of Identity*, ed. Craig Calhoun, 175–97. Oxford: Blackwell.

Metge, Joan. 1986. *In and Out of Touch: Whakamaa in Cross Cultural Perspective*. Wellington: Victoria University Press.

Meulenbelt, Anja. 1994. *Über die Unmöglichkeit der Liebe zwischen Mann und Frau*. Reinbeck: Rowohlt.

Meyer, Thomas. 1989. "Wandlungen im familialen Geschlechterverhältnis. Neuere Befunde empirischer Erhebungen." *SOWI* 18.4:260–5.

Middlebrook, Christina. 1996. *Seeing the Crab: A Memoir of Dying*. New York: Basic Books–Harper Collins.

Moderne Hausfrau. 1995. *Aktuelle Informationen für die Frau in Haushalt und Beruf.* 7/8.

Mora-Lebrun, Francine. 1986. "Marie de France héritière de la lyrique des troubadours: L'exemple du Chaitivel." *Travaux de linguistique et de littérature* 24.2:19–30.

Motyl, Alexander, ed. 1992. *Thinking Theoretically about Soviet Nationalities: History and Comparison in the Study of the USSR*. New York: Columbia University Press.

Moynihan, Daniel Patrick. 1993. *Pandaemonium: Ethnicity in International Politics*. Oxford: Oxford University Press.

Mukai, Linda Pratt, and Janis Fischer Chan. 1996. *Living with Dying: A Personal Journey*. San Anselmo: Butterfield Press.

Müller, Ursula. 1994. "Feminismus in der empirischen Forschung: Eine methodologische Bestandsaufnahme." In Diezinger et al. 1994, 31–68.

Nabokov, Vladimir. 1980. *Lectures on Literature*. San Diego: Harvest Book.

New York Times. 1996. 3 September, Business Day, D1.

Nicolson, Harold. 1955. *Good Behavior, being a Study of Certain Types of Civility*. London: Constable.

Noakes, J., and G. Pridham, eds. 1988. *Nazism, 1919–1945*. Vol. 3, *Foreign Policy, War and Racial Extermination*. Exeter: University of Exeter.

Noll, Peter. 1991. *Diktate über Sterben und Tod*. München: Piper.

Offit, Avodah. "Are You Ready for Virtual Love? A Psychiatrist Looks at Cybersex." Available at http://web2.airmail.net/wlaraven/

Ostrander, Sheila. 1967. *Etiquette etc.: A Concise Guide with a Fresh Look*. New York: Sterling.

Pearson, Geoffrey. 1983. *Hooligans: A History of Respectable Fears*. London: Macmillan.

Pitman, Sara. 1996. "From Keyboards to Human Contact: Love Relationships through Computer-Mediated Communications." Available at http://edie.cprost.sfu.ca.

Porter, Cecil. 1972. *Not without a Chaperone: Modes and Manners from 1897 to 1914*. London: New English Library.

Post, Emily. 1922. *Etiquette in Society, in Business, in Politics and at Home*. New York: Funk and Wagnalls. Rev. eds.: 1923, 1927, 1931, 1934, 1937, 1942, 1950, 1960; replica of first ed.: 1969.

– 1965 [1968]. *Emily Post's Etiquette*. Rev. Elizabeth L. Post. New York: Funk and Wagnalls. Published as *The New Emily Post's Etiquette*, 1975, 1984, 1992.

Price, Reynolds. 1995. *A Whole New Life: An Illness and a Healing.* New York: Plume, Penguin.

Ranger, Terence. 1983. "The Invention of Tradition in Africa." In *The Invention of Tradition,* ed. Eric Hobsbawm and Terence Ranger. Cambridge, New York: Cambridge University Press.

Rapport der Regeerings-Commissie inzake het Dansvraagstuks. 1931. Gravenhage: Algemeene Landsdrukkerij.

Reid, Elizabeth M. "Cultural Formations in Text-Based Virtual Realities." MA thesis, University of Melbourne. Available at http://www.ee.mu.oz.au/papers/emr/.

Renan, Ernest. 1990. "What Is a Nation." Trans. Martin Thom. In *Nation* and *Narration,* ed. Homi Bhabaha, 8–22. London and New York: Routledge.

Resnick, Paul. 1997. "Filtering Information on the Internet." *Scientific American,* May. Available at http://www.sciam.com.

Retzinger, Suzanne. 1991. *Violent Emotions.* Newbury Park: Sage.

Richardson, Anna Steese. 1927. *Etiquette at a Glance.* New York.

Richardson, Colin Ryder. 1995. *Mind over Cancer.* London: W. Foulsham.

Roth, Guenther. 1971. "Max Weber's Generational Rebellion and Maturation." *Sociological Quarterly* 12:441–61.

Rundell, John, and Stephen Mennell, eds. 1998. *Classical Readings in Culture and Civilization.* London: Routledge.

Russell, Steven B. 1996. *Jewish Identity and Civilising Processes.* London: Macmillan.

Sackstetter, William. 1991. "Least Parts and Greatest Wholes: Variations on a Theme by Spinoza." *International Studies in Philosophy* 23:75–87.

Sallis-Freudenthal, Margarete. 1977. *Ich habe mein Land gefunden: Autobiographischer Rückblick.* Frankfurt am Main: Suhrkamp.

Salumets, Thomas. 1999. "Poetry and the Human Sciences: The 'Other' Norbert Elias." *Interlitteraria* 4:19–40.

Sardar, Z., and J.R. Ravetz. 1995. "Cyberspace: To Boldly Go." *Futures* 27.7:695–98.

Sauer, Birgit. 1994. "Was heißt und zu welchem Zwecke partizipieren wir? Kritische Anmerkungen zur Partizipationsforschung." In Biester et al. 1994, 99–130.

Scheff, Thomas. 1990. *Microsociology.* Chicago: University of Chicago Press.

– 1994. *Bloody Revenge.* Boulder: Westview Press.

– 1997. *Emotions, Social Bonds, and Human Reality: Part/Whole Analysis.* Cambridge: Cambridge University Press.

– and Suzanne M. Retzinger. 1991. *Emotions and Violence: Shame and Rage in Destructive Conflicts.* Toronto: Lexington Books.

Schlesinger, Arthur M., Sr. 1946. *Learning How to Behave: A Historical Study of American Etiquette Books.* New York: Macmillan.

Schliff, Sebastian. 1977. *Gutes Benehmen – Kein Problem!* München: Humboldt-Taschenbuchverlag.

Schluchter, Wolfgang. 1996. *Paradoxes of Modernity: Culture and Conduct in the Theory of Max Weber.* Trans. Neil Solomon. Stanford: Stanford University Press.

Schneider, Carl. 1977. *Shame, Exposure, and Privacy.* Boston: Beacon.

Schröter, Michael. 1997. *Erfahrungen mit Norbert Elias: Gesammelte Aufsätze.* Frankfurt: Suhrkamp.

Schröter, Ursula. 1995. "Ostdeutsche Frauen im Transformationsprozeß: Eine soziologische Analyse zur sozialen Situation ostdeutscher Frauen (1990–1994)." *Aus Politik und Zeitgeschichte* 20:31–42.

Schutz, Alfred. 1962. "Concept and Theory Formation in the Social Sciences." In *Collected Papers I: The Problem of Social Reality,* ed. Maurice Natanson. The Hague: Nijhoff.

– 1967. *The Phenomenology of the Social World.* Trans. George Walsh and Frederick Lehnert. Evanston, Ill.: Northwestern University Press.

– 1974. *Der sinnhafte Aufbau der sozialen Welt: Eine Einleitung in die verstehende Soziologie.* Frankfurt: Suhrkamp.

Searle, John R. 1969. *Speech Acts.* London: Cambridge University Press.

Seiler, Joachim. 1996. *Lügenzeit: Wenn der Partner an Krebs stirbt.* München: Verlag C.H. Beck.

Sennett, Richard. 1980. *Authority.* New York: Knopf.

– 1994. "Das Ende der Soziologie." *Die Zeit,* 29 September.

Seton-Watson, Hugh. 1977. *Nations and States: An Inquiry into the Origin of Nations and the Politics of Nationalism.* London: Methuen.

Shaver, P., S. Wu, and J. Schwartz. 1992. "Cross Cultural Similarities and Differences in Emotion and its Representation." *Review of Personality and Social Psychology* 13:175–212.

Shea, Virginia. 1996 "The Core Rules of Netiquette." Available at http://www.albion.com/netiquette/corerules.html.

Shin, Nan (Nancy Amphoux). 1986. *Diary of a Zen Nun.* New York: E.P. Dutton.

Simmel, Georg. 1971. "The Metropolis and Mental Life." In Levine 1917, 324–39.

– 1978. *The Philosophy of Money.* Trans. Tom Bottomore and David Frisby. London: Routledge.

Skinner, Quentin. 1978. *The Foundations of Modern Political Thought.* 2 vols. Cambridge: Cambridge University Press.

Smith, Anthony. 1986. *The Ethnic Origin of Nations.* Oxford: Basil Blackwell.

– 1995. "Gastronomy or Geology? The Role of Nationalism in the Reconstruction of Nations." *Nations and Nationalism* 1.1:3–23.

Smith, John. 1996. "Network Etiquette (Netiquette)." Available at http://ourworld.compuserve.com/homepages/bobby_elliot.

Smith, Page. 1966. *As a City upon a Hill: The Town in American History.* New York: Alfred A. Knopf.

Smythe, Benjamin Roth. 1986. *Killing Cancer: The Jason Winters Story.* Las Vegas: Vinton Publishing.

Sombart, Werner. 1967. *Luxury and Capitalism.* Ann Arbor: University of Michigan Press.

Sontag, Susan. 1979. *Illness as Metaphor.* New York: Vintage-Random House.

Spiegel, Der. 1993. "Gesellschaft, Manieren, 'Verbale Krawatten.'" 47.7:243.

Stacey, Jackie. 1996. "Conquering Heroes: The Politics of Cancer Narratives." In *Cancer: Through the Eyes of Ten Women,* ed. Patricia Duncker and Vicky Wilson. London: Harper Collins.

Stearns, Peter N. 1989. *Jealousy: The Evolution of an Emotion in American History.* New York: New York University Press.

– 1994. *American Cool: Constructing a Twentieth Century Emotional Style.* New York: New York University Press.

– and Carol Stearns. 1986. *Anger: The Struggle for Emotional Control in America's History.* Chicago: University of Chicago Press.

Stein-Hilbers, Marlene. 1989. "Frauen und Männer: Erste Anzeichen eines Wandels von Geschlechterverhältnissen." *SOWI* 18:221–7.

Stone, John, and Stephen Mennell. 1983. *Alexis de Tocqueville on Democracy, Revolution, and Society.* Chicago: University of Chicago Press, 1980.

Stone, Lawrence. "Interpersonal Violence in English Society, 1300–1980." *Past and Present* 101:22–33.

Streeck, Wolfgang. 1997. "Regimewettbewerb: Vorläufige Überlegungen zu einem zukünftigen Schlüsselbegriff." *Wissenschaftszentrum Berlin,* 25 February.

Stüber, Lotte. 1995. "Im Visier: Frauen auf Rädern." *Die Tageszeitung,* 18 May.

Sweeney, Ester Emerson. 1948. *Dates and Dating.* New York: Women's Press.

Tainter, Joseph A. 1988. *The Collapse of Complex Societies.* Cambridge: Cambridge University Press.

Tausch, Anne-Marie. 1995. *Gespräche gegen die Angst: Krankheit – ein Weg zum Leben.* Reinbek: Rowohlt Verlag.

Taylor, George Rogers, ed. 1956. *The Turner Thesis concerning the Role of the Frontier in American History.* Boston: D.C. Heath.

Templeton, Brad. 1996. "Dear Emily Postnews." Available at http://www.clari.net/brad/emily.html.

Terry, Eileen. 1925. *Etiquette for All, Man, Woman or Child.* London: Foulsham.

Thielscher-Noll, Helma, and Hans Gerhard Noll. 1994. *Ich brauche dich: Mein Leben mit Krebs.* Moers: Brendow Verlag.

Thürmer-Rohr, Christina. 1989. "Mittäterschaft der Frau – Analyse zwischen Mitgefühl und Kälte." In *Studienschwerpunkt Frauenforschung am Institut für Sozialpädagogik der TU Berlin, Mittäterschaft* und *Entdeckungslust,* 87–103. Berlin: Orlanda.

– 1994. *Verlorene Narrenfreiheit: Essays.* Berlin: Orlanda.

Tilly, Charles. 1961. "Reflections on the History of European State Making." In *The Formation of National States in Western Europe*, ed. Charles Tilly. Princeton: Princeton University Press.

Tocqueville, Alexis de. 1961. *Democracy in America*. Trans. Henry Reeve. Vol. 2. New York: Schocken.

Tomkins, Silvan S. 1963. *Affect/Imagery/Consciousness*. Vol. 2. New York: Springer.

Treibel, Annette. 1993. "Engagierte Frauen, distanzierte Männer? Überlegungen zum Wissenschaftsbetrieb." In Klein and Treibel 1993, 21–38.

– 1995. *Einführung in soziologische Theorien der Gegenwart*. Opladen: Leske & Budrich.

Troubridge, Lady L. 1926 [1931]. *The Book of Etiquette*. Kingswood: Windmill Press.

– 1939. *Etiquette and Entertaining*. London: Amalgamated Press.

Turner, Frederick Jackson. 1962. "The Significance of the Frontier in American History." In *The Frontier in American History*. New York: Holt, Rinehart & Winston.

Umgangsformen Heute. 1988. *Die Empfehlungen des Fachausschusses für Umgangsformen*. Niedernhausen: Falken.

van Benthem van den Bergh, Godfried. 1971. *The Structure of Development: An Invitation to the Sociology of Norbert Elias*. Occasional Paper no. 13. The Hague: Institute of Social Studies.

Vanderbilt, Amy. 1978. *The Amy Vanderbilt Complete Book of Etiquette*. Rev. and expanded by Letitia Baldrige. New York: Doubleday.

van Osta. 1996. "Nationalisme en Natievorming, 1815–1870: Italie en Duitsland." In *Veränderende Grenzen, Nationalisme in Europa, 1815–1919*, ed. L.H.M. Wessels and A. Bosch. Heerlen: Nijmegen and Open Universiteit.

van Stolk, Bram, and Cas Wouters. 1984. "Die Gemütsruhe der Wohlfahrtsstaates." In Gleichmann et al. 1984, 242–60.

– 1987. *Frauen im Zwiespalt: Beziehungsprobleme im Wohlfahrtsstaat, Eine Modellstudie*. Frankfurt am Main: Suhrkamp.

Viroflay, Marguérite de. 1916. *Plichten en Vormen voor Beschaafde Menschen*. Amsterdam: Cohen Zonen.

Visser, Margaret. 1991. *The Rituals of Dinner: The Origins, Evolution, Eccentricities, and Meaning of Table Manners*. New York: Grove Weidenfelt.

Wachtel, Joachim. 1973. *1 x 1 des guten Tons heute*. München: Bertelsmann Ratgeberverlag.

Wacquant, Loïc. 1992. "Décivilisation et diabolisation: La mutation du ghetto noir américain." In *L'Amérique des français*, ed. T. Bishop and Christiane Faure. Paris: Éditions François Bourin.

Wadler, Joyce. 1994. *My Breast*. New York: Pocket Books,

Wander, Maxie. 1996. *Leben wär' eine prima Alternative*. München: Deutscher Taschenbuch Verlag.

Weber, Eugen. 1976. *Peasants into Frenchmen: The Modernization of Rural France*. Stanford: Stanford University Press.

Weber, Max. 1930. *The Protestant Ethic and the Spirit of Capitalism*. London: Allen & Unwin.

– 1949. *The Methodology of the Social Sciences*. Ed. E.A. Schils and H.A. Finch. New York: Free Press.

– 1958. *From Max Weber: Essays in Sociology*. Ed. and trans. Hans Gerth and C. Wright Mills. Oxford: Oxford University Press.

– 1973. "Die 'Objektivität' sozialwissenschaftlicher Erkenntnis." In Max Weber, *Soziologie, Universalgeschichtliche Analysen, Politik*, ed. Johannes Winckelmann, 186–262. Stuttgart: Kröner.

– 1978. *Economy and Society*. 2 vols. Berkeley: University of California Press.

Wetterer, Angelika. 1992. *Profession und Geschlecht: Über die Marginalität von Frauen in hochqualifizierten Berufen*. Frankfurt am Main: Campus.

– 1994. "Rhetorische Präsenz – faktische Marginalität: Zur Situation von Wissenschaftlerinnen in Zeiten der Frauenförderung." *Zeitschrift für Frauenforschung* 12.1/2:93–110.

Wilber, Ken. 1991. *Grace and Grit: Spirituality and Healing in the Life and Death of Treya Killam Wilber*. Boston: Shambala.

Williams, John R. 1987. *Goethe's Faust*. London: Allen and Unwin.

Wilterdink, Nico. 1991. *Ongelijkheid en interdependentie: Ontwikkelingen in welstandsverhoudingen*. Groningen: Wolters-Noordhoff, 1993.

Winter-Uedelhoven, Hedwig. 1991. *Zur Bedeutung der Etikette*. Frankfurt/Main: R.G. Fischer.

Wobbe, Theresa. "Eine Frage der Tradition: Wissenschaftspolitische Überlegungen in historischer Perspektive." In Biester et al. 1994, 122–40.

– and Gesa Lindemann, eds. 1994. *Denkachsen: Zur theoretischen und institutionellen Rede vom Geschlecht*. Frankfurt am Main: Suhrkamp.

Wolter, Irmgard. 1990. *Der Gute Ton in Gesellschaft und Beruf: Überarbeitet von Wolf Stenzel*. Niedernhausen: Falken.

Woodiwiss, Anthony. 1993. *Postmodernity USA: The Crisis of Social Modernism in Postwar America*. London: Sage.

Wouters, Cas. 1976. "Is het civilisatieprocess van richting veranderd? [Is the civilizing process changing direction?]" *Amsterdams Sociologisch Tijdschrift* 3:336–7.

– 1977. "Informalization and the civilizing process." In *Human Figurations: Essays for Norbert Elias*, ed. P.R. Gleichmann et al., 437–53. Amsterdam: Stichting Amsterdams Sociologisch Tijdschrift.

– 1986. "Informalisierung und Formalisierung der Geschlechterbeziehungen in den Niederlanden von 1930 bis 1985." *Kölner Zeitschrift für Soziologie und Sozialpsychologie* 38:510–18.

– 1986. "Formalization and Informalization: Changing Tension Balances in Civilizing Processes." *Theory, Culture & Society* 4.2/3:1–18.

- 1987. "Developments in Behavioral Codes between the Sexes; Formalization of Informalization, The Netherlands, 1930–1985." *Theory, Culture & Society* 4.2/3:405–29.
- 1990. "Social Stratification and Informalization in Global Perspective." *Theory, Culture & Society* 7.4:69–90.
- 1991. "On Status Competition and Emotion Management." *Journal of Social History* 24.4:699–717.
- 1992. "On Status Competition and Emotion Management; The Study of Emotions as a New Field." *Theory, Culture & Society* 9.1:229–52.
- 1994a. "Konformitätsdruck und Profilierungszwang: Zwischen Identifikation und Individualisierung – Ambivalenzen des Affektmanagements." *Frankfurter Rundschau*, 11 January.
- 1994b. "Manners." In *Encyclopedia of Social History*, ed. Peter N. Stearns, 436–8. New York: Garland.
- 1995a. "Etiquette Books and Emotion Management in the 20th Century: Part One – The Integration of Social Classes." *Journal of Social History* 29:107–24.
- 1995b. "Etiquette Books and Emotion Management in the 20th Century: Part Two – The Integration of the Sexes." *Journal of Social History* 29:325–40.
- 1998a. "Etiquette Books and Emotion Management in the 20th Century: American Habitus in International Comparison." In *An Emotional History of the United States*, ed. Peter N. Stearns and Jan Lewis, 283–304. New York: New York University Press.
- 1998b. "How Strange to Ourselves Are Our Feelings of Superiority and Inferiority?" *Theory, Culture & Society.* 15.1:131–50.
- 1998c. "Balancing Sex and Love since the Sixties Sexual Revolution." *Theory, Culture & Society* 15.3/4:187–214.
- 1999. *Informalisierung: Norbert Elias Zivilisationstheorie und Zivilisationsprozess im 20. Jahrhundert.* Opladen: Westdeutscher Verlag.
Wrobel, David M. 1993. *The End of American Exceptionalism: Frontier Anxiety from the Old West to the New Deal.* Lawrence: University Press of Kansas.
Zachert, Christel, and Isabell Zachert. 1996. *Wir treffen uns wieder in meinem Paradies.* Bergisch Gladbach: Lübbe Verlag.
Zorn, Fritz. 1994. *Mars.* Frankfurt/Main: Fischer Taschenbuch Verlag.
Zwaan, A.C.L. 1996. "Duits Nationalisme tijdens het tweede Keizerrijk." In *Veranderende Grenzen, Nationalisme in Europa, 1815–1919*, ed. L.H.M. Wessels and A. Bosch. Heerlen: Nijmegen and Open Universiteit.

INDEX